The Good ?

by John Ironmonger

Based upon source material by Ray Heaton
and John Ironmonger, with additional research
by Sue Ironmonger.

Illustrated by G. L. Grandy

📖 HarperCollins*Publishers*

HarperCollins*Publishers*
London · Glasgow · Sydney · Auckland
Toronto · Johannesburg

First published 1992
© John Ironmonger, 1992

ISBN 0 00 219921 1

Printed by Butler & Tanner, Frome, Somerset

Contents

Acknowledgements

I should like to offer my special thanks to my wife Sue for all her research and for her invaluable insights. I am most grateful to the many zoo directors, curators, and especially keepers who have helped, often unknowingly, in the preparation of this guide; particular thanks are due to Ray Heaton who visited every zoo in the guide at least once, and most on numerous occasions, and who also provided many long hours of help and advice on the manuscript. I am most grateful to Roger Wheater, director of Edinburgh Zoo, and to Val Cooper and Trevor Dale.

HOW TO USE THIS BOOK

The Good Zoo Guide is divided into six sections:

Part 1

How Green are Our Zoos?
This chapter looks at the reasons zoos give for keeping wild animals. How valid are their claims?

Part 2

Keeping Animals in Zoos and Wildlife Parks
This chapter looks at the different groups of animals kept in British zoos, from gorillas to goldfish, from elephants to emus.

Part 3

The Good Zoo Guide Star Ratings
How do you tell a good zoo from a bad zoo? How do you compare a huge safari park with a small city zoo? This section explains the star ratings used in the book.

Part 4

The Good Zoos
Thirty-one zoos which we consider the best in Britain – their history, their specialities, their good points, their weak points.

Part 5

An index to the mammals in the best zoos, listing nearly five hundred mammal species represented in the Good Zoos and where to see them.

Part 6

Where to see animals in Britain
A county by county list of more than 130 zoos, safari parks, wildlife parks, bird gardens, butterfly houses, and aquaria; how to find them, and what to see there

The 31 Good Zoos of Britain

- Highland
- Blair Drummond
- Glasgow
- Edinburgh
- Belfast
- Blackpool
- Knowsley
- Chester
- Welsh Mountain
- Dudley
- Twycross
- Norfolk
- Banham
- West Midlands
- Woburn
- Whipsnade
- Colchester
- Penscynor
- Cotswold
- Windsor
- London
- Bristol
- Chessington
- Howletts
- Longleat
- Marwell
- Port Lympne
- Cricket
- Drusillas
- Paignton
- Jersey

Part 1
Introduction

How Green Are Our Zoos?

Can you remember the very first time you ever went to a zoo? Didn't the animals seem amazing? The very first time you ever saw an elephant – how huge it seemed, how unbelievable its trunk was, how extraordinary it was that this great fantastic creature was actually there, sharing the world with you. If you live close to a zoo, then for you it is probably still 'The Zoo'. It may still have affectionate memories for you, memories of strange exotic creatures, and curious smells; a place full of beasts with a power to fascinate, intimidate, or amuse.

But perhaps your memories of the zoo are not so pleasant. Perhaps your last impression of the zoo was not of an astonishing place full of playful monkeys and towering giraffes, but of the sad and listless eyes of a poor wild animal imprisoned in a hopelessly unsuitable cage. For zoos are not always exotic and exciting places. They may be cruel, dank, and depressing. And however startling our first impressions of the zoo might have been, we soon begin to look at the world with clearer, more critical eyes. We no longer visit the zoo to marvel at the sheer size of the elephants or to gasp at the jaws of the lions, and we start to question the ethics of it all.

Britain has over eighty mammal collections that might properly be called zoos, and there is a huge variation in their quality. Most of us can intuitively recognise a bad zoo when we have the misfortune to visit one. Yet there seem to be very few rules to help us determine which zoos, if any, deserve to be called 'good zoos'.

To begin with, is there really such a thing as a good zoo at all in the 'Green Decade' of the nineties? Can zoos really justify their existence in the light of the new environmental realism that we all have to face, or do they simply exist to satisfy a rather old fashioned appetite for the curious and the macabre? Is there really a case for caging animals any more, especially now that we have television wildlife programmes to satisfy our thirst for knowledge of the wild world, and we have theme parks to take the family to on a Sunday afternoon? Today we are all becoming 'green consumers'. We have green supermarkets, and green products from washing powder to petrol. How green are our zoos?

If you begin to ask zoo directors these questions, you will soon come across a fairly standard reply. Modern zoos, they will explain, are no longer the consumers of wild animals and the fairground attractions that they once were. Today's zoos are sanctuaries for rare and endangered animals, they are educators of our children, teaching us all to love and appreciate the wildlife of our planet, and they are centres of academic research. Well they would say that, wouldn't they.

This book aims to discover whether there is any truth in these claims. Zoos stake a claim to four fundamental objectives – conservation, education, research, and recreation. But just how these objectives are perceived, and what emphasis is accorded to each one, varies considerably from zoo to zoo. These days recreation tends to be considered insufficient justification for depriving animals of their freedom. Half a century ago it may have been quite acceptable to keep a solitary animal in close confinement just for our amusement, but perceptions have changed. Today we expect more of our zoos. We hear of 'Animal Rights'. We think of animals as being 'exploited' – a concept unknown during the formative years of British zoos. So we must look towards conservation, education, and research if we are to justify our modern zoos. But are these really just a smokescreen, a fiction behind which nothing has really changed?

This book takes each of these issues in turn, and explores the way that British Zoos are facing up to them. If we take zoos at their face value, we should be able to judge, albeit subjectively, whether they pay more than lip service to conservation, education, and research. If they do, then perhaps, just perhaps, they deserve to be called 'good zoos'.

And surprisingly, or unsurprisingly, depending upon your prejudices or your point of view, the evidence suggests that there are still plenty of good zoos in Britain. Some of them undoubtedly deserve to be listed among the best zoos in the world. Others at least deserve more local recognition. The best British zoos are bold and innovative. They are not shackled by the vestigial ideas of the post-war years. They do not believe that the only way to attract visitors is to keep just the nursery-book species. They understand that every animal has its own peculiar environmental, behavioural, and emotional demands, and they design their enclosures accordingly. They understand too that the human animals, as visitors to the zoo, must have their needs catered to as well. Most of all they recognise that many of the world's animals are now in imminent danger of extinction, and that zoos may represent the only way to escape the eternal condemnation of every future generation of mankind for allowing these unique species to disappear forever. In a very real sense these zoos are among the 'greenest' institutions in this country.

Many of these issues are complex and controversial. But there is a growing consensus that there are good zoos. They deserve our patronage, and we in turn can learn from them, and can gain a great deal of pleasure from visiting them. This book attempts to identify those good zoos.

Conservation

The word 'Conservation' is bandied about a lot these days. It is a fashionable word, like the word 'green'. It is a word that suggests a rather selfless dedication towards protecting wildlife and wild places. A lot of zoos use the word conservation to describe their role in society. 'Our Aim is to Assist in the Conservation of Endangered Species by Captive Breeding' proclaims a sign at one menagerie that is not included as a good zoo in this guide. It is a questionable claim.

But who can blame hard-pressed zoo directors for climbing onto the green bandwagon. It only costs a few pounds, after all, to put up a sign claiming to be a 'conservation zoo', and from then on any zoo can bask in the reflected glory of those few collections which really are committing resources towards breeding endangered species. The word conservation has become common and cheap. The act of conservation, alas, is rare and brutally expensive.

To begin with there is the cost of the animals themselves. Even in these days of breeding loans and cooperative species management, animals are still bought and sold. The rarer the animal, the higher is the asking price. The entire animal stock of the Zoological Society of London at Regent's Park and Whipsnade was valued in 1958 at £174,618. Today a single female okapi might fetch over £150,000 if sold. Add to that the cost of transport, the building of special crates, quarantine expenses, insurance, dealer's profits and a huge amount of paperwork. You may begin to realise that starting a zoo for endangered species is far from cheap. When John Aspinall chose to bring two Sumatran 'woolly rhinos' from Indonesia to his zoo at Port Lympne in 1986, the operation is said to have cost him almost two million pounds.

And then there is another, subtler, cost. This is what John Knowles of Marwell Zoo calls 'deficit financing'. It works like this: imagine that a scimitar-horned oryx costs, say, £50 a week to maintain in food, housing, keeping, and veterinary costs. A doubling of your herd will double your costs, but visitors like to see a lot of species, not a few huge herds. They are apt to become bored by a succession of cages all occupied by an identical cat asleep in an identical corner. A good zoo director will know that numbers are almost always critical to breeding success in the long term. But a herd of thirty oryx will attract not one more visitor than a herd of fifteen, or a family of four. So how does a zoo justify the keeping of these 'uneconomic' groups?

The answer is that justification has to be made on conservation, not on economic grounds. Deficit financing means that popular animals like monkeys, sealions, penguins and giraffe generate the income by attracting visitors, and the surplus goes towards maintaining the 'uneconomic' herds that have less popular appeal.

There is one major drawback to this approach, and it has to do with competition. If the zoo down the road has the same popular animals as yours

Przewalski's horse

14

but does not choose to spend its money on conservation-sensitive creatures, then down comes its gate price, up goes its market share, down comes your market share, and out of the window go all your conservation ideals. The brutal law of the market place prevails. In the final analysis, the big crowds go to a zoo for a good day out, not for the warm glow they might get from having contributed towards saving an endangered animal; and while it is true that fourteen million Britons go to a zoo every year, they do have over one hundred collections to choose from, to say nothing of a growing number of theme parks and stately homes, and competition can be fierce. These days it is as much as many zoos can do to stay in business from one wet summer to the next, let alone to commit substantial amounts of their scarce resources towards keeping a species that the public has probably never heard of, just because it is endangered.

So you see why it is cheaper just to put up a sign.

All of which is bad news for conservation, and ultimately bad news for the zoos themselves. Because, despite everything, captive breeding of endangered species, once the bête-noire of many conservationists, is rapidly becoming more and more important. Consider the Humboldt's penguin. Almost everywhere you go you can see Humboldt's penguins, and more than twenty collections exhibit them. Their popularity in zoos has been, in part, due to their abundance in the wild, and back in the old collecting days they were fairly easy to come by. They come from the Pacific Coasts of South America where they feed in the fertile coastal waters and nest in burrows on the shore. Over the past decade the wild population has collapsed dramatically. Over-fishing, coastal development, and pollution are blamed for the penguins' decline, and a recent estimate put the wild population at two thousand pairs, with a continuing fall expected. What this illustrates is that the time-honoured complacency of many zoos that some species will always be in plentiful supply is now on shifting sand. Nowadays hardly any species can be taken for granted, not even penguins; and if the zoos don't breed them, then there will soon be plenty of empty penguin pools up and down the country.

So, in a crude fashion, the zoos themselves have a nettle to grasp, just to keep themselves in stock into the next century. But, alas, the problem goes a great deal deeper than that. There is now a real likelihood that many vertebrate species will soon only exist in captivity.

The human population of the world is to blame. The World Bank has estimated that population will level off at around ten to twelve billion towards the end of the next century. Most of the expected increase will be in the poorer countries of the world, often countries rich in wildlife. Just consider the impact that four billion people have already had upon Planet Earth, and multiply that effect by three: three times the demand for food and farmland and fresh water and firewood, three times the demand for raw materials, housing, and roads. Imagine the effect that this is going to have upon the rate of forest destruction, (already proceeding at fifty acres a minute), on over-fishing, pollution, poaching. The spectre of such a world may seem alarmist, but perhaps we could all do with a little alarmism. Freud wrote that we should 'think the unthinkable,

15

and then plan for it.' But how do you plan against the imminent wholesale extinction of hundreds, maybe thousands, of animal species?

One plan might be to keep a safe reservoir of every species likely to become threatened, in safe havens, closely managed to protect against in-breeding and disease. This is another way of saying perhaps we should keep animals in zoos. A recent report predicts that we shall need to keep around two thousand species of large terrestrial animals in captivity for five hundred years or more if we are to save them forever from extinction. It is a tall order. But can it be done?

To begin with, we would need a reasonable captive population of each species. This is necessary to prevent inbreeding. Curiously, populations can often survive well even if they all derive from a very small number of founding parents. Every Arabian oryx alive is descended from a single herd of nine and every Père David's deer from a herd of eighteen. But if the number of animals stays low for more than a few generations, the problems of inbreeding may prove fatal. The solution is to establish a large zoo population of each threatened species as swiftly as possible, and then to circulate animals between the zoos to keep the populations genetically diverse and healthy. Zoologists disagree about the minimum size of a zoo population needed to provide a secure future, but the consensus seems to be that at least one hundred breeding individuals are essential and over three hundred would be desirable.

There are estimated to be slightly more than a quarter of a million animals in the zoos of the world. If every one of these were to be included in an organised captive-breeding programme, and if populations were to average around 275 individuals, simple mathematics show that no more than 925 species could be saved. Gerald Durrell once called zoos 'Stationary Arks'. It looks as though they will be crowded. In fact, if they are to function success-fully, we may need twice as many.

However, in the United Kingdom we already have around 50,000, animals in our zoos, about a fifth of the world's zoo population. Maybe we have more than our fair share. Some zoo directors clearly think so. It all comes back to the question of competition. So long as the public is sufficiently uncritical there will be plenty of zoos to satisfy the demand for lions and llamas and all the other common species that breed so prolifically in captivity that they are both cheap to acquire, and are of little conservation value. In a very real sense these zoos are acting in a manner that is directly contrary to their often stated conservation aims. By competing directly against the good zoos, they deny them the income they need. They also help to create a climate of opinion that regards zoos at best as places that do no more than indulge our curiosity, and at worst as animal prisons and consumers of wildlife.

All of this leaves serious zoos looking for alternative sources of finance. Gate receipts will not finance conservation until the public becomes more discerning.

The government in Britain does assist two zoos. They are London Zoo and Whipsnade, the two zoos of the Zoological Society of London. The support has so far enabled these zoos to direct some resources towards conservation projects. A number of zoos have also benefited from tourist board, or devel-opment agency grants. This can help provide some of the financing that the

16

real conservation work demands. Elsewhere the only real evidence of dedication to captive breeding has come from the personal commitment of enterprising or wealthy men: men like the late Sir Peter Scott who founded the Wildfowl Trust at Slimbridge, and whose contribution towards rescuing the Hawaiian Goose from the very brink of extinction has been the inspiration for many other projects: men like Gerald Durrell, the bestselling author, John Knowles, a wealthy farmer, or John Aspinall, a millionaire club-owner. It is a sad indictment of British zoos to have to say that without men like these we would have very little to be proud of in this field.

The potential role of zoos as agents of conservation has not always appealed to all conservationists. Essentially all that zoos can do is to preserve a population of animals in close captive management, while the real source of the problem, habitat destruction or over-exploitation, goes unchecked. A common argument against this form of species preservation goes like this: all the money invested and spent annually on zoos would be far better spent actually preserving habitats. Surprisingly, perhaps, few zoo people would dispute this fact. However, it is rather like arguing that all the money spent upon slimming aids would be better spent helping to alleviate world hunger. The alternative is an artificial one. The fourteen million zoo visitors in Britain who spend around £4 each for their day out are doubtless canvassed by the World Wide Fund for Nature for donations, but that is not how they choose to spend their money on a summer Sunday. We would do better to recognise that there are zoos that do spend our money wisely, and to direct our visits towards them. That is what this guide aims to help us do.

When habitats come under threat, it is invariably the bigger animals that go first because their demands upon the environment are the greatest. These are creatures that zoos are often in a position to help. Already there have been some astonishing successes. Without captive management we would no longer be sharing our planet with Père David's deer, American or European bison, Przewalski's horse, Arabian or scimitar-horned oryx. Island species are also important candidates for captive conservation. Species saved include the Hawaiian goose, the Jamaican boa, and the Mauritius pink pigeon. Some re-introductions have already taken place, but in the short term we should not expect too many of these. After all, if animals have become extinct in a habitat, the reason for the extinction needs to be removed before the species can be returned. Nevertheless, good zoos have proven that they can be a reservoir for endangered species. Now they face up to their greatest challenge, to sustain up to two thousand species, in close management, perhaps for centuries.

In Britain there are encouraging signs. The best of these is the effort being made by the National Federation of Zoological Gardens, which represents over fifty collections, to coordinate breeding programmes for the most crucial species, and by the Joint Species Management Programs, which aim to focus the attention of good zoos upon sharing their precious animals to improve their long-term chances of survival. Good zoos now take their role as a conservation resource very seriously. Many more animals are now swapped or placed on breeding loans than ever before. Success in breeding even traditionally difficult species like cheetah is now rapidly improving. The vast majority of zoo animals were themselves bred in captivity. They belong to the early generations of a time-bridge that may have to span several centuries before their distant descendants once again tread the wild soils of their native lands.

The Vocabulary of Extinction

The journey from abundance to extinction can be a very rapid one. It took less than fifty years for the passenger pigeon to fall from being the most abundant species of bird on earth, to becoming extinct. So when we say that an animal species is 'In Danger of Extinction', how far along this road has it travelled, and how much further does it have to go?

To help discuss these issues, conservationists use the following terminology:

A species is *abundant* if, like mankind or the brown rat, it seems destined to be around for the foreseeable future.

A species is *extinct* if, like the passenger pigeon or the quagga, there have been no confirmed sightings for fifty years.

A species is *endangered* if its continued survival is unlikely should the factors causing its reduction in number continue to operate. The black rhino is an *endangered* species; so is the Siberian tiger, and the Californian condor.

A *vulnerable* species is one that is likely to become *endangered* soon if the cause for its decline continues. The African elephant is a *vulnerable* species, and so is the jaguar, and the white eared pheasant.

A species is *Rare* if, like the giant panda or Goeldi's monkey, its distribution is very localised, but in no immediate danger.

Education

There is a small natural history museum in Colchester, where a common sight is a party of school-children, all armed with pencils and drawing paper, intent upon sketching the stuffed animals in the showcases. A few miles down the road they could sketch living animals at the zoo. But so far as the law is concerned stuffed animals are educational and living animals are entertainment (which is why zoos have to charge VAT while museums do not).

Not so many years ago, a visit to the zoo was unashamedly for fun. School trips to the zoo were seen as a good end-of-term excuse to let children enjoy themselves for once, comfortable in the knowledge that while they may be making ribald remarks about the colourful hindquarters of the primates, there would be no danger that they might actually break anything, they would not have to be kept too quiet, and while a few might become temporarily lost, the zoo itself would act like one enormous enclosure from which escape should be highly unlikely.

These days however, zoos have discovered 'Education', and school trips to the zoo may never be the same again. So what exactly are zoos trying to educate us in? And why should they be making such an effort?

Motives are probably a good place to start. It is easy to be suspicious when

18

an establishment that takes your money at the gate suddenly takes a strong moral stand on a subject like education. Education, like conservation, can be a very convenient label for poor zoos to use in an effort to justify their existence. It cost very little to produce an 'Education-Pack' of photocopied drawings for children to colour, or a simple quiz for school parties to complete. Then any zoo can claim to fulfil an educational role, and who are we to know better?

We often hear it said that television is now the best medium for teaching children (and adults, too) about wildlife. In many ways it is difficult to argue with this proposition. But then again, television is so forgettable. We see so much of it. Most children watch several hundred hours of television every year, so that an episode of a wildlife series, however brilliant, soon fades into the recesses of memory. By contrast a visit to a zoo or a safari park is so memorable. Who can ever forget the baboons climbing over the car, or the roar of a hungry lion, or the playfulness of a pair of otters? A face-to-face confrontation with an elephant is so unlike anything that television could ever offer that it beggars comparison. Only in the flesh, so to speak, can you realise just how tall a giraffe is, just how agile monkeys are, just how colourful are the parrots. There is something about the solid, three dimensional, living, moving animal with all its smells and noises that imprints itself upon the mind, and for children the distinction is even more emphatic. Take children bird-watching and they will soon learn to identify different birds. Show them an educational video and they still won't distinguish a starling from a sparrow. Something about the experience and sense of occasion that children feel when they see a live animal, even if it is only in a zoo, cannot be replaced by other teaching aids. This is the key to the powerful educational potential of good zoos. Children (and adults) visit a zoo emotionally prepared to assimilate a lot of new information, and the circumstances ensure that much of that information will be retained. So the onus falls upon the teacher and the zoo itself to ensure that this opportunity is used to the best advantage.

Good zoos recognise the responsibility they have to educate while they entertain. Perhaps the most important indicator of commitment here is the information provided on each enclosure. While no one expects an encyclo-paedia of information alongside every cage, an accurate, legible label is essential. What appears on the label tends to vary considerably from zoo to zoo. An illustration of the animal in its native habitat perhaps, a distribution map, life style, main source of food, litter size, gestation time, and so on. It helps if the label adds something unique or interesting about the animal concerned. Capybaras become more memorable when you learn that they are the world's largest rodents, spider monkeys when you learn to watch for them swinging by their tails, Przewalski's horses when you learn that they are extinct in the wild. A good guide book can complement the signs, but should never replace them.

Many zoos now have an education department, a classroom, full time educational officers, and extra teaching support in the summer. Edinburgh Zoo has pioneered a scheme called 'interlink' which combines the resources of the zoo, local museums, and the botanic gardens to create educational courses. Like several other zoos it offers teachers a range of courses from day trips with infants to intensive courses for A-Level students, and even undergraduates. In 1991 over 50,000 students were involved with structured courses at Edinburgh Zoo. Schools are also offered educational 'packs' to issue to children, and most good zoos will offer advice to teachers on the most appropriate areas of study for that zoo.

We have tried, in our zoo ratings, to judge the educational service offered by the good zoos. Zoos are a resource that our schools probably undervalue. They have a lot to offer, and in the end the zoo visit will probably be remembered longer than a whole year of classroom lessons.

Recreation

Most zoos define their aims as 'Conservation, Education, Research, and Recreation'. Sometimes they substitute the word 'Entertainment', but note how they nearly always list it last. We all know that zoos are recreational places; this is the real reason that fourteen million of us go to the zoo every year – to have a good day out. Yet fashionable opinion has taught us to be faintly ashamed of enjoying a zoo *too* much. We should not, we seem to believe, enjoy seeing animals deprived of their liberty. So zoos will often pretend that recreation is a subsidiary objective to all those noble ones.

Of course there is an element of humbug in this. Zoos have to survive, and unless they enjoy the patronage of a benevolent millionaire, they do it by offering us a good day out. Leaving aside all of the fringe attractions that a zoo can use to accomplish this – funfairs, discovery centres, camel rides, and so on – the real point at issue is the animal collection itself. Can this be made more attractive without compromising all those other ideals?

There is an old fashioned view which seems to hold that recreation and welfare are in conflict. Under this theory cages should not be too big otherwise they appear empty. Too many dens and hiding places conceal the animals from the paying public. Too large paddocks reduce the impact of herd animals to specks upon the horizon. Too little variety in the collection is unexciting for the visitor. Zoos that have been developed with this theory in mind tend to have large, diverse collections within small, simple enclosures. Let us call them Type 'A' zoos. They might include London, Bristol, Edinburgh, Glasgow, Colchester, Dudley.. to name only a few.

But then there is a second point of view, almost directly opposed to the first. We could call this the Type 'B' attitude, which believes that an enclosure designed to offer the most to the animal is intrinsically more interesting to the visitor. Never mind that the animals might be hidden or far away. They look freer, happier, and the experience of the zoo is fundamentally more optimistic and encouraging. Few zoos are really Type 'B'. Safari parks often try to be, and John Aspinall's zoos at Howletts and Port Lympne also tend strongly towards this view, to the extent that visitors will almost certainly never see a clouded leopard in any one of Howletts' numerous breeding enclosures: the animals just never emerge in daylight. A Type 'A' collection would shut at least one outside. If nothing else, it would prove they had one. At a Type 'B' zoo you need patience. They are not museums with exhibits on display. They are enclosed habitats, where, with luck, you might spot a wild animal.

So which strategy is right? Visitor statistics might suggest that the first is more successful; but the second surely represent the way that public opinion is moving. If this is correct, then the small city zoos have had their day, and the future lies with big estate zoos where, perhaps, binoculars will be loaned out at the gate as the best way to enjoy the day.

What does all this have to do with recreation? Well, ultimately the most enjoyable zoos are those which seem to care the most about their animals. This does not have to mean that the animals are all off-show; but it does mean healthy contented animals, not bored and listless ones. This guide judges the recreation value of zoos predominantly upon the satisfaction value of their animal collection. Yes, this does mean variety, but not variety at the expense of space, or at the expense of keeping animals in sensible numbers.

Of course there are many other ways in which zoos try to be recreational. There are several good zoos where you could easily imagine enjoying the walk even if there were no animals there at all. The Cotswold Wildlife Park you might enjoy for the trees and the parkland, Chester Zoo you might enjoy for the gardens, Dudley for the castle, or Port Lympne for the views and the house. Some zoos take recreation to an extreme, like the Chessington World of Adventures with its theme park setting. At others the animals are just one part of a whole package of entertainments, as at Longleat where you can lose yourself in the largest hedge maze in the world or visit one of England's historic houses. We may take account of these when we consider the recreation value of any zoo; but bear in mind that at this extreme the recreation is really rather peripheral to the zoo.

Some zoos have found imaginative ways of integrating recreation into the zoo, to add value to the visit. Jersey provides children with a climbing frame alongside the gorillas, to encourage them to copy the gorilla behaviour. Marwell has periscopes alongside the giraffes – to 'see the world from a giraffe's height'. Several zoos have miniature railways, and the best tend to be those that also provide a good view of the animals. Chester Zoo has a boat ride and a monorail. Dudley has a chair lift.

There is also a growing fashion for contact sessions with animals. London Zoo has regular meet-the-animals events in its open air marquee. Whipsnade and The Welsh Mountain Zoo have falconry displays. Most zoos with sealions make a big event out of feeding time, and Edinburgh Zoo, of course, has its penguin parade. All of these things enhance a day out at the zoo, and help to make it a more memorable event. So long as they do not unfairly exploit the animals, (and of course different people will interpret this in different ways), then they are helpful, educative, and yes, entertaining.

Zoos need to entertain. It need not conflict with their greater ideals. Good zoos become exciting and entertaining places to visit because their animals inspire awe and wonder, and because they help us to appreciate the animals with some variety, some beauty, some imagination. These are the elements we have looked for in the good zoos in this Guide.

Research

If a human being falls ill and visits a hospital, a whole host of experts will be at hand to treat his condition. The laboratory will know the normal ratio of red blood cells to white blood cells, will know the normal levels of sodium or calcium in the plasma, will know what microbes or parasites to look for. The physician will know what medicines to prescribe, and how much, and what outcome to expect. But what happens when a wallaby falls ill? Or a parrot, or a blue tongued skink? What might be normal for a mongoose lemur might be different for a Mayotte lemur. A bug that seems to have no effect upon an ocelot might kill a clouded leopard. Why?

And why do some animals breed so readily in captivity, while others seem so reticent? Does food have anything to do with it? Or is it design of cages? Or something else?

The gerenuk is a graceful long-necked gazelle from the arid thorn-bush regions of Eastern Africa. Zoos in America that kept gerenuk despaired of ever breeding them. Then it was discovered that the female gerenuk signals her receptivity to the male through a scent in her urine. In the wild, gerenuk are quite independent of water, and scarcely ever drink. The urine of a wild gerenuk is highly concentrated. Zoos, out of misplaced kindness, gave their animals plenty of fresh water. The result was a dilute urine far too feeble to attract the male. Once the problem was diagnosed, the solution was simple – take away the water and the animals should breed. They did.

There are literally thousands of lessons like this one, and countless more waiting to be learned. Some can be learned through sheer luck, some through years of trial and error, but most require the application of the scientific method – in short they require research. Veterinary surgeons need to know the normal haematology of penguins, curators need to know the social preferences of marmosets, the best diet for red pandas, or the best incubation temperatures for Bateleur eagle eggs.

Very few good zoos can afford to devote realistic sums of money towards defined programmes of research. But they can nonetheless encourage research in a number of ways. To begin with they could offer training to keepers in the scientific method, could encourage them to keep accurate records and observations of the behaviour, health, and growth of the animals in their charge, and could then offer them a medium in which to publish any significant findings. Jersey Zoo goes so far as to employ a large percentage of keepers with university degrees, and has an exhaustive record-keeping system that provides a historical record of everything that has happened to every animal – the detailed observations and outcome of every illness and treatment, how animals were sedated and moved, what they eat, how they behave towards one another, and so on. You never know what might prove to be useful. So record it all.

Good zoos share the information they gather. Some employ their own full-time veterinary staff, both to treat sick animals, and to study ways of maintaining animals in a healthy state. They support and solicit research from universities or research establishments nearby. Behavioural research is particularly suited to zoos. One way to measure how 'happy' zoo animals are is to study and compare their behaviour in the wild, and their behaviour in the zoo. If they are spending the same proportions of their time doing the same sort of things, then they are probably okay.

Just as zoos are undervalued as an educational resource, so they seem to be undervalued as a research resource. How can we understand our world if we fail so abysmally to understand the creatures that share it with us? Good zoos can, and should, do a lot more to help improve our understanding. They will benefit. The animals will benefit. Our great-grandchildren will benefit. And ultimately the planet will benefit.

Animal Welfare: Are Zoos Cruel?

The most common accusation levelled against zoos is one of cruelty. Is it cruel to keep animals in a zoo?

The RSPCA, guardian of the nation's conscience in these matters, is ambivalent in its attitude towards zoos. Officially it is neither pro-zoo, nor anti-zoo. Instead it claims to support good zoos and to oppose bad ones. Most zoo visitors are similarly even-minded about the issue. And yet the question is valid nonetheless. Is it possible that we have somehow become inured to the concept of animal captivity, in the same way perhaps as two centuries ago we might have accepted the concept of slavery, or as the Romans accepted the principle of human sacrifice as entertainment? Will future generations look back upon our own as barbaric because of our treatment of zoo animals?

Like so many of the issues that surround zoos, a lot depends upon your assessment of the extremes. Who, for example, would take offence at the sight of a well-fed Exmoor pony grazing in an acre field? Few people would see cruelty there. Yet who would not feel sorry for a tiger in a circus trailer, endlessly pacing before the bars. By understanding that there is a spectrum of possible conditions of captivity from national parks to battery pigs, and by appreciating that we all have a threshold beyond which we will point the finger and say 'that is cruel' – we can begin to delimit the types of zoos that we can accept. Of course there will be those will condemn even the captive moorland pony, and for them no zoo will ever meet with their satisfaction. There is nothing wrong with this attitude. It is a perfectly rational point of view, and those that hold it are genuine animal lovers with a real concern for animal welfare.

But most zoo keepers are genuine animal lovers too. They believe that animals in their charge are contented and as 'happy' as their wild relations. Certainly zoo animals do tend to live longer lives, to feed better, and to suffer from fewer parasites or diseases. They live without the fear of predation; they live without famine. And the freedom, that they also live without, is seen by people like Gerald Durrell as a purely human construct, largely irrelevant to the day to day lives of animals.

So how should we determine whether a zoo enclosure is cruel or not? Zoologists can try to assess how similar the behaviour of a captive animal is to a wild animal of the same species – but it does not necessarily follow that, for example, a wolf that sleeps all day in a zoo cage is less happy than a hungry wild wolf whose time is spent searching for food. Similarly it may be unreasonable to assume that animals are happiest in an environment that mimics their own wild habitat. John Knowles of Marwell Zoo theorises that animals like the scimitar-horned oryx, which normally pick out a meagre existence in the semi-desert scrubland of the Sahara, do so not because they choose or enjoy this harsh environment, but because they have been forced to the fringes by species better equipped to out-compete them elsewhere. According to this theory the scimitar-horned oryx should be in heaven among the lush meadows of Hampshire – as indeed they seem to be. The lions at zoos like Chester are offered the option every winter day of centrally heated accommodation, or the chill winds of Cheshire. They virtually always choose to brave the elements, even preferring ice and snow to the warmth indoors – a reminder perhaps that although we think of lions as tropical animals, they once roamed throughout Europe, and their current range is directly due to human intervention.

For the visitor, trying to assess cruelty is made all the more difficult because we do not always know, and cannot always see, what becomes of the animals at night when all the people have gone home. Very often this is when the real process of confinement takes place. Many zoo enclosures are designed primarily for daytime occupation, with the primary design requirement of the sleeping quarters being to separate animals and keep them from physical harm until the keepers return in the morning.

For years zoos have responded to accusations of cruelty by adopting a defensive attitude. They have used a 'we know best' approach, lecturing their visitors in an attempt to persuade us all to accept their definitions of what is cruel and what is not. But, Canute like, the tide has begun to engulf them. Public attitudes have changed faster than zoo cages. Cages that were hailed as liberating and progressive ten years ago are now seen by visitors as unacceptable. This is undoubtedly frustrating for the zoos, but if they are to survive they will have to understand that the customer is always right. They will have to learn to measure public attitudes and to keep their collections one step ahead of the moving window of public opinion. And in the end zoos ought to be prepared to accept that there may be species (like the dolphin perhaps, or the polar bear) for whom they cannot realistically recreate the fundamentals of life. If they wish to avoid accusations of cruelty then they will need to put their money where it can best be used, to help species that can best benefit with the best regard to welfare.

Part 2
Keeping animals in zoos and wildlife parks

Keeping animals in zoos and wildlife parks

There are more than 50,000 animals in British zoos, wildlife parks, bird gardens and aquaria, and Britain has more zoos open to the public than any other country, except for the United States. Within the international zoo community, British zoos are highly regarded. A great many innovations in zoo design, and in animal management techniques, began here.

Below, we consider some of the most important species that you can currently see in good British zoos. How are they faring? Are our zoos still setting standards for the rest of the world to follow, not only in animal welfare, but also in breeding and conserving endangered species? Is there more that we should be doing? Are we, perhaps, trying to do too much? There are no real answers, beyond simple opinions, and perhaps history alone will tell if our zoos succeed or fail. But there are some good signs, and there are some bad signs. Perhaps the success of zoos in Britain will depend upon which signs the zoos, and public opinion choose to follow.

Gorillas

Zoo conditions have changed dramatically for gorillas in recent years, as our understanding of their biology has developed. Gorillas were not described by science until 1847, and very few made their way alive to Britain for Victorian zoos to display. Since they were spared the centuries of barbaric exhibition suffered by chimpanzees and orang utans, the history of gorillas in zoos is quite well documented. At first it looked as if gorillas would never survive in zoos. The first five at London Zoo all died soon after their arrival, and the Council

Gorilla

of the Zoological Society determined for a while not to send for any more. After the first World War, however, the zoo did occasionally play host to a gorilla named John. He was the family pet of a Miss Alyse Cunningham, and he apparently shared her flat in Sloane Street, slept in a bed, went of his own accord to the bathroom, and lived as a Londoner for several years. He may have inspired the zoo to try again with gorillas. But apart from Miss Cunningham's several gorillas, contemporary accounts of the species in captivity unanimously record their nature as 'sullen, gloomy, ferocious, and quite untameable.'

In the years leading up to the second World War, scarcely one gorilla a year left Africa for Western zoos. After the war the trade began to increase. By 1954 there were 56 gorillas in Europe and America, and by 1960 there were 160. They were still perceived as being ferocious and sullen, and were always held in small, heavily barred cages, usually alone. The public image of the gorilla was still of a brutal, aggressive monster, not of a peaceful, sociable vegetarian, and zoo cages did nothing to correct this misunderstanding.

But now things are changing. Today there are around seventy gorillas in nine British zoos (all the Western Lowland subspecies), and two zoos in particular, Howletts Zoo and Jersey Zoo, have between them set new standards for the keeping of gorillas against which all other zoos must now be judged. The new standards arise from a simple but fundamental observation. Wild gorillas do not live alone. They live in large social groups. So why not keep them that way in a zoo? Howletts and Jersey tried it, and the sullen psychotic ape became once again the peaceful, gentle, browser. Howletts now keep around thirty- five gorillas in one large enclosure. It is little more than a huge caged gymnasium, its floor strewn deeply with straw. In this adventure-play-ground of a cage there is room for the whole range of social interactions that field workers observe in the wild. The huge silver-back males control the harem of females while the younger males vie for superiority. Baby gorillas are carried about by their mothers, and a gorilla birth is now a routine event at Howletts.

Gerald Durrell has created a similar social environment at Jersey in a large outdoor compound with steep, barrier walls within which the eight or more gorillas thrive under the watchful eye of the zoo's best known inhabitant, the huge but gentle 'Jambo'.

There is little doubt that the success of these two enclosures has blown a wind of change through many British zoos. Some like Chester have chosen to stop keeping gorillas, suddenly aware of the shortcomings of their housing. Others are attempting to copy one approach or the other. The new cage at Chessington is broadly similar to the Howletts cage, while the new £600,000 gorillarium at Port Lympne is a high-tech masterpiece, borrowing heavily from Howletts but adding a new dimension of height to the captive environment. And although few zoos have enough individuals for a genuine social troupe, the breeding successes now achieved with the species begin to make the future look promising.

Chimpanzees

There are over 150 chimpanzees in 30 British zoos. They are one of the 'staples' of the traditional zoo, and few zoos apart from safari parks and specialist collections have chosen not to have at least a pair on display. Chimpanzees have been held in various grim conditions in captivity for several centuries. London Zoo's first chimpanzee arrived in 1835, less than a decade after the zoo opened, and although neither that animal nor many of its numerous successors survived for more than a few months, the zoo continued to buy and display chimpanzees to the obvious appreciation of the public. The image of the chimpanzee became quickly established as playful and intelligent. 'Anyone who has seen a gorilla (and a chimpanzee) at the zoo will realise the intellectual difference,' wrote one naturalist. The director of London Zoo's aquarium, E. G. Boulenger, saw the chimpanzee as '.. more responsive to the demands of civilization than are certain tribes of savages that disport themselves to this day on the banks of the Amazon River.'

With such a press, captive chimps were always in great demand. Despite their appalling survival record, large sums of money were paid for them. London Zoo paid £300 for a young chimp in 1845. It lived for seven months.

In 1927 the new monkey house at London Zoo was opened, and hopes were raised for a an improvement in the survivability of chimpanzees, and perhaps even for a breeding success. The chimps did indeed live a little longer, but it wasn't until 1935 that the first baby chimp was born. Lessons were learned, and standards slowly improved. Ape houses became better designed. Cleanliness and hygiene improved. More distance (or glass) was placed between the chimps and the public to protect the animals from human diseases to which they are extremely prone, and the health and longevity of the chimpanzees gradually improved.

Today good zoos are continuing to improve their chimp accommodation.

Chimpanzee

Like gorillas, chimps are social animals and they should be kept in large social groups wherever possible. Zoos that have done this are rewarded not only by a real improvement in the psychological welfare of the chimps, but also in the exciting spectacle of a troupe of apes interacting with each other in very much the same way that they do in the wild. In social groups chimps can groom one another, they can play, they can fight, and they can learn a whole range of behaviours from one another. In particular, since a great many zoo chimps have been hand-reared by humans, hand-reared mothers can learn from other chimpanzee mothers how to raise their own young. In order to more closely mimic their wild behaviour, chimpanzees need a great deal of room to rush around, and a lot of three-dimensional space for climbing and swinging. Probably the only zoos to provide both in abundance are Chester, with its network of islands and its large indoor playground, Belfast with its huge outdoor compound, and Monkey World in Dorset. The latter acts as a rescue centre for chimpanzees confiscated from Spanish beach photographers and from research laboratories, and is releasing young chimps into a four-acre compound.

Other zoos are beginning to look closely at their chimp accommodation; close to Chester the Welsh Mountain Zoo opened a new chimp complex in 1990 and Colchester Zoo opened a spacious new house in 1991. Whipsnade's chimps now have a large outdoor area fenced only by electric fencing. With examples such as these there seems little doubt that captive conditions for these intelligent, social apes will continue to improve.

Orang utans

There are two subspecies of orang utan, one from Borneo and the other from Sumatra. Despite clear anatomical differences, the two will interbreed producing hybrid animals of neither one subspecies nor the other. Modern zoo management frowns, rightly, upon this sort of cross-breeding, and today both races are carefully managed in captivity, as their endangered status demands, to ensure true breeding, and a healthy mixing of genes.

Orang utan

Orang utan adults are solitary in the wild, although youngsters may be quite happily kept with parents for several years, and pairs seem to cope well together in captivity. However a solitary animal in a zoo should not necessarily be considered distressing. Possibly the most important provision to be made for orangs is sufficient climbing. In the wild these apes rarely descend from the trees. They are poorly adapted for walking on the ground, and are much more at home high up in the tree canopy. Tree stumps are not much good for them. Ropes and branches are more suitable, and zoos with orang utans that provide them have at once an entertaining and delightful exhibit of an endangered species that will almost certainly need effective captive breeding to ensure its continued survival.

Gibbons

Gibbons are apes, not monkeys. They are relatives of chimpanzees, gorillas, orang utans, and men. There are nine different species of gibbons and probably more than twenty subspecies, so that if the zoos of the world were doing their jobs properly then they would need to keep around twenty different self-sustaining populations just to be on the safe side.

Eight of the nine gibbon species are represented in the good zoos in this guide (only the hoolock gibbon is absent), although only the lar gibbon and the siamang are represented in reasonable numbers. Gibbons are a traditional exhibit in zoos, and when displayed well they can be superb. They are remarkable athletes, masters of a unique mode of locomotion called brachiation that involves swinging from arm to arm like trapeze artists with extraordinary speed and skill. Several zoos, among them London, Edinburgh, and Chessington keep gibbons in long aviary-like cages which show their abilities off to good effect. Paignton Zoo has pioneered the use of gibbon islands, and in the mild Devon climate they remain outdoors, sleeping in large nest boxes high in the trees. Britain's best gibbon collection, at Twycross Zoo, uses long (but not very tall) cages with indoor glass-fronted rooms. Twycross keeps seven species, and demonstrates its commitment by keeping numbers of young and non-breeding individuals to help sustain a good zoo population, even though gibbons are demanding of cage space, and are difficult to run together unless they are a family group or an established pair.

The largest of the gibbons is the siamang, a black woolly ape that uses its extended throat-sac to produce haunting warbling calls. Siamang are well represented at Howletts Zoo in excellent, well roped, rustic cages.

All of the gibbons are threatened by the rapid destruction of rainforests in South-East Asia. They are climax species which need vast areas of forest in which to survive, and as human population and commercial logging encroaches on the forests so the importance of good zoo management of these animals increases, with the hope of future reintroduction into the wild. Zoos are still a long way from this goal with most gibbon species, although the efforts of collections like Twycross and Howletts give some hope for the future.

Monkeys

When visitors to zoos are canvassed for their opinions, they usually admit to having enjoyed the monkeys most of all. Clearly this cannot apply to every zoo, since not every zoo keeps monkeys. Also, since many visitors wrongly consider chimpanzees, gibbons and orang utans to be monkeys, the poll is rather stripped of its validity. Nevertheless there is no doubt that monkeys are popular, and they are certainly entertaining. Probably it boils down to a combination of their comic resemblance to humankind, their acrobatic skills, and to the fact that they are almost always active while other zoo animals just seem to sleep in a corner.

Excluding the apes, there are an astonishing *one hundred and six* different species or subspecies of primates in British zoos. It is doubtful whether more than a handful of people could correctly identify them all on sight. They vary from the little pygmy marmoset and the fat-tailed dwarf lemur to the mandrill and the hamadryas baboon. They include several Red Data Book species, like the golden lion tamarin whose home in the Brazilian Atlantic Rainforest has been practically eliminated, the leaf-eating douc langur from South-East Asia which was almost exterminated by the effects of the recent wars, and the lion-tailed macaque from India which suffers from poaching and habitat destruction. There are also a great many common species. They include the familiar and the unfamiliar, like capuchins, squirrel monkeys, lemurs, bush babies, marmosets, colubus, patas monkeys, and macaques.

With such a variety, it is not altogether fair to generalise about the best zoo conditions for primates. There are bound to be exceptions to every rule. Nevertheless, there are some general things to look out for. Perhaps the most important factor with most (but not all) species is the social group. Most monkeys are social animals and they will suffer if kept alone or in very small groups. London Zoo has shown in the Sobell Pavilion how the welfare of the monkeys has improved with the expansion of the groups, and this principle is being adopted now by all good zoos.

Talapoin monkey

31

Most monkeys need heated indoor accommodation to help them cope with the British climate, and good zoos have a system of indoor and outdoor cages. Glass is a useful barrier now widely used on indoor rooms. Many monkeys can be kept on grass, and although it is rarely practical to keep monkeys in trees because they will strip both leaves and bark, this can be used to good effect with some species, as Banham Zoo has demonstrated on their squirrel monkey islands. Climbing is a crucial requirement, and generally the more climbing facilities available, the better. Height is a dimension often forgotten in designing monkey cages, and zoos that have constructed very high outdoor cages have discovered a way of dramatically increasing the space available for the monkeys without taking any more ground area. At the same time this allows visitors to observe monkeys from the same viewpoint that they would have on safari, by looking upwards.

Safari Parks were quick to discover that monkeys were a major attraction. Cars always linger longer in the monkey jungle than they do even among the lions. The species best suited are the ground-living monkeys, baboons and rhesus monkeys, and although many parks have had teething problems (some of the monkeys became rapidly adept at stripping cars of aerials, vinyl roofs, and wiper blades), the monkey troupes in Safari Parks have generally thrived well.

There is an obvious problem that British zoos will have to face soon. A hundred and six different types of monkeys will require concerted management if they are to survive for many more generations without the necessary importation of more individuals to bolster up the gene pools. With many species this is not a problem. Sufficient individuals already exist, at least for the time being. Other species that only exist in Britain in very low numbers, often at only a single collection, are quite clearly in jeopardy.

Cats

There are thirty five recognised species of cats and a whole host of subspecies or races. They range from the massive Siberian tiger (the largest recorded was a 348 Kg/ 845 lb male) down to the rusty spotted cat of Southern India and Sri Lanka which averages less than 1.5 kg / 3 lbs in weight. For this reason zoologists tend to talk about 'big cats' and 'small cats', and there is general agreement about which cat falls into which category.

There are seven big cats: lions (most zoo lions are African lions, but some zoos keep the endangered Asiatic lion), tigers (the most common of the seven surviving subspecies is the Indian or Bengal tiger, the rarest are the Javan tiger, the South Chinese tiger, and the Caspian tiger all of which may well now be extinct), leopards (there are seven sub species, all endangered), jaguars (eight sub species all vulnerable to extinction), snow leopards (endangered), cheetah (vulnerable), and the smallest of the 'big' cats, the clouded leopards (vulnerable).

Lions and tigers are among the staple 'nursery book' species at practically every zoo. Very few animals can arouse the same feelings of awe and majesty as these great beasts. Yet lions and tigers have often fared appallingly in zoos,

Tiger

have been kept in tiny, squalid cages, and have had little or no veterinary care. Much of their troubles came from their reputation, which understandable portrayed them as immensely powerful ruthless killers. Stories of animals like the Champawat man eater, a tigress who was reputed to have killed 438 people in eight years (and was finally shot by Jim Corbett in 1911) added to the grotesque fascination shown towards these animals.

Lions and tigers are much better treated today. Once zoos and safari parks had recognised that big cats did not need great iron bars to keep them out of harm's way, this lead to the provision of much more space. Chester Zoo was the first British zoo to make the radical, and at the time highly controversial, move of keeping lions behind chain-link fencing. The technique worked, despite the worst fears of its critics, and it started a move away from traditional cages towards today's open safari parks and moated lion dens.

Today it has been estimated that there are more lions per square mile in Britain than there are in Africa, and anyone who has visited Longleat and seen the huge prides that stalk the lion park will probably accept the truth of that statement. But it does illustrate a catch-22 of zoo conservation: in order to attract visitors an animal has to be well known and easily recognised (like lions); but to become well known the animal is likely to be common (unlike clouded leopards); and if the animal is common and breeds well then there is less justification for keeping huge numbers of them in captivity (like lions). The upshot of all this is that most zoos, good and bad, produce a surplus of animals like African lions, and in reality there is not enough room for them all. Most zoos will have to 'put down' its surplus animals from time to time. The tabloid newspapers may make a sensation of this, but in reality it is no different to our annual destruction of tens of thousands of unwanted puppies and kittens. In the end it may be the best management policy. What is more questionable, and harder to prove, is whether bad zoos deliberately breed lion cubs every spring as an attraction to visitors, only to destroy them at the end of the season once their usefulness is over. Good zoos protect against this by the old fashioned but reliable technique of contraception. But isn't it equally strange that even as we hear about the need for zoos to act as refuges for hundreds of disappearing species, so many British zoos have big cats who are neutered or on the pill.

33

Look out for some of the other big cats when you visit a zoo. The tables in Part 5 list some of the rarer or lesser seen cats. Consider rewarding a zoo with a visit if it keeps and breeds snow leopards (Marwell, Banham, and Port Lympne for example), or cheetah. Cheetah have been kept by man for possibly two thousand years. Arabs, Abyssinians, and Mogul emperors used cheetah to hunt antelope. And yet for centuries no cheetah was ever recorded as having cubs in captivity. In 1950 Professor Hediger of Zurich zoo declared that the cheetah was a 'non-breeder' in zoos. Not long after this, an Italian who owned a female cheetah as a pet, ignorant of the fact that captive cheetahs would never breed, took her to his local zoo to meet their male. She rewarded him with a cub. The mould had been broken, and zoos began to try to repeat the success. Now many zoos have bred cheetah, among them Philadelphia, Oklahoma, Toledo, and Longleat; but none have had the success of Whipsnade which has now bred well over one hundred and thirty cheetah. Their formula for success seems to depend upon their respect for the independent, solitary nature of the cheetah. The sexes are not introduced too often, the enclosures are well away from other species that might disturb them, and their dens are rarely cleaned out. Above all, Whipsnade has *dedicated* itself towards the breeding pro- gramme, unlike other zoos with cheetah which still seem resigned to their non-breeding status.

The small cats include some of the most delightful animals you will see in a zoo: animals like the delicate margay, the beautiful ocelot, the lithe jagua- rundi. Almost all the small cats have suffered as a result of the demand for their furs, and many are now vulnerable or endangered in the wild. Zoos could almost certainly play a useful role in holding a population of the smaller cats, but with so many species and so few individuals, the future of many in zoos is uncertain.

Elephants

Britain's first zoo elephant arrived in London in 1254. It was a present to Henry III from Louis IX of France. Crowds flocked from so many miles to see the amazing creature, which was housed in the Tower of London, that a special shelter had to be built to accommodate the sheer number of visitors. His popularity was matched a little over six hundred years later by London Zoo's 'Jumbo' who became such a huge attraction for Londoners that there was a great public outcry when he was sold to an American circus. But in spite of the popularity of elephants, and in spite of their almost domestic use in Asia, very few have ever been bred in captivity. There is one very good reason for this: very few zoos that keep elephants keep an adult bull. Of the sixty or seventy elephants in British zoos, less than ten percent are bulls. More than a dozen zoos keep Asian elephants, and only Port Lympne Zoo Park, Woburn Wild Animal Kingdom, Cricket St. Thomas, Belfast Zoo and Chester Zoo, keep adult bulls. Rather fewer zoos keep the larger and more difficult African elephant, and of these, only Howletts Zoo keeps adult bulls.

It is not as though the breeding of elephants is unreasonable or uneconomic.

The first zoo-bred elephant in Britain was a male, Jubilee, born at Chester Zoo in 1977. African Elephants have bred twice at Howletts Zoo in Kent. And at both zoos the resulting upturn in visitors reflected the great public interest in seeing a baby elephant. So given a pair of elephants, and good feeding, housing, and management, nature ought normally to take its course, and we all ought to be rewarded with the incomparable sight of baby elephants fairly regularly in British zoos.

So why does it not happen like that? The simple answer is that adult bull elephants are probably the most difficult and dangerous of all animals to keep. There is a saying among European zoos that for every calf born, a keeper has been killed. This may no longer be true, but the danger is very real all the same. It is essential therefore for any zoo that hopes to breed its elephants to provide a secure bull corral. Bull elephants, in the past, have broken out despite a variety of barriers, including deep moats and high fences. It is a tall order, perhaps, to expect every zoo that wants to keep elephants to have to cope with these problems. How much easier it would be for them, after all, just to keep cow elephants and to let other zoos take the risks. But good zoos should not allow themselves to fall into the trap of thinking like this. Either they should be making positive plans to keep both sexes, or they should be negotiating breeding loans with other zoos; or else, perhaps, they should, like Edinburgh Zoo or like Chessington, be deciding no longer to keep elephants at all.

African elephant

One incident that illustrates something of the difficulty of keeping adult bull elephants was the sad death of an amiable African Bull, Jumbolino, at Chester in 1976. Jumbolino died after being pushed by a matriarchal Asian cow elephant into a steep sided moat. Another death to occur in a similar way was the notorious death of Dixie at London Zoo. Where an elephant is able to fall into a moat and injure itself, perhaps fatally, then this type of barrier must be unacceptable. Elephants are such heavy animals that they can easily sustain serious fractures if they fall.

Better alternatives exist. Some collections use railings as barriers, and moats with a sloping approach could perhaps be used more often. Chester has replaced its inside moats with railings, and all of Aspinall's extensive accommodation at Howletts and Port Lympne is fenced. Electric fencing is used to good effect at many safari parks. But dangerous looking moats still exist at several major zoos. Elephants are intelligent, and emotional animals. They require companionship, sensitive handling, and plenty of space. Not all zoos can, or do, provide all three of these.

Where strong fences and crushes are used, a 'zero handling' policy can be employed. But some collections, favour building up a closer association between elephant and keeper with daily training and handling. Tame elephants can mean closer contact for the public. London's baby elephants are escorted around the zoo every day to meet the visitors. Colchester's baby African elephants put on a daily show. But there is another advantage for a zoo that trains its elephants. Zoos unable to keep a bull can more easily transport their females for mating. This is the plan for London's cow elephants. In Europe elephants are regularly sent to be mated at other zoos. Copenhagen's bull entertains cows from as far away as Basle in Switzerland. Today this technique is being adopted by British zoos. Chester's Jubilee is already playing host to cow elephants from other zoos, although he has yet to father his first calf. To sustain a population of around thirty of each species within British zoos would require no more than one or two calves to be born and reared each year. Surely this is an achievable target.

Rhinos

'If the rhino was clever enough to submit to man and do a job of work as a combined agricultural tractor and plough... there would be room for him. But he has a bad habit of charging blindly, so the only answer to him is a rifle-bullet.'

The quotation comes from a 1927 book, *The Zoo Unbarred* by L. G. Mainland of the Daily Mail. Has any animal suffered as much from the pig-headed ignorance of humans as the poor rhinoceros? In the Far East, millions still believe that rhino horn possesses magical medicinal qualities, and in North Yemen a rhino horn handle for a young man's dagger is still supposed to enhance his virility. So rhinos are hunted to within a whisker of extinction, and all the programs to 'Save the Rhino' become no more than valiant attempts to hold back the tide.

Can zoos help at all? To answer this we should first define the problem. There are five living species of rhinoceros (mankind has already dispatched a European and a North American rhino). **White rhinos** (the 'white' comes from the Dutch word for 'wide', referring to their wide lips) are fairly common in zoos. About half of Britain's good zoos keep them. Whipsnade has a magnificent herd that breed quite frequently. They are a herd animal, and already owe their existence to conservation management. At the beginning of this century the southern race of the white rhino was down to a few dozen animals, all in the Umfolozi Valley of Natal. Thanks to careful protection the descendants of that group make up most of the white rhinos on earth. The exceptions are the dozen or so northern white rhinos, now closely guarded in reserves, who are all that remain from a population of a thousand or more less than ten years ago.

Black rhinos (with narrow lips) are now far more threatened. Their population has fallen from twenty thousand to less than six thousand in a decade. They are solitary animals and have never bred particularly well in zoos. In fact their captive population has been slowly falling as their death rate has exceeded their birth rate. But research and careful management may halt this decline. Four good zoos keep black rhinos. They are London, Whipsnade, Chester, and Port Lympne. Recently two black rhino calves, both female, were born in London and in Chester.

Great Indian rhinos, once common in northern India and Nepal, are now restricted to small populations in forest reserves. Their decline has been halted, and now like so many wild species their future depends upon continued political stability in their countries of origin. There are very few in European zoos, and only four in Britain (three at Whipsnade – a pair and their female calf – and an older, now fully-grown calf at Chester). Nevertheless the species seems to breed readily in captivity, and there is good reason to expect a safe reservoir population will become established in zoos.

Until very recently you would have had to explore the forests of Indonesia if you ever wished to see a **woolly rhinoceros**. There is a record of a female woolly (or 'Sumatran') rhino arriving in London Zoo in 1872 (she lived for thirty three more years); and a second was held at Calcutta Zoo in 1889. The only animal you could perhaps have seen since was a male who died at Copenhagen Zoo in 1972. With a world population numbered only in the hundreds, scattered in upland forests in Malaya, Thailand, Borneo and Sumatra, this the smallest of the living rhinos has been little known, and rarely seen or photographed. But on Friday 24th May 1985 a historic agreement was signed in Jakarta by officials of John Aspinall's zoos (the Howletts and Port Lympne Foundation) and the Indonesian government, for a project to conserve the Sumatran rhino. The project centred around 'doomed' rhinos – animals in isolated forests due to be felled for agriculture. A grim fate normally awaits such animals, but Aspinall's plan was to capture all the doomed rhinos and

White rhino

place them in breeding colonies in Indonesia and in Britain. So it was that in April 1986 a young male woolly rhino, 'Torgamba', arrived at Port Lympne Zoo in Kent. It is doubtful whether any zoo animal has ever been so cosseted. While a permanent twelve acre enclosure was being prepared, Torgamba, and a mate that arrived in August 1986, were kept at a private farm with their own heated swimming pools, luxurious mud baths, and sun ray lamps. They were fed upon three buckets of exotic fruits a day (flown in twice a week at a cost of £1,000 a time), and even their fresh hay was dipped in pineapple juice to make it more accept-

37

Black rhino

able. Branches were cut for them from a carefully tended, unsprayed woodland: deep wood-chippings were provided to mimic the forest floor, and the animals were watched and cared for twenty four hours a day. The rhinos became immediately tame, and greatly loved by their keepers. Today visitors have a chance to see these unique beautiful animals for the first time in Britain since 1905. If they breed, and there is every chance that they will, then it will be a first for the species in any zoo, and may well herald a safer future for one of the world's most endangered mammals.

The fifth, and most endangered species of rhino is the **Javan rhino**. There are perhaps fifty surviving individuals in the Udjung-Kulon reserve in Java, and a smaller number in the Leuser reserve in Sumatra. There are no Javan rhinos in any of the world's zoos.

A controversy surrounds the recommendation of American zoologist, Dr Ulysses Seal, that twenty rhinos should be captured from Udjung-Kulon and brought into captivity. Seal argues that without captive management, there is only one direction that the Javan rhino population can go, and that is towards extinction. His critics counter, with some justification, that no one knows if the rhinos will breed in captivity, no one knows how to keep and manage them, and no one knows how to capture them in the first place. If zoos could fund a compromise project to capture a single pair and keep them locally to put these reservations to the test, then this might help support a decision in one direction or another. It might also demonstrate the good intentions of the zoos. The worst decision would be one made purely for political or financial reasons.

The cruel contrast between mankind's ignorant, systematic extermination of rhinos, and the gentle nature of the animals themselves is very obvious when you see them well kept in a zoo. Zoo rhinos tend to become tame and affectionate. They will often allow visitors to reach across the barriers and scratch them, and they always develop a very close bond with their keepers. Rhinos, like gorillas, are misunderstood, gentle giants. If good zoos can help to save them, then they deserve our support.

Small mammals

Several zoos have small mammal houses, or some accommodation to exhibit just a few rodents or bushbabies or fruit bats to balance their collection a little.

Of course if zoos were really representative of the animal kingdom as a whole then a quarter of all their mammals would be bats and a third would be rodents but this is clearly not the case. Perhaps this illustrates something of the selective nature of the type of conservation work that zoos can do. It isn't only zoos that are guilty of this though. We all value African elephants more than we value kangaroo rats or hutias, and perhaps we are right to do so. But it does mean that there are probably dozens of endangered rodents and bats whose plight we are quite unaware of.

Another feature of the small mammals in zoos is the fact that so many of them crop up at just one collection. Take a look at the table on pp. 000-00 and see how few zoos keep small mammal species in any numbers. As an example you can see that out of twenty-four zoo exhibits of rats and mice, seventeen are at London Zoo. In fact London is the only good zoo that can seriously claim to specialise in small mammals (along with a lot of other things of course), and London's small mammal house is an experience in itself.

Many small mammals are nocturnal, and zoos have discovered what a good exhibit they can be if they are kept in nocturnal houses with day and night reversed. Almost without exception the animals are kept behind glass, and in some cases, like London again, even the burrows are half-glassed so that you can see the animals asleep 'underground'. It is a pity that so few zoos take rats and mice, squirrels, and bats seriously. They do deserve our attention, and Jersey Zoo has shown with its Jamaican hutias and volcano rabbits that real conservation work can be undertaken with even the most unlikely little creatures.

Grazing mammals

There are seventeen deer species grazing in Britain's good zoos, forty-two antelopes, and various other hoofed animals like camels, giraffes, pigs, and horses. They include some of the rarest and most endangered animals on earth. The Red Book of Endangered Species includes Grevy's zebra and Hartmann's mountain zebra, Przewalski's horse, the Malayan tapir, babirusa, vicugna, Formosan sika deer, addax, Barbary sheep, dama gazelle, lechwe, gaur, anoa, Arabian and scimitar-horned oryx, and markhor all on the endangered list. They are all present in British zoos, and most of them are doing fairly well.

In many ways zoos are in a good position to serve the grazing animals. For a start these animals are always likely to be at some risk in the wild because the majority of them are edible, and many of then are prized by hunters who still like to prove their prowess by gunning down a deer. Secondly, they are relatively easy for zoos to accommodate. You don't need too many purpose-built concrete edifices to house a herd of deer, just a spacious field, and some rudimentary stabling. Most (but not all) species fare better in a herd, often the larger the better, and although there are veterinary problems that many species encounter, in general the management problems that grazing animals present tend to be issues like what to do with surplus males.

British good zoos have a long and enviable reputation for their keeping of

Scimitar oryx

hoofed animals. Père David's deer were rescued from extinction by the eleventh Duke of Bedford in his deer park at Woburn and have since been sent back to a reserve in China by Woburn, Whipsnade and Chester Zoos; scimitar-horned oryx were bred and reintroduced into the wild by Marwell, Whipsnade and Edinburgh Zoos; London and Marwell cooperated with American Zoos on the project to breed and reintroduce Arabian oryx to the wild in Jordan; and several zoos are now looking at the possibility of sending Prezwalski's horses back to Mongolia. The record of cooperation is encouraging, and gives hope not only for future reintroduction projects with hoofed mammals, but with every other group of animals as well.

Zoos that specialise in grazing mammals will usually be spacious, and will keep large and healthy herds. Look out for them particularly at Whipsnade, Marwell, Howletts, Port Lympne, Edinburgh, Chester, the Cotswold Wildlife Park, and the safari parks, among others.

Dogs and other carnivores

'The Carnivores' are a related group of animals which include all of the cats, large and small, the bears, the dog family (which includes jackals, coyotes, foxes, and wolves) the raccoon family (which includes the pandas even though these are not carnivorous animals), the weasel family, the civet family (which includes genets, meerkats and mongooses), and the hyaenas.

The largest member of the dog family are the wolves, and the commonest species, the grey wolf, can often be seen in zoos. Up to thirty two subspecies or races of the grey wolf have been described, and it is likely that most zoo wolves in Britain are something of a mixture of the various races. Sadly not one British zoo keeps pure European wolves. Wolves live in packs and ought really to be kept in packs in captivity. Good zoos, like Port Lympne, Whipsnade and the Highland Wildlife Park will have a wolf wood, plenty of space, a

Maned wolf

healthy group of animals, and the wolves will look well and breed well. This requirement does mean that any zoo contemplating keeping wolves really needs to have a good sized wood to begin with; either that or they need to plant a wood, which does mean planning for the wolves rather a long time in advance.

Maned wolves are not wolves at all, and they look, as one zoo describes them, like 'a red fox on stilts'. They are South America's largest member of the dog family, and are little known, and rarely seen. Their wild population is now vulnerable, and the captive population is frail. Eighty percent of captive and wild maned wolves suffer from a genetic disease, cystinuria, and in addition they are susceptible to the common diseases of domestic dogs. Several British zoos now keep them, and Marwell Zoo has successfully bred them. This is a species that is secretive, and you may have to be patient to see them. They will need careful management in zoos if their numbers are to grow.

African hunting dogs are no relation to domestic dogs, despite their name and appearance. They are one of the most critically threatened species of carnivore, and can breed well in zoos, although not many British zoos yet keep them. Good groups are kept at Marwell and at Port Lympne.

Several species of foxes are kept in British collections, although surprisingly few of our native red fox (except at Highland Wildlfe Park and Norfolk Wildlife Park). Some foxes, like the Arctic fox, seem to do very well in zoos, and they make popular exhibits.

Other, smaller carnivores in zoos vary from the familiar, like raccoons, otters, and mongooses, to the less familiar red pandas, coatis, martens, and honey badgers, and the practically unknown cacomistles, kinkajous, linsangs, zorillas, and wolverines. They are often very entertaining animals in zoos, and although few have any particular conservation value, many are now fairly self sustaining in captivity.

Bears

The image of the captive bear, chained by the ankle, muzzled and teetering on two legs for the pleasure of the crowd, is one that seems to be ingrained in our collective memories. Bears have been captured and made to perform since the

41

days when the brown bear shared most of Europe with us. British bears were often trapped for the circuses in ancient Rome, and for most of recorded history the bear has been a popular animal only so long as it was chained and humiliated, and unpopular enough to slaughter wherever it roamed wild.

Has anything changed? Critics of circuses and zoos would argue not. Bears are still rather shabbily treated in many collections, are often kept in pits or concrete cells totally unsuited to their behavioural demands. It seems that many zoos are still prejudiced by the incarnation of the performing bear rather than by the wild, magnificent animal.

Several species of bears are kept in British zoos. Sadly the European brown bear is now rarely seen, although some zoos have the North American brown bear, and some keep hybrid bears whose subspecific origin is no longer really known. The Asiatic black bear, recognisable by the cream coloured v-shape on its chest, and the South American spectacled bear with its notable face markings are also kept in several zoos. All these bears are essentially forest dwelling omnivores. They need room to roam, trees to climb, pools to swim, caves to hide in. Whipsnade and Glasgow probably come the closest of the traditional zoos to providing such enclosures, although some of the safari parks, like Woburn provide splendid wooded areas where the bears seem totally at home, and where they are a pleasure to watch.

In 1988 there were eighteen polar bears in United Kingdom zoos. Today there are ten (two adults and two recent cubs at Edinburgh, a single male at Chester, two at Chessington and three at Belfast). Nina and Misha, the two bears who once drew huge crowds at Bristol Zoo, were put down in January 1992. Ten bears is a small number when compared to the the world captive population of more than 400, but nonetheless British zoos have come under more attack for their keeping of polar bears than of any other animal. Polar bears are the largest terrestrial carnivores. Their wild status is classified as

Polar bear

42

Vulnerable, and although bans on commercial hunting have led to an increase in the wild population, a good case can still be made for keeping a reservoir population in captivity. Unfortunately, British zoos do not have a good record of breeding this species, or of raising young bears to adulthood.

Several factors are believed to be important in breeding polar bears. They need a small dark den which will mimic the maternity den that a wild she-bear will dig in the snow. Not every zoo provides such a den. Once cubs are born they must be completely undisturbed. A disturbed mother may kill her cubs. There has been a suggestion, that British winter temperatures may not fall low enough to encourage breeding, but more important may be a period of fasting to correspond with a similar period experienced by a wild she-bear.

There have been polar bears born in British zoos; Edinburgh Zoo has made considerable capital out of its recent 'Wee Sweetie' and its most recent cub was born in 1992; but an average of around one bear a year needs to be born and raised to sustain existing numbers. At present this is not being achieved.

Another problem experienced by many zoos is the stereotypic pacing and head-weaving displayed by several bears. This type of behaviour is distressing to watch, and although it does little for the reputation of zoos to keep animals that behave in this way, few zoos seem to have any idea how it might be avoided. The problem does seem to be more prevalent in bears that are born or kept in a pit, and it may be associated with the frustrated desire to look out. There has been a recent suggestion that the problem might relate to toothache; or it may be simply due to boredom, and there is no doubt that most polar bear enclosures are small and dull when compared to the cages of other large carnivores.

Polar bears were once among the most popular animals in British zoos. Today they are increasingly seen by the zoos themselves as an embarrassment, and it seems likely that by the end of the century there may be none left in Britain. This has been a notable victory for Zoo Check, who first drew attention to the plight of the bears. Disappointingly, no zoos have tried to introduce radical new accommodation for the bears – although there are plans for a possible Artic exhibit at London Zoo. So, given our poor record with these bears, their departure must be a welcome one.

Aquatic mammals

Aquatic mammals in zoos are not a distinct zoological group, but might include the 'real' aquatic mammals, whales and dolphins, as well as 'swimming mammals' like seals and sealions, otters, and rodents such as beavers, coypus, and capybaras. Other mammals that might sometimes be thought of aquatic could include hippopotamuses, tapirs, and even water buffalos, or polar bears. Clearly there are difficulties in generalising about a group of animals this diverse.

Dolphins and whales

Dolphins and whales are a group of animals that attract a great deal of controversy whenever they are kept in zoos. Today the only good zoo in this guide to exhibit them is Windsor. In recent years Whipsnade, Knowsley, Woburn and the West Midland Safari Park have all relinquished their dolphin exhibits. Conservationists object to the principle of keeping animals which show very little chance of breeding in small pools, and which often involve hazards to the animals in capture from the wild. The severest critics of dolphinaria in recent years have been organisations like Greenpeace and the Whale and Dolphin Conservation Society. They have pointed out that the life expectancy of captive dolphins is less than seven years, compared to thirty years or more in the wild. They draw attention to the dramatic difference between the freedom and space of the open seas, and the cramped limitations of a tiled pool. Dolphins and whales live in a sonic environment, communicating and navigating with clicks and whistles and echo-location. What a harsh and sterile and featureless environment the best of zoo pools must be to such an animal when compared to the open oceans. Dolphins and whales are intelligent, sensitive, social animals. Hundreds of them are still captured from the seas every year for Sea Worlds and Dolphinaria all around the world, and the survival rate of captured dolphins is pitifully low. The most unfortunate asset that the dolphin possesses, the conservationists say, is its smile. It is not a human smile, despite its appearance, and it creates the impression of a happy, contented animal. The truth may be very different.

Britain, however, is no longer a significant consumer of wild dolphins. A recent government report drew up new guidelines demanding deeper and wider pools wherever dolphins are kept, and the investment that this entails is only being met at Windsor. Zoos with dolphins assert that their animals are ambassadors for their species in the wild, and few people can fail to be moved by the almost unbelievable skill and intelligence of dolphins in a dolphin show. Not everyone is convinced, however, and controversy about the morality or otherwise of keeping captive dolphins is bound to continue. Some European and American zoos have succeeded in breeding and rearing dolphins in large pools, and this includes Windsor Safari Park where the Atlantic bottle nosed dolphins have bred several times since 1984.

Killer whale

Seals and sealions

With the move away from dolphins, some zoos and safari parks have brought in sealions to fill their empty pools. Like dolphins sealions can be trained to perform for the crowds. Two points of view seem to be held about the best way to keep and display sealions. The more traditional zoos believe that both sealions and visitors prefer regular circus shows – balancing balls, performing handstands, and barking for fish. They will argue that the sealions clearly enjoy the shows, and can sometimes point to breeding successes to justify their attitude. Zoos that have taken this approach include the Welsh Mountain Zoo and most of the safari parks.

Other zoos prefer untrained sealions, in family groups. Zoos that have taken this approach, like Chester, Blackpool, London, and Edinburgh, also end up with an enormously entertaining exhibit, particularly if the sealions have a large, deep, landscaped pool. The attraction at these zoos comes from the natural activity and boisterous interaction of the sealions. Family groups in large pools can be used at feeding time, to give an entertaining display, and this type of 'sealion encounter' can often teach us more about the biology and behaviour of the animals than any number of circus tricks will ever do.

Perhaps, however, each school of thought could learn from the other. A live commentary at feeding time could enhance the experience at some zoos, while zoos that keep performing sealions could benefit from enlarged pools, and natural beaches.

There are around fifty California sealions and a dozen Patagonian sealions in British Zoos. Only one or two of each species are born and reared every year, probably not enough to maintain the current zoo population. To breed sealions successfully a zoo really needs a quiet breeding beach, and offshow pens with some means of separating the adults. Good zoos are now cooperating in a management scheme for sealions which aims to improve the breeding successes by the sensible grouping of animals at good facilities.

Other swimmers

Mammals and birds that swim have the potential to be exciting, dynamic, zoo exhibits. But although many zoos have underwater viewing for their penguin pools, this idea is not often copied for their swimming mammals. In fact, many zoo enclosures rather under-value the swimming behaviour of animals like tapirs, capybaras, or even talapoin monkeys. Large bodies of water in an enclosure can be difficult and often expensive to maintain in a clean and safe way, and many zoos tackle this problem in a rather half-hearted way. Pools are often either too small, or make very little provision for effective viewing.

Birds

There are well over a hundred places in Britain where you can see captive birds. They include almost all the zoos, as well as scores of bird gardens, parks, country homes, and specialist collections. Between them they hold well over a thousand species and subspecies of birds (the National Federation of Zoologi-

Scarlet macaw

cal Gardens lists 1,005 species among its member zoos). Altogether there are probably more than 35,000 individual birds in collections in Britain – a fairly substantial number. Less than half of the species breed regularly, which means that many of the remaining five hundred species will probably rely upon wild caught birds to sustain their numbers in captivity. This may be a disheartening statistic, but it conceals the fact that most of the species that *do* breed, breed well; and things are improving for many of the rest.

Britain's best known bird collections are the various centres of the Wildfowl and Wetlands Trust which keep the best and most complete collections of waterfowl in the world. The Trust's centre at Slimbridge in Gloucestershire is the only place on Earth where you can see all six species of flamingo (four breeding well). The Trust also provides essential protected wintering areas for vast numbers of migrating waterfowl in Britain, and their work with endangered species – captive breeding and reintroducing birds into the wild – has been hugely successful, and highly influential.

Other specialist collections in Britain include several falconry centres which breed birds of prey. They will usually mount falconry displays for visitors, and several have put their falconry techniques to good effect in reintroduction programmes. A number of bird gardens have large and successful collections of tropical birds. Among the best are the World Pheasant Association collection at Childe Beale near Reading, Bird World at Farnham in Surrey, Harewood Bird Gardens near Leeds, and Paradise Park at Hale in Cornwall.

Critics of zoos will often make an exception for places like Slimbridge and Childe Beale. Yet these are just as much zoos in the strict dictionary definition, as places like Bristol or London Zoos; and although we have chosen not to include specialist bird collections in this guide, this is not to overlook their growing importance in conservation.

Parrots

Birds have always been important exhibits in zoos, and traditionally the more showy and brilliant the plumage, the better the exhibit, so far as zoo directors were concerned. Other birds that have found favour in zoos have often been those with 'anthropomorphic' features – birds that strut or shuffle around on two legs like cranes or storks or penguins; birds that have huge forward-facing eyes like owls; and birds that can actually talk, like parrots and mynahs. These have all become regular exhibits in zoos, and none more so than the parrots which seem to combine everything that a zoo visitor wants to see. Yet parrots worldwide are now an alarmingly threatened group of birds, and ironically their very attractiveness is often the cause of their decline as trappers mine the forest populations to satisfy the desires of collectors. Over 150 parrot species are kept in Britain, many in populations only in single figures; and although many, like the macaws, breed well, others like the African grey parrot are dreadfully difficult to breed. Good zoos will need to pay more attention to the breeding of their parrots; at present it is often easier and cheaper just to buy parrots from a dealer, but no zoo should keep animals that it cannot hope to breed.

Waterfowl and flamingos

Every public park has its duck pond, often with an assortment of ducks for the public to admire and feed. In zoos waterfowl are popular exhibits, helped by the fact that a number of different and colourful species can all be kept on the same pond, and they can often be used to fill in vacant corners and empty aviaries. In order to breed waterfowl however, a degree of commitment is necessary. Many duck species will interbreed, so these species often need to be aviary bred. Geese often need a large pen for each pair in order to form pair bonds, and nest rearing is often so difficult to manage that it is usually easier to incubate the eggs and hand-rear the chicks. This requires trained staff and good equipment – more than many zoos might have.

A number of zoos devote space to endangered waterfowl. Jersey Zoo has bred Meller's duck (an endangered mallard from Madagascar), and white winged woodduck from S. E. Asia, and waterfowl form an important part of the collection at London, Chester, and Cricket St Thomas, among others.

Only in recent years have flamingos been kept in the sort of single species flocks that now seem to prevail at many zoos. Most zoos are now making real efforts to provide nesting areas, and to adjust their flocks to the best sex ratios and age structures. Flamingos will rarely lay eggs in small flocks, and some

Scarlet ibises

47

zoos are experimenting with mirrors to create the illusion of a larger flock. Unless such flocks are built up, the chances of establishing sustaining populations in Britain seem unlikely.

Tropical birds

Large free flight bird houses feature in many of the good zoos. At Chester a huge tropical house contains palms, ponds and waterfalls, and is home to weaver birds and brightly coloured starlings. There are good tropical bird houses at Cricket St Thomas, London, Bristol, and the Cotswold Wildlife Park, and a whole host of birds, toucans and hornbills, tanagers, pittas, quetzels, and sometimes even humming birds and sun birds on display. The delicacy and desirability of tropical birds has always meant large and often illegal importations of birds, and although good zoos are now more selective about the birds they keep, they do often benefit indirectly from the illegal trade when birds are deposited with them by H. M. Customs. There are to date very few sustained breeding schemes for popular tropical birds other than some parrots and pheasants, and zoos would do well to address this, not only for the benefit of the birds, but also to keep their bird houses well stocked up into the next century.

Birds of prey

There are one hundred and nine different species of hawks, falcons, eagles, vultures, owls, and other birds of prey in British zoos; but despite some large impressive aviaries, not many collections are successful in hatching and rearing birds of prey. London and Chester have had some recent success with Andean condors due to a dedicated programme of incubation and hand rearing, but most of the smaller species, and even the owls often breed best in secluded aviaries, out of sight of humans and other birds. This tends to mean that specialist collections have much more success in breeding raptors than the zoos, who cannot provide this sort of accommodation.

Some zoos now mount falconry displays, and these can be both entertaining

Eagle

Penguin

and educational, particularly shows like Whipsnade's which includes naturalistic behaviour and a well informed commentary.

Penguins

Most zoos keep penguins, but not many zoos keep them well. Like most of the birds in zoos, a substantial degree of commitment is needed to breed penguins. Humboldt's penguins, for example, need sandy burrows to lay their eggs, and a quiet off-show area to rear the chicks. Hand rearing of young chicks is often essential because although wild birds will feed their young fish from their crops, it is difficult in zoos to repeat this. This is because without the long swim and walk back from the sea, the fish does not have long enough to predigest. Where zoos are committed to breeding, they can be very successful. Chester Zoo, Penscynor, and Whipsnade hatch about sixty chicks a year between them; but few of the remaining zoos with Humboldt's penguins manage to rear any.

Of the more rarely seen penguins in zoos, nowhere has more success than Edinburgh Zoo which annually hatches around thirty gentoos and usually a small clutch of rockhoppers and king penguins. Edinburgh Zoo's new penguin pool, opened in 1992, is probably the best place to see penguins in Europe.

Reptiles and fish

No one can be really sure how many different species of reptiles or fish there are in British zoos. In both cases the largest collections are at London Zoo which at any one time has around a hundred different reptiles, and almost two hundred different fish. Chester Zoo comes a close second in both categories with 62 reptile species, and 163 fish. Both zoos have fairly traditional aquariums and reptile accommodation, but both are making a very good effort to

Nile crocodile

49

Python

breed the reptiles in particular. This is important because both groups of animals tend to be largely ignored when zoos publish or discuss their breeding successes and failures. A great many reptile and fish species, probably well over three quarters, never breed at all, and their zoo populations are often bolstered, ironically, by illegally imported animals, confiscated and donated to the zoos by HM Customs.

Undoubtedly the best reptile collection, so far as breeding success is concerned, is Jersey Zoo which devotes considerable effort to hatching and rearing a whole variety of endangered snakes, lizards, and tortoises. There are also good collections at Edinburgh, Colchester, the Cotswold Wildlife Park, Dudley Zoo, the Welsh Mountain Zoo, Glasgow Zoo, and Paignton Zoo. Look out for signs that indicate that the animals are breeding.

Part 3
The Good Zoo Guide
Star-Ratings

The Good Zoo Guide Star Ratings

How do you compare a huge urban zoo like London Zoo with a Safari Park like Longleat? Or how would you rate a small children's zoo like Drusillas in comparison with a huge estate like Port Lympne? Whatever yardsticks you may devise, in the end there has to be a generous helping of subjectivity. Some zoos are pleasant places to visit. Others are not. One zoo might create a bad impression with small pokey cages, and another with litter-strewn pathways. One distressing exhibit might destroy the positive appeal of a dozen good ones, while one outstanding exhibit might encourage a disregard for less acceptable parts of a collection.

And what about the question of conservation? A spacious and beautiful zoo might keep nothing more significant than llamas and wallabies, while another, less beautiful, concentrates upon rarer and more endangered species. So, since this is a guide after all, and a guide should allow some measure of discrimination, how should we decide which zoos to include, and which to exclude? And how should we indicate our own preferences among the chosen zoos?

The Zoos in the Good Zoo Guide

There are a great many licensed animal collections in this country, not all of which bear the name 'zoo', but many of which belong within the dictionary definition of a zoo (a place where wild animals are kept for exhibition and study). This definition implicitly rules out private collections where the public are not admitted. For the purposes of this guide we have made two more quite fundamental distinctions:

The first is to limit the scope of the Good Zoo Guide to 'responsible' collections, and as a measure of responsibility we include collections that either belong to the National Federation of Zoological Gardens of Great Britain or who annually submit details to The International Zoo Yearbook. Many zoos, of course, qualify on both counts.

The second distinction is to include only mammal collections. There are several excellent 'bird zoos' in Great Britain where the majority of the occupants are captive birds. They include the establishments run by the Wildfowl and Wetlands Trust at Slimbridge in Gloucestershire, at Martin Mere in Lancashire, at Washington, Tyne and Wear, and at Arundel in Sussex. They also include a number of very good bird gardens, such as Bird World at Farnham, and specialist collections like the Hawk Conservancy at Weyhill in Hampshire. This criterion for exclusion also covers aquariums and vivaria for the same reasons. Despite the fact that these collections are undoubtedly zoos within the strict dictionary definition, we cannot help feeling that most visitors do not see them as zoos, but understand the role they play in the captive breeding of non- mammal species. We have chosen not to consider them as zoos. We do, however, consider safari parks, wildlife parks, urban zoos, and country estate zoos. All of these are zoos, and we do not distinguish between them.

So, having established which places qualify for inclusion, the questions that we have asked ourselves for each may be summarised as follows:

- What animals does the zoo keep? Are they of conservation value? Does the zoo represent a genuine conservation resource?

- How many animals of each species does the zoo hold? Does the zoo attempt to keep significant numbers of each species, or are they predominantly kept in twos or threes?

- How well housed are the animals? Is their welfare fully considered? Do they have sufficient space? Is the space appropriate to their behaviour?

- How well are the animals breeding?

- How dedicated does the zoo appear to be to the 'less visible' aims of education and research? Is there an education department? Are there good interpretive signs on the enclosures? Is there an inexpensive and informative guide book?

- What sort of day-out does the zoo represent? Is it an attractive and pleasant place to visit? Are there clean cafeterias, playgrounds, shops and toilets? Are there well tended gardens? Is it tidy? What additional facilities has the zoo provided for the benefit of visitors?

- Does the zoo offer good value for money?

These are all questions that visitors may ask themselves when they visit a zoo. Obviously, the answers given will vary considerably with individual judgment, with subjective feelings about zoos in general, and with changing years and even seasons. To give an idea of our own impressions, we have awarded from one star (unimpressive) to four stars (the best) under each of the following categories:

Conservation.
A measure of the commitment of a zoo towards its role as a conservation resource. A maximum of four stars are awarded to zoos who concentrate their efforts upon Red Data Book species, who keep species in appropriate numbers for maximum breeding successes, and who co-operate in national and international schemes for species preservation. Good zoos see conservation as their primary role.

Enclosures
A measure of the emphasis placed upon animal welfare by the zoo. Good zoos house their animals in spacious enclosures, with housing designed around the behavioural needs of each species. Social animals are kept in groups. Solitary animals are kept alone. There are veterinary facilities on site. The animals are in excellent health, they are happy, they show no signs of stereotypic behaviour or of boredom. A large percentage of the species kept breed regularly. No animals are kept in inadequate or distressing accommodation. Diets are appropriate and carefully regulated. Good zoos are well staffed, and enclosures are clean.

53

Education

A measure of the zoo's commitment towards its duty to educate. Many good zoos have an education department with qualified teachers and a classroom or interpretational centre. They produce educational material and promote a full range of educational tours to schools and colleges from a primary level to degree level. All enclosures are clearly labelled with the common and scientific names of the species, and further information of interest is provided. A clear and comprehensive guidebook is available with background information about the major species or animal groups kept.

Recreation

A measure of how good the zoo is as a outing. Good zoos offer an unforgettable day-out to casual visitors, families, and enthusiasts. They are attractive, clean, friendly places. They make the very best of their location, and provide all the little extras that make a visit to the zoo so special; train rides or boat rides, playgrounds, shops, cafes, picnic areas, gardens and so on. The side-shows do not overwhelm the zoo, but the variation they provide avoids the danger of a visit becoming boring, and caters for the energies of children. In many instances the recreational provisions will be educational, associated in some way with the animal collection. This category also takes account of the way that enclosures have been designed for the benefit of visitors, to allow optimum viewing without adversely affecting the animals.

Research

A measure of the efforts that zoos are making to learn from the animals they keep, and to publish their findings for the benefit of other zoos and ultimately for the animals themselves. Good zoos carry out non-invasive research designed to improve our understanding of animal behaviour, physiology and reproduction. The fruits of this research will help other zoos improve their success in breeding, and will improve standards of animal husbandry. Even when zoos do not employ dedicated research staff, good zoos are anxious to share the lessons they have learned with other zoos.

Part 4
The Good Zoos

BANHAM ZOO

The Grove, Banham
Norwich NR16 2HB
Telephone: 095 387476

How to find it:
Leave the A11 Thetford to Norwich road at
Attleborough and take the B1077 / B1113 to
Banham. The zoo is signposted from there.

Open: All year from 10.00 am

Prices: adult £5.00; child £3.00; OAP £3.00

Area: 10 hectares / 25 acres

	Species	Animals
Mammals	44	340
Birds	78	242
Reptiles	12	49
Amphibians		
Fish		
Total	134	631
Conservation		★★★
Enclosures		★★
Education		★★
Recreation		★★
Research		

Banham Zoo began life as a collection of pheasants and parrots which opened to the public in 1968. In 1971 it became 'Banham Zoo and Woolly Monkey Sanctuary', thanks to a splendid colony of woolly monkeys that arrived that year. Today it is simply 'Banham Zoo', and although it still holds one of the finest collections of monkeys in Europe, these are no longer the sole attraction at what has become a diverse and interesting collection.

The zoo occupies an open site of around 25 acres, surrounded by an expanse of arable farmland. The site is well maintained, clean, and attractive, and it makes for an easy stroll among the animals and gardens. Most cages and aviaries look new, and many have indoor areas which can be viewed through glass. There is a large car park with an adjacent garden centre, farm shop and pet shop, and every month they hold Norfolk's largest car boot sale here.

Monkeys and gibbons are one the main attractions within the zoo, and Banham has a very good reputation for keeping and breeding a large number of species. The guide book for the zoo uses the symbol of a ringing alarm clock, its hands set at five minutes to midnight, to highlight the species for whom time is running out; brightly coloured Diana monkeys from West Africa, the imp-like little black Goeldi's monkeys from the Upper Amazon, large acrobatic siamang gibbons from Malaya and Sumatra, ring-tailed lemurs from Madagascar – these are all creatures for whom the alarm is sounding, and all have bred at Banham. The cages for the monkeys are rather variable in their design. Some, like the enclosures for the ruffed lemurs are very spacious, others, like the silver leaf langurs and some of the gibbons are rather unexciting. This hasn't prevented the langurs or the gibbons from breeding here, but perhaps for a zoo that specialises in primates, the accommodation could allow for more climbing, with more space and more height. The siamang gibbons, in particular, look

Ring-tailed lemur

as if they would all appreciate much more room to swing about, as gibbons like to do. A new gibbon complex is planned for 1994-5.

There are several groups of marmosets and tamarins here, and each species seems to be kept in good sized groups. Perhaps the best are the emperor tamarins, recognisable by their droopy white moustaches, and the tiny pygmy marmosets, smallest of all the living monkeys.

One group of monkeys that have a superb climbing area are the black-capped squirrel monkeys from Bolivia. They have what must be the best monkey island in any British zoo, a wild cluster of trees that hides a dozen or more little monkeys within its dense canopy. The 'monkey jungle is-land' is away at one corner of the zoo, down a peaceful woodland walk where there are wallabies, flamingos, waterfowl, and cranes including the easily recognisable crowned crane from East Africa. This area of the zoo has been well landscaped with splendid walkways, and you find yourself having to look around for animals in the trees and the undergrowth (don't animals seem far more exciting when you have to search for them than they do when presented in a sterile cage with no concealment?).

Two other exhibits at Banham vie closely with the monkey jungle for special recognition. The maned wolves have an excellent wooded com-pound, perhaps half an acre or more in size, and the pair of wolves look splendid. Alongside is an information kiosk (what an excellent idea), a shelter from which you can watch the animals, and where a tape recording provides plenty of information about them. From it you can learn that the maned wolves have bred successfully here, and that their cub has now departed for another zoo. This idea of ready information on tape is copied again in places around the zoo, to very good effect.

But for many visitors the pride of Banham Zoo are the snow leopards. They are the only large cats at the zoo, a bold decision when most visitors expect at least tigers and lions; but the decision is a calculated one, and it allows Banham to devote the effort and space to these endangered cats that many zoos devote to less threatened creatures. Their enclosure is large, clean, and interesting, there is glass-fronted viewing inside and out, and if you have the good fortune to visit at a time when the leopardess has cubs to care for, as she did in 1989, then you may find yourself in for a very long stay at this enclosure.

Other cats at Banham include ocelots and Geoffroy's cats in good new cages. There are a wide variety of grazing mammals, like the Grevy's zebra, sika deer, and camels, and there are chimpanzees in a compound which does not really reflect the best about Banham Zoo.

The bird collection is large, and well housed. Apart from the water fowl and flamingos, there is a huge assortment of owls, one of the finest collections in the country, including the little burrowing owl, hawk owls, various eagle owls, and a captive bred pair of great grey owls, the first pair ever to be seen in this country. There are also plenty of parrots, kookuburras, emus, and Rothschild's mynahs, among many others. There is also a small reptile house.

A new £100,000 penguin pool opened in 1992 features around thirty blackfooted penguins and provides good underwater viewing.

For children Banham has a large education centre for a small zoo, and there is a playground with climbing frames, and a pet's and farmyard corner which is open and clean, but mainly consists of rabbits and goats.

Banham is a new zoo, but its heart and its intentions seem to be in the right place. It is a pleasant place to visit, its collection of animals is well balanced and focussed upon species that it can manage well. Until September 1991 visitors to Norfolk could choose between two splendid collections of monkeys. Less than thirty miles west of Banham, just North of Thetford, was Kilverstone Wildlife Park with its unrivalled collection of South American primates, and particularly of spider monkeys. But Kilverstone closed its gates after only eighteen years of operation, citing poor visitor numbers and lack of cash. Most of the rarer monkeys departed for zoos in the USA. Banham may be the unwitting beneficiary. Kilverstone, in its hey day, would attract up to two hundred thousand visitors a year. Many of these might now go to Banham. If they do, they will find a less specialised collection, with fewer endangered species than Kilverstone. But they will find an interesting, positive, zoo that deserves to succeed, to build and improve, as it will surely continue to do so.

CITY OF BELFAST ZOOLOGICAL GARDENS

Antrim Road
Belfast   BT36   7PN
Telephone: 0232 776277

How to find it:
Signposted on the A2 Antrim Road North of
Belfast.

Open: All year from 10.00 am

Prices: adult £3.9; child £1.80; OAP free;
Winter reductions

Area: 24 hectares / 60 acres

	Species	Animals
Mammals	60	230
Birds	48	250
Reptiles	5	36
Amphibians	1	1
Fish	10	40
Total	124	557
Conservation		★★★
Enclosures		★★★
Education		★★★
Recreation		★★★
Research		★

Belfast Zoo might be forgiven for feeling like Britain's forgotten zoo. Like so many of Northern Ireland's attractions, it is virtually unknown on the British mainland except among zoo enthusiasts, and Ulster emigrés. Yet it ranks as one of the finest and most attractive zoos in the British Isles; is is a zoo with a collection of growing conservation value, it has a sound reputation for breeding and managing a wide range of species, and it plays a valuable role in the community of Northern Ireland. A quarter of a million people visit every year, and almost all of these are loyal, regular visitors from the province's population of a million and a half.

The Bellevue Zoo (as it was originally known) began as an attraction within The Bellevue Pleasure Gardens, on the spectacular hillside of Cave Hill, north of the city of Belfast. The Pleasure Gardens themselves were the idea, in 1913, of Belfast City Tramways, part of the Belfast Corporation. They were looking for a way to encourage passengers onto the trams, and were hoping, too, to provide a new recreational resource for the citizens of Belfast. They developed 32 acres of the hillside in fine Edwardian fashion, with a network of zig-zag pathways, extensive planting of trees and shrubs, a tea house, and a floral hall. The gardens became a popular destination for day trips, and two decades later the temptation to enhance the attraction to include a zoo, at a time when zoos like Whipsnade, and Chester, and Paignton were opening their gates, proved irresistible to the Corporation. In 1933 a private collection of animals at the Pleasure Gardens drew more than two hundred thousand paying visitors, and the Corporation decided that the enterprise ought to be officially embraced. In September of that year the decision was made, and twelve acres of the gardens were swiftly developed at a cost of £10,000. On March 28th 1934 Bellevue Zoo opened, and the optimism of the Corporation was rewarded as visitors arrived in their thousands. 284,713 visitors came in the very first year of operation.

But then came the war, and the fortunes of the zoo declined. Most of the 'dangerous' animals were destroyed, and many of the rest were disposed of. The zoo struggled on through the post war years, but it was a sad and ailing collection. In 1962 the Parks and Cemeteries Committee took over the running of the zoo from the Transport Committee, and the future of the zoo came up for debate. The small 12 acre zoo had no real potential for improvement, and the options seemed to be either to move the animals to a new site, or to close the zoo down. The City Council owned 750 acres of adjoining land, and so eventually they made a larger tract of the hillside available alongside the old zoo. It was a perfect location, with a high escarpment rising up to provide a breathtaking view across the city to Belfast Lough and the sea. The man responsible for converting the wild hill into an attractive modern zoo was the zoo manager, John Stronge. Plans were drawn up in the 1970s, and the new Belfast Zoo opened in 1978. Stronge was trained as a horticulturist, and his influence shows clearly in the layout and design of the zoo. Everywhere there are plants and trees and shrubs, and the park has been landscaped so that the pathways weave and wind and every bend reveals a surprise. Fences are hidden within hedges, creating the impression, here and there, that the animals are unconfined. And as the paths meander gently up the hill, so they reveal more and more of the magnificent views.

The animal collection at Belfast is broadly mixed, reflecting its history as a city zoo. There are elephants and polar bears, lions, tigers, sealions, and penguins, chimps, and gorillas, and camels – a whole variety of instantly recognisable creatures. All are imaginatively housed, and generally, all are doing well. The bottom of the hill houses a variety of enclosures around a waterfowl pond. There are spider monkeys in this part of the park, with a small but interestingly appointed island. Two antelope paddocks hold beautiful Indian blackbuck, and gemsbok. Sitatunga, graceful African antelope, are housed in a sloping, grassy paddock, and another holds a group of red lechwe, a vulnerable antelope from Central Africa.

With zoos elsewhere scurrying to divest themselves of their polar bears, Belfast Zoo has no such intention for its three bears. Their enclosure may be no larger than many disused bear pits elsewhere, but it has been landscaped against a high rocky crag allowing the polar bears to climb high and to look out over the sea. The bears make the very most of the enclosure, and they seem to be well balanced, and playful, using the high rocks to dive from into the pool beneath.

A modern, slate-roofed building is home to ostrich, and to zebra and giraffe that run together. It also houses Asian elephant, and the zoo has recently obtained a bull elephant, Luka.

One of the best features of the new zoo is the chimpanzee and gorilla house, opened in summer 1991 by Jane Goodall. The chimps and gorillas have similar accommodation – a large, landscaped outdoor area, walled, with glass viewing windows. The chimp enclosure, indoors and out, is a rich playground, strewn with ropes and trunks, scramble-nets and branches, and even sporting some live trees, which the chimps have so far spared. The enclosure is home to a social group of nine chimps, and the group is growing. The pair of gorillas is a new addition, and they have yet to breed.

The penguin pool holds a good mixed group of gentoo penguins, rockhopper penguins, Magellanic penguins, and king penguins. The birds, fifty six in all, were all reared from sixty eggs that were collected from the Falkland Islands in 1990 and 1991. The pool has good underwater viewing.

A notable breeding success for Belfast in 1992 was achieved with the Californian sealions, and this is one of the only zoos to provide underwater viewing for these beautiful creatures.

At the very top of the hill are the spectacled bears looking out over the crags. Belfast is one of only two British Zoos to keep these bears as a part of an international breeding programme (the other is Jersey Zoo), and they were rewarded with their first cub in February 1992. There are mara here as well in a grassy pen.

Winding back down the hill, the path takes you past tigers against a craggy backdrop with a commodious pool, hyaena in a sloping field, and endangered Asian lions. There are delightful red pandas high in the trees, prairie marmots, and here and there are little densely planted cages for marmosets and tamarins – including golden lion tamarins.

A free flight aviary provides a walk-through opportunity to see birds like spoonbill, egrets, and storks, and ibis nesting high above a waterfall, up on a rocky bank.

Ring tailed lemurs roam free in the zoo. You may be lucky to spot them. There is an excellent farmyard that is popular with local children, a small nocturnal house, some reptiles, and a small play area. There are plans, if funding becomes available, to convert the old Floral Hall into an education/environmental resource centre.

A spacious new monkey house opened in 1992 has richly branched outdoor runs, and is home to Diana monkeys (vulnerable), black and white colobus monkeys, lion tailed macaques (endangered), and black lemurs (vulnerable). The choice of monkeys for the new house is an indication that Belfast Zoo sees its role as being more than just a recreational resource for the people of the province. John Stronge is determined that the zoo should also become a leading conservation centre.

Much of the original 1930s zoo still stands, although it is now closed to the public, and has long ceased to hold animals except for occasional quarantine and veterinary cases. Perhaps one day it could re-open without any living occupants as a museum – its cramped and heavily barred cages an uncomely reminder of the way we once kept and feared wild creatures. But, for now, Belfast Zoo provides an illustration of the way that zoos have changed, making splendid use of the sixty acres it now has, with plans for a further fifty steep and rocky acres to use, perhaps, as an Alpine park for animals like ibex, chamois, and markhor. The zoo has been fortunate to have the support of the City Council who have been generous in subsidising the growth and development of the collection. They have created a fine zoo, one that the people of Northern Ireland can be proud of, and one that the people of mainland Britain are unfortunate to miss.

BLACKPOOL MUNICIPAL ZOOLOGICAL GARDENS

East Park Drive, Blackpool
Lancs
Telephone: 0253 65027

How to find it:
Leave the M55 at Exit 4 and turn right.
Follow signs to Stanley Park and Zoo.

Open: All year from 10.00 am

Area: 13 hectares / 32 acres

Prices: adult £2.95; child £1.50; OAP £1.40.

	Species	Animals
Mammals	36	185
Birds	70	259
Reptiles	4	63
Amphibians		
Fish	1	36
Total	111	543
Conservation		★
Enclosures		★★
Education		★★★
Recreation		★★
Research		

There has been a zoo in Blackpool since 1874, twenty years before the Blackpool Tower opened. Then for nearly eighty years the zoo was within the famous tower itself, and it was presumably the Tower Zoo that featured in Stanley Holloway's 'Albert and the Lion'. But the Tower was a wholly unsuitable home for a zoo, and in 1971 Blackpool Corporation set about moving the zoo to a new home two and a half miles from the Golden Mile. The site had been the location of Stanley Park Aerodrome, and since 1953 it had been the showground for the Royal Lancashire Show. When the show moved in 1971, it seemed an ideal opportunity to use the site for the new municipal zoo. But municipal zoos are rare in Britain, and a special Act of Parliament had to be passed to enable the new zoo to be built.

The zoo opened its doors to the public in 1972 to general public acclaim. It is a simple, open, zoo, and occupies 32 acres. Twenty years after its opening, the landscaped zoo has matured, and there are bank, copses, and shrubberies that give interest to what was once flat grassland. Some of the original airport buildings are still in use; the old airshow stand is used by the excellent education department and zoo offices, and the elephants and giraffe occupy a large, converted hangar. The zoo is modestly sized, and easy to walk around. There is also a good miniature railway which goes half way around the park, and a children's adventure playground.

As you might expect from a resort zoo, Blackpool zoo keeps most of the popular 'ABC' species – animals like elephants, gorillas, sealions,

lions, tigers, and penguins. It is a non specialist collection, but seems to keep all of its animals well. The enclosures are adequate, and clean, although some are rather unimaginative in their designs. The big cats have large, grassy, square pens, the elephants have a rather cramped compound, and a good herd of camels occupy a fairly small hardstanding. More imaginative is a rocky precipice that dominates a central lake, and is home to markhor, a vulnerable mountain goat with magnificent spiral horns. There is a rocky penguin pool where gentoo penguins breed, and an attractive, modern monkey house with very good groups of capuchins, squirrel monkeys and vervet monkeys. Gibbons and spider monkeys have a new house with access to small islands in an oval lake, and the orang utans, chimpanzees and gorillas have modern, although fairly simple, enclosures.

The sealion pool at Blackpool is one of the largest in the country. The sealions here are entertaining and look well, although they might benefit from more natural beaches.

If Blackpool specialises at all, then it is with marsupials. Once there was a good collection of tree kangaroos here, and although these are now gone, there are Parma wallabies, wallaroos, red- necked wallabies, and marsupials as unfamiliar as potoroos, quokkas, and cuscus.

There are good paddocks for grazing animals, represented by bisons, llamas, zebus, damara zebras, and several cranes; and there is a good group of delicate Arabian gazelle. There are good waterfowl ponds around the zoo, and an aviary full of African grey parrots.

Blackpool is still Europe's busiest seaside resort. It deserves a good zoo, and it is a credit to the town corporation that they have succeeded in creating one.

Lion

BLAIR DRUMMOND SAFARI AND LEISURE PARK

Nr Stirling
Scotland FK9 4UR
Telephone: 0786 841 456

How to find it:
Seven miles North of Stirling on the A84 and
from Exit 10 on the M9

Open: Daily during Summer months from
10 am.

Prices: adult £5.00; child £3.00;
OAP £3.00.

Area: 48 hectares / 119 acres

	Species	Animals
Mammals	23	161
Birds	4	47
Reptiles		
Amphibians		
Fish		
Total	27	208
Conservation		★
Enclosures		★★
Education		★
Recreation		★★★
Research		

Blair Drummond Safari and Leisure Park, once known as *Scotland's* Safari
Park, was opened on the estate of Sir John and Lady Muir, near Stirling,
in 1970. It was the first attempt to bring the safari park concept of African
and Asian animals to Scotland, and like several of its English forebears,
considerable use was made of the expertise and the animals of Jimmy
Chipperfield. The park is well signposted off the A84 Stirling to Doune
road, and it occupies around 120 acres of fairly flat green pastureland,
overlooked by the fairy tale turrets of Blair Drummond House.

Like most safari parks, the visitor drives a tortuous winding course
through a succession of fenced paddocks, within which a whole variety of
species roam relatively freely. At Blair Drummond the roads wind almost
too often, as if the designers have tried too hard to compensate for a rather
smaller overall area, compared to say, Woburn, Longleat, or Knowsley.
To add to the confusion, the route into the safari park itself takes you right
around the perimeter of the park so that you do see something of a preview
of what awaits you, before you even enter the first enclosure.

Nevertheless, once inside, there is a fair mix of species to be observed.
The first animals you may see are the African elephants in a spectacular
new elephant house that opened in 1992, and which allows access to visitors if the elephants are not outside. The elephants have a large outdoor
paddock, a huge pool which holds 55,000 gallons of water, and a sand pit
with 800 tons of sand. You may see them sliding down the muddy hillside
with their back legs outstretched behind them, an activity which zoo director Angela Rennick describes as 'their favourite game'. The clay mud
keeps their skins in good condition. The elephants, like several others in
British zoos, are rescued youngsters from the culling programme in Zim-
babwe. The park now has room to keep six, and at the time of writing there
are three, two cows and a young bull. Since the decisions of both

Edinburgh and Glasgow Zoos to close their elephant houses, these three are the only resident elephants in Scotland.

The first paddock holds a rather curious combination, including sika deer (from Japan), eland and lechwe (from Africa), Pere David's deer (from China), bactrian camels and yaks (from Asia) and Emus (from Australia). Despite their diverse origins however, the group semm to blend together in a quite satisfactory way. The monkeys are rhesus macaques, a more popular choice for monkey jungles than baboons. They will climb on your car, carrying babies in their arms, and are bound to make the trip through this part of the park the most entertaining of the tour.

The lion area is fairly large, and there is now an elevated walkway where visitors can look down upon the lions. The pride is only small (six lions at the time of writing), but perhaps this demonstrates sensible management of a species whose numbers can rapidly expand in safari park conditions. There are several young Siberian tigers in a separate enclosure. These originate from John Aspinall's collection, and perhaps they are an indication that Blair Drummond is beginning to take an interest in conservation-sensitive species.

The final paddock holds American bison, fallow deer, zebras, and dromedary camels –another geographic mix. But the visit is not yet over because now is the time to leave the car for the sealion show, to see the Humboldt's and black foot penguins in a large new pool, meerkats in a well appointed enclosure, ring tailed lemurs, otters, and capuchin monkeys, all within the children's zoo area. There is also a walk-through area with ponies, donkeys, goats, llamas, wallabies, and rheas, among other favourites. Finally, once the rides and amusements are exhausted, there is the opportunity to take a boat ride out along a waterway to the chimp island where Blair Drummond has been proud to see mother-reared chimps. The island is spacious, and new climbing features have recently been added to enrich the environment.

Altogether Blair Drummond is a well appointed and attractive day out. Children will enjoy the monkeys and of course the funfair, and meanwhile the park is slowly establishing itself as a responsible animal collection.

BRISTOL, CLIFTON AND WEST OF ENGLAND ZOOLOGICAL SOCIETY

Clifton
Bristol BS8 3HA
Telephone: 0272 738951

How to find it:
From the city centre follow sign to Clifton.
The zoo is on the B4468 about 2 miles from
the cente of town.

Open: All year from 9.00 am

Prices: adult £4.50; child £2.20.

Area: 5 hectares / 12 acres

	Species	Animals
Mammals	67	444
Birds	109	418
Reptiles	27	162
Amphibians	2	15
Fish		
Total	205	1039
Conservation		★★
Enclosures		★★
Education		★★★
Recreation		★★
Research		★★

The Bristol, Clifton, and West of England Zoological Society was founded on September 18th 1835 by an eminent West Country physician, anatomist, philosopher, and one-time grave robber, Dr Henry Riley. Riley was a collector of fossils who clearly had a yearning to collect living specimens as well.

Together with fellow members of the Bristol Institution, a learned society of the day that included such luminaries as Isambard Kingdom Brunel and the Frys, he established a Zoological Society. Its aims, as he put it, were to 'promote the diffusion of useful knowledge by facilitating observation of the habits, form, and structure of the animal kingdom; as well as affording rational amusement and recreation to the visitors of the neighbourhood.'

Two hundred and twenty 'proprietors' were each persuaded to become shareholders in the new venture, in exchange for which they were later allowed free admission to the gardens. A sum of £3,574.4s 8d. was spent buying twelve acres of farmland from a former mayor of Bristol, and a further £3,384.18s.8d. was spent upon landscaping, building and road making for the new Zoological Gardens. The man responsible for the design was Mr Richard Forrest, a greatly admired landscape gardener who also created the gardens for the Duke of Westminster at Eaton Hall. Forrest's designs for the gardens, the large central lake, the expansive lawns, and the siting of enclosures around a perimeter wall all remain very largely unchanged to the present day, and a century and a half later, visitors would almost certainly recognise the zoo from nineteenth century plans.

On Monday July 11th 1836, the public were admitted to the gardens for the first time, a decade before the London Zoo was to open its gates to paying visitors. The 'Clifton Zoological Gardens' as they were then known, soon became known simply as the 'Clifton Zoo', and thus the word 'zoo' found its way into the English Language. Besides being a place where the citizens of Bristol could see exotic creatures for the first time ever, the zoo also became a centre for fashionable recreation. By the end of the century the Society was earning more than half its income from 'amusements', and a list of these reads like a carnival poster. There were, at various times, elephant and camel rides, boat trips, hot air balloons, flower shows, musical concerts, penny-farthing races, mock battles and gymnastic displays. There was tennis, croquet, archery, and even golf. At times there were firework displays, agricultural shows and fetes. Altogether it was a recipe for success that was destined to establish the zoo firmly as an essential part of Victorian society.

For a century and a half, Bristol has had a zoo with an enviable reputation. Many notable firsts were achieved here. The first chimpanzee ever conceived and born in captivity made his appearance in 1934. The first black rhinoceros ever to be born in Britain (and the first of five to be born at Bristol) arrived in 1958, the first okapi in 1963, and the first lowland gorilla in 1971. The zoo has achieved a string of successes with primates, and now regularly breeds lion-tailed macaques, diana, de Brazza, and colobus monkeys. Success too came in the field of public relations, and for years the zoo featured regularly in television's 'Animal Magic' which made animals like Dotty the ring-tailed lemur famous throughout the country.

Bristol Zoo no longer offers the carnival atmosphere that made it so popular in Victorian times, but the zoo is still popular with its regular visitors. Newcomers, however, might find the zoo rather disappointing in view of its larger than life reputation. Twelve acres, unfortunately, may no longer be sufficient for the educated and discerning public of the nineteen nineties, and Bristol Zoo now suffers from the legacy of design left by Richard Forrest of Acton. Very few of the zoo's acres are actually given over to animals at all, with the majority taken up by the gardens, lawns, and lake. There is a feeling of pleasant urban parkland about the place, very much like a walled park or arboretum. Trees are very much in favour and are well labelled. There are limes, sweet chestnut, rowan, Corsican pines, and tall deodar cedars among many others.

The animals are largely distributed in houses around the walls. The first you might encounter are the big cats in cages rather too small. The Ape House is no more encouraging. Outside the apes have an artificial rocky slope, and indoors glass-fronted dens with concrete moulded trees and steps. The gorillas and orangs look invariably bored in this rather sterile concrete environment.

The Reptile House is better. Built in 1980, it is dedicated to Reginald Greed who was director of the zoo for forty five years until 1974, and who was the father of the present director. It is an imaginative house, housing huge pythons and Nile crocodiles.

The new 'World of Water' opened in 1989 is a welcome addition to the zoo. It brings the concept of the aquarium very much up to date, combining five large 'landscaped' tanks with a 'walk-through' coral reef tank and a number of smaller tanks.

One of Bristol's highlights is the nocturnal house, said to be the first ever opened at any zoo. It shows quite a variety of night time animals including African fruit bats in a realistically designed cave.

The monkey house is perhaps the best feature of Bristol Zoo. Although fairly small in area, it holds only a few species, but holds them well, in twenty foot high well branched outdoor enclosures, in family groups. The monkeys include the extremely endangered lion-tailed macaques, rarely seen entellus langurs, and lovely silvery leaf monkeys. Next door is a run of marmoset cages with some rarely seen species.

Probably the one feature at the zoo that has attracted more than its fair share of adverse publicity, was the polar bear pit. Bears have bred here, but the pit itself was just that; a pit. The last two polar bears at Bristol, Misha and Nina, were put down in January 1992. The zoo has no plans to replace them. Two further pits have now been filled in, and the new sandy enclosure that results holds endangered Arabian gazelles.

For many years Bristol Zoo was known best for its okapis. The Society has now relinquished their control of these animals in the best interests of a cooperative breeding programme involving other zoos, but there are still okapis at Bristol in a short hardstanding. Pygmy hippos also have a long association with the zoo, and they occupy a 'designer' compound with a small concrete pond and a periphery pool. The elephant house is adequate, although the compound is entirely concrete. The house is shared with giraffe, which have a successful history at Bristol.

The seal pool looks as if it was once designed for shows, but now holds a group of endearing southern fur seals. There are small paddocks with

Fruit bat

tapirs, zebras and kangaroos, and several aviaries including one rather effective circular aviary home to several birds of prey.

One of the most curious enclosures at Bristol is the Monkey Temple, built in 1928 when monkeys were associated in the popular mind with Kipling's ruined temples. A concrete temple stands on top of an octagon of six high concrete steps, and the whole is sunk into a circular walled pit around which visitors can congregate. The temple holds a group of around thirty crab-eating macaques in an active, if bizarre troupe. It has been suggested that all the monkeys in the pit have lost the very tips of their tails. It is a consequence, apparently, of the flip-flap doors of the temple which occasionally catch the end of the tail as a monkey nips through. If true, it may give some reason for second thoughts about the monkey temple.

A building in the centre of the park houses the main offices, and a tropical bird hall. Outside there is a small children's area with guinea pigs, rabbits, sheep, goats and calves – but not to touch.

There is a small penguin pool, with a variety of species, and a curious compound which holds penguins, marmots, and mara. The final exhibits at the zoo, if you proceed clockwise around the park, are the grey gibbons and black and white Eastern colobus in splendid high enclosures, and an attractive new lemur house which in glass fronted runs features both black and brown lemurs, mongoose lemurs, and red and white fronted lemurs.

The newest enclosures at Bristol are a series of islands set in the large central lake. The £250,000 islands are home to ring tailed lemurs and marmosets, and they also hold new aviaries. A new gibbon enclosure is also planned for the islands.

Altogether Bristol Zoo is a slightly uncomfortable survivor from the Victorian age. It has been a great pioneer in animal management techniques, and there has been a great history of success. The Society seems to take seriously its conservation obligations, and the gardens are attractive and well tended. But somehow this is not quite enough. In 1966 the Society purchased a large estate eight miles north of Bristol, The Hollywood Tower Estate, and the intention was to use it as a new country site for the zoo. For various reasons the plans floundered, and Bristol Zoo remains in Clifton. How much better might it have been for the reputation of the zoo however, if a bold decision had been made, and the zoo had been moved. In 1990 a twenty-year plan was announced for the zoo to gradually move away from keeping larger animals. The perimeter exhibits will all be linked with a covered walkway, making them more accessible during the winter months; the monkey temple is to be redeveloped as an enclosure for Sumatran tigers. This should in time help to preserve the reputation of the zoo. Nevertheless, Bristol still remains popular with a huge number of annual visitors, it contributes soundly to species management schemes, and recent additions to the zoo, like the reptile house, the monkey house, and the splendid aquarium, mean that it will probably continue to attract visitors just as it has now for 155 years.

CHESSINGTON WORLD OF ADVENTURES

Leatherhead Road, Chessington
Surrey KT9 2NE
Telephone: 037 27 27227/729560

How to find it:
5 miles north of Leatherhead on the A243
Half a mile from Chessington South Station
Exit M25 Junction 9

Open: From March 28, daily 10.00 am
onwards until November

Prices: adult £10.50; child £9.50; OAP £9.50.

Area: 14 hectares / 35 acres

	Species	Animals
Mammals	49	156
Birds	88	226
Reptiles	20	45
Amphibians	4	5
Fish		
Total	161	432
Conservation		★
Enclosures		★★
Education		★
Recreation		★★★
Research		

You come across the Chessington World of Adventures in the middle of
London's green belt on the Kingston to Leatherhead road, and you can tell
at once from the rows of coloured flags and acres of car parks that this is
no ordinary zoo. You might be forgiven for believing that Chessington is
no more than a glamorous fairground – a nineties theme park with animal
sideshows; but as soon as you pass through the gates you learn that this
impression is not altogether true, and Chessington does have claims to be
a serious animal collection.

Most people remember Chessington simply as Chessington Zoo, an attractive and entertaining collection of animals that has been a summer
day-out for Londoners for three generations. The Zoo was opened to the
public in the summer of 1931 by the late Mr. R. S. Goddard in the grounds
of Chessington Manor. The manor itself has an illustrious history. Originally built in 1348, it became a school for Officers of Archery, and was
visited by Queen Elizabeth I. During the Civil War it became a Royalist
stronghold, and was burnt to the ground by Cromwell's army. When it was
finally rebuilt in 1660 it was renamed 'Burnt Stub'. Now it has a commanding position in the centre of the theme park, a venue for conferences,
Jacobean banquets, and business lunches.

Chessington is now owned by the Tussaud Group, a leisure company
best known for its ownership of Madame Tussaud's and the London
Planetarium. Their other interests include Warwick Castle (the most
visited stately home in Britain), Alton Towers, and Rock Circus at the
London Pavilion. Chessington is their only zoo. In 1987 the zoo had a
change of name and became the Chessington World of Adventures, a
name which seemed to reflect the decline in popularity of the traditional
zoo, and highlighted Chessington's attempts to broaden its market appeal.
Several million pounds were spent converting what was once a zoo and a

funfair into a Disney-style theme park with a monorail (the 'safari sky-way'), a 'Wild West Town', and a host of funfair rides and amusements.

But let us ignore the theme-park aspects of this zoo for the time being. A winding pathway takes you around the park, and the first impression is of a bright, clean, interesting zoo. A lot of wood has been used in the construction of enclosures, and in landscaping the public areas – old railway sleepers, conifer trunks, pine posts, rope, and thatch. The effect is natural, soft, and rather unexpected given the futuristic, technicolour logo that greets visitors to the park. It is not a large zoo, and the walk around is undemanding, but the designers have made it unregimented with something new and surprising around every corner. It is a clean, well maintained, and well staffed zoo, and it shows.

Depending upon the direction you choose at the gate, the new ape house will either be the first impression you receive of the animal collection, or else the climax of the tour. Either way it is an indication that the zoo may still see its role as more than just an adjunct to the theme park. Opened in 1984, the ape house accommodates gorillas and chimpanzees in surroundings modelled on John Aspinall's ape house at Howletts. The cage is a fair bit smaller than Howletts great Gorillarium, and has no slides or swings, but then it holds far fewer apes. Some time will be required to build up the group, but the first gorilla birth in 1990 must have given the keepers here great cause for optimism. It is a good ape house, and provides plenty of diversions for the animals, on a floor covering of deep straw. The other apes at Chessington, the lar gibbons, have a splendid long enclosure at the opposite end of the zoo, full of vegetation, with plenty of opportunity to display their unique brachiating locomotion to good effect.

Other primates, the monkeys and lemurs, are housed in a newly enlarged area of the zoo – , the monkey walk. Here you can see Celebes macaques, lovely little white-throated capuchins, and Barbary apes, among others. The monkey walk is attractive, well laid out, and fun. There are good outdoor pens, not particularly spacious, but well appointed, often planted with grass, and scrupulously clean. Honeysuckle climbs over the covered walk-way, and there is a little hedge of bamboo between each outside cage, affording each group of monkeys some privacy from the monkeys next door. Elsewhere, black and white colobus monkeys have a super tall outdoor cage well equipped with ropes and branches.

Many of the best known and best loved zoo animals may be found somewhere at Chessington. There are giraffe, penguins, camels, lions, polar bears, tigers, sealions, and gorillas. The giraffe inhabit a tall, clean, giraffe house with a rather small concrete paddock, and the giraffe have bred here. The polar bears are a young pair, but they look healthy and content which is not always true of this species in captivity. Their enclosure allows for underwater viewing of the bears in a cool, blue, underground viewing room, although you will be lucky to catch them taking a dip.

Cats are well displayed here, although none of the cages are particularly generous with space. Indeed the limitations of space do keep many of the enclosures below a comfortable size, and there is an impression that more room could have been used for some of the animals. The cats include jaguars, and snow leopards, which despite being close to the noise of the fair, have bred in 1990. Tigers are well displayed in a long, luxurious enclosure.

Until recently there were three elephants at Chessington, but the zoo had the misfortune to lose two within a short period of time, and being left with a single cow elephant gave managers the opportunity to reconsider the keeping of these animals. The elephant house had never been spacious, and the public did not take well to the sight of a solitary elephant. So eventually the decision was taken, and it was undoubtedly the right one. The final elephant departed in 1991, and the elephant house was closed. There are beavers with crystal clear water, and otters in a small but interesting compound. Sealions have a typical and rather unexciting pool.

The old bird garden had to move to make way for theme park rides, but Chessington has modelled a new home for its bird collection in 'Bird Land', a thoughtfully designed area with plenty of water, wooden bridges and walk-ways. The birds, a large and varied collection, include many familiar species, such as flamingos, owls, storks, and parrots. The flamingos in particular have a delightful pool, grassed around and landscaped with a rocky backdrop. Ibis have a similar enclosure, and the penguins have a small but attractively landscaped pool, with underwater viewing, a rocky bank, and a pebble beach. Andean condors, one of the largest living flying birds have a high outcrop of rock on which to perch.

There is a new and attractive reptile house which is part of the wild west town, decorated as 'Snakebite Saloon'. Inside it lives up to its name with several large snakes including a beautiful yellow anaconda.

The best feature of the theme park, so far as the zoo is concerned, is the safari skyway – a bright yellow monorail ride which glides high above many of the zoo enclosures. There is a recorded commentary that supplies information about the animals beneath. The rest of the theme park tends to occupy the perimeter of the park, and the theme (since there has to be one) is a loose collection of geographical associations. Thus the park's best roller coaster (the 'Vampire') is in Transylvania, the runaway train is in the Wild West, and the Dragon River Water Ride is in the Mystic East. There is a circus too, and appropriately enough it is Tamara Coco's circus without animals.

Do funfairs and zoos really mix? It is a difficult question to answer. Where does a zoo like this spend its operating surplus – on better enclosures, or on more rides? Does it trivialise the serious nature of the modern zoo to present animals alongside sideshows as if they were both objects of human entertainment, and nothing more? How do we know if the zoo management sees the animals as anything more than another way to win visitors and earn money? Chessington World of Adventures seems to have struck a balance acceptable to its shareholders, and it is certainly popular. Despite the huge shift in emphasis of recent years from the zoo to the theme park, it has managed to maintain a good animal collection, attractively if not lavishly housed. If you want to visit a good zoo, you would do better driving north to Regent's Park, east to Howletts or Port Lympne, or south-west to Marwell. If however, you want to take the family for an exciting and entertaining day out, you should certainly get that at Chessington.

THE NORTH OF ENGLAND ZOOLOGICAL SOCIETY CHESTER ZOO

Chester Zoo, Upton by Chester

Telephone: 0244 380280

How to find it:
Take the M53 in to Chester and turn right on the A41 towards Birkenhead. The zoo is well signposted off the A41 about 2 miles north of Chester.

Open: All year from 10.00 am

Prices: adult £5.50; child £3.00; OAP £3.00.

Area: 45 hectares / 111 acres

	Species	Animals
Mammals	87	741
Birds	183	798
Reptiles	67	341
Amphibians	14	190
Fish	137	1317
Total	488	3387
Conservation		★★★
Enclosures		★★★
Education		★★★★
Recreation		★★★★
Research		★

Chester Zoo is one of the foremost zoos in Europe. In the sheer size and diversity of its collection, in the compelling innovation of its design, and in the breathtaking beauty of its gardens, it has had a profound influence upon the style and development of zoological gardens all around the world.

It may seem remarkable that a small Roman city in the North of England should possess such an outstanding zoo, but then the founder of Chester Zoo was a remarkable and redoubtable man. His name was George Mottershead, and he was one of the last great animal collectors of this century. The son of a Cheshire nurseryman from Shavington, near Crewe, he began collecting animals as a child, the sort of animals that arrived unexpectedly in packages of exotic plants – lizards, spiders, and all manner of insects. When he was nine years old his father, Albert, took George and his brother to see the animals at Manchester's Belle-Vue Zoo. It was 1903, and zoos were dank and unsavoury places then. In particular, one image engraved itself upon George Mottershead's mind; it was the image of an elephant, shackled, confined behind bars, and compelled to ring a bell to beg for food. It was a pivotal experience that would determine Mottershead's destiny, and would lead him to declare his life's ambition – to build a zoo without bars.

The Great War almost put an end to that ambition. A German bullet damaged Mottershead's spine, and he was confined to a wheelchair for several years. But his collection of animals grew nonetheless, and eventually he began to search for a suitable home for the zoo he dreamed of building. Oakfield House in Upton, a leafy suburb of Chester, with its nine acres of gardens and its easy access to the railways and to the busy centres of Manchester and Liverpool, seemed the perfect place. The local council did not easily consent to the idea of having wild animals on their doorsteps, and lofty voices were raised in protest. But Mottershead prevailed, and Chester Zoo had its inauspicious public opening in 1931.

The early years were not easy ones for the young zoo. George Mottershead and his family made huge sacrifices to ensure the survival of the growing collection. It was a time that Professor Lord Zuckerman of London Zoo called 'an era of decay' for zoos. Yet Chester Zoo grew and flourished. 'Always Building' was the motto of the zoo, and true to that sentiment Mottershead began to purchase every plot and parcel of land that he could that bordered onto the estate. Within a few decades the zoo had grown to 111 acres, and zoo farms, houses, and car parks accounted for more than four hundred additional acres of land. Today that figure may have shrunk very slightly with the sale of some of the land to help support the zoos finances, but Chester is still a large zoo by the standard of most city zoos, and it ranks as the second largest collection of animals in the country housing almost three and a half thousand animals.

Here at Chester, many of the great concepts in zoo design were born and nurtured. Mottershead was a zoo pioneer, strongly influenced by the revolutionary ideas of Hamburg's Carl Hagenback who virtually invented the modern zoo, and by Heine Hediger who introduced the science of ethology – the study of animal behaviour – into the design of animal enclosures. At Chester Mottershead seized upon Hagenback's idea for moats and ditches as an alternative to Victorian ironwork, and extended their use throughout the zoo, often with species that Hagenback had not considered. Most notable perhaps were the great apes. When chimpanzees were released into their new enclosure at Chester in 1956, a group of grassy islands separated from visitors by no more than a twelve foot strip of water, Mottershead and his keepers could only cross their fingers and hope. Nobody knew in those days if chimps could swim. It turned out that they could not (or would not), and today the chimp islands are a centrepiece of Chester Zoo, holding a social troupe of around twenty almost exclusively zoo-bred chimps. Chimpanzees are social creatures, and in the wild they live in community groups 15 – 120 animals strong. Very few zoos have either the facilities, or indeed the animals to mimic these conditions, but Chester not only provides the space, it also keeps all of its animals together in the largest chimp colony in Britain, and undoubtedly one of the finest captive groups in the world. The new chimp house, a high conical-roofed building opened by the Princess of Wales in 1988, is a masterpiece of design. It allows the chimps almost twice the island space they traditionally had, and then provides perhaps the best indoor chimpanzee area in Europe. The climbing indoors is a huge wooden construction, slung this way and that with thick ropes, and reaching high into the roof. The chimps can play indoors or out, whichever they choose, and the visitor can sit and watch them, whatever the weather. Good signs provide information about the chimps, and there is such a complex, political social structure to watch – an all-powerful dominant male, arrogant young upstart males, nursing mothers, adolescents, infants, elder statesmen, matriarchs, four generations in all – if you go to Chester Zoo and only stay to see the chimps, you will have had your money's worth for sure.

Also behind moats are successful breeding groups of Sumatran and Bornean orang utans on islands leading off a large and purpose-built orang house. The spacious indoor accommodation seems slightly wasted, and could perhaps be improved with the addition of more climbing facilities. Nevertheless, the orangs make a terrific impression as the first animals most visitors see.

Chester Zoo has eleven miles of tarmac pathways, and certainly demands more walking than any other British zoo, except perhaps Whipsnade. There is no economical route to see the whole zoo without having to walk a very long way. You should allow a whole day to do justice to this zoo; or better still, visit twice. Large pushchairs are hired out at the main entrance, and their use is recommended to families with young children.

The difference between Chester and most other urban zoos seems to be the emphasis upon space. The central lion enclosure, for example, is a wooded acre with thirty or forty trees, surrounded by chainlink fencing. The fencing was another Chester innovation. It was introduced at a time when lions were kept only behind heavy iron bars, and Chester's enclosure was built in the face of extreme local opposition. Again however, the idea proved more than adequate, and it set a new standard for the keeping of big cats that was copied worldwide. It was the enclosure at Chester that finally persuaded Wiltshire County Council to sanction Britain's first lion park at Longleat in 1966.

Almost every group of animal that you might expect to find in a zoo is represented at Chester. The Californian sealions are spectacular, drawing huge appreciative crowds at feeding times, and they have an off-show breeding beach where young sealions have been born. The huge giraffe house, once famed for holding the world's tallest measured giraffe, now holds a small mixed group of Masai and Rothschild's giraffe, with a spacious outdoor paddock. The penguin pool with its large picture windows for underwater viewing is magnificent, and enormously popular. There are around thirty Humboldt's penguins here, and the zoo has boldly resisted the usual temptation of trying to create the impression of an Arctic environment with concrete and tile, and instead has provided a generous sandy beach, which accurately reflects the true wild environment of these birds. There is a large offshow area for the penguins too, and Chester has an excellent breeding record. Flamingos wade beautifully in a large central lake. Rhinos (black and Indian), are in low walled, moated paddocks, so too are Brazilian tapirs. The pair of black rhino, Parky and Esther, are both captive bred and their first calf, Emma, was born in February 1991.

Elephants have long been associated with Chester. George Mottershead, true to his vision, was one of the first zoo directors to keep these animals unshackled, and the housing of elephants was a problem that he approached with characteristic directness. 'In most zoological gardens', he wrote, 'the largest of all animals have to be content with perhaps the smallest amount of room in proportion to their size.' This was not to be the case at Chester. The new elephant house, built in 1959, was a showpiece covering 20,000 square feet, leading to a moated paddock over an acre in size. It is a bold, cathedral-like building, heated indoors in the winter months, with colourful indoor displays of flowers, and it is a wonderful place to get close to some fully grown elephants. It was Mottershead's ambition to establish his zoo as a significant breeding centre for elephants, and he lived to see the birth of Jubilee, an Asian bull whose arrival during the Queen's Silver Jubilee celebrations of 1977 earned him his name. He was the first elephant to be conceived and born in Britain. Today Jubilee is separately corralled from the other various elephants at Chester, many of whom come here on breeding loans in the hope their occasional sojourns with him might prove fruitful. He is still the best known character at the zoo and still receives birthday cards by the score. If he succeeds in fathering a calf this will be the first second generation elephant birth in Europe.

Another example of the thinking on a grand scale that characterises this zoo is the quite astonishing tropical house. Built in 1964, this building is almost sixty feet high, with a floor area of around 40,000 square feet. As well as housing the reptile collection the building also features quite luxuriant undergrowth of tropical palms, rubber trees, hibiscus, bougainvillea, banyan, and a display of orchids, set around an artificial waterfall. Heating costs prevent zoo gardeners from growing all the tropical species they would dearly like to grow in this building, but the effect is impressive nonetheless. Free flying birds occupy the building, and these include weaver birds whose intricately woven nests hang pendulously from the high palms. Dwarf crocodiles and Johnson river crocodiles and Mississippi alligators occupy steamy pools. The rest of the reptile collection is huge, in splendidly landscaped vivaria along one wall of the open hall, and down one side of a long, dimly lit, corridor. Chester is one of the few zoos that takes the breeding of reptiles seriously, and there is a lot that goes on behind the scenes. One species that bred in 1990 were sunbeam snakes, a scarcely known species from South East Asia. This may have been the first ever zoo breeding of this snake, but since it is a burrowing species it is not even displayed. The zoo holds a record for breeding endangered Madagascan tree boas, has been successful with amphibians, like the red-eyed tree frog from South America, and regularly breeds a long list of snakes, lizards, tortoises and amphibians. There are some huge pythons, boas, and anacondas, a host of venomous rattlesnakes, vipers, and mambas, and lizards large and small.

The western end of the zoo is largely devoted to paddock animals. A beautiful herd of Père David's deer graze here, and there are Przewalski's horses, eland, black buck, and gnus, along with many others including onagers, ostrich which breed here, wallabies and axis deer, and a spectacular herd of reindeer on a rocky hardstanding. There are some huge American bison, llamas, alpacas, and guanacos, but perhaps the most delightful grazers are the charming little prairie marmots, rabbit-sized social rodents from North America. A colony of around two hundred of them occupy a network of burrows that have spread from one paddock, underneath the tarmac pathway, to reappear in another.

Also at the western end of the zoo is a small nocturnal house, featuring the 'rarest bat in the world', the endangered but beautiful Rodrigues fruit bat. There are kinkajous too in this house, bushbabies, and little shambling echidnas – spiny relatives of the duck-billed platypus from Australia. The cat house holds a dozen species, from the delicate little margay to the magnificent black leopard, and the rare jaguarundi. The cat runs are glass fronted and not particularly large, but are nonetheless interesting in their style and design. Nearby is the monkey house, another grand building, planted indoors with high bougainvillea, and featuring several species of monkeys in glass-fronted cages. Most of the cages have doors that lead to enclosures outdoors. The cages are, however, a little unimaginative in their design, and there is a slight 'museum' atmosphere about the place. Outside the enclosures could be greatly improved if they were to be doubled in height with the addition of more ropes and branches. There is a wonderful group of spider monkeys here, as well as endangered lion-tailed macaques, ruffed lemurs, de Brazza monkeys, and little talapoin monkeys. Ring-tailed lemurs seem to do extraordinarily well at Chester, and there are often over forty at the zoo, their number shared between the monkey house and a densely wooded lemur island where they can often be seen on summer days luxuriating in the sun.

Birds are very well featured at Chester with over one hundred and seventy species on display. There are thirty five members of the parrot family, many displayed in a large purpose-built parrot house, and these include a breeding group of the rarely-seen blue-eyed cockatoo. A walk-through temperate bird-house holds a wide variety of species, and there are large aviaries for birds of prey, including vultures, eagles, and Andean condors which have been hatched and hand-reared here. There is also a range of rustic, but perhaps slightly inadequate aviaries for a wide variety of owls, and several waterfowl ponds and canals home to dozens of species of ducks and geese and swans.

There is so much to see and do at Chester Zoo, so many groups of animals or enclosures that deserve a mention, that it is difficult to avoid producing simply a long list of animals that should not be missed. The list would have to include the cheetah, the Siberian tigers in a large new enclosure, otters, wapiti, camels, coatis, a beautiful herd of red lechwe which are a vulnerable antelope species from Central Africa, endangered Arabian gazelles, kangaroos, Arctic foxes, capybaras, porcupines, and coypus. The list goes on, and a more thorough list can be found at the end of this book. There is a large and rather old-fashioned aquarium that has recently been extensively renovated, a small children's zoo with pygmy goats and pigs, a simple children's play-ground, and a leisurely canal boat ride.

There are no fairground attractions to detract from the experience of visiting the animals, but 1991 saw the opening of a spectacular monorail which carries visitors aloft over several of the paddocks. It is a generous ride, covering a fair portion of the zoo. A recorded commentary provides information on the animals beneath. For a zoo of Chester's size, with so much required walking, the monorail, and the canal boat ride, are a welcome diversion, and a less taxing way of seeing some of the far flung corners of the zoo. As an educational zoo, Chester has a head start because of the sheer size and breadth of its collection. But education does play an important part in the life of the zoo, and there is both a full time education officer, and a teaching staff to cope with the huge annual influx of school parties. The signs around the zoo are attractive copies of watercolour paintings by wildlife artist G. L. Grandy, commissioned especially for Chester Zoo, but now marketed widely to other zoos in Britain and overseas. They provide a comfortable, consistent and informative style of labelling on every one of the thousand or more enclosures around the zoo.

Chester Zoo once claimed to attract more Britons through its gates than any other zoo. American authoress Emily Hahn who visited most of the world's major zoos, agreed that Chester Zoo has an appeal that is difficult to explain. 'If I am asked why Chester is my favourite,' she wrote in her book 'Zoos', 'I can only say that it is the prettiest zoo I ever saw.' Pretty, it undoubtedly is. The gardens are laid out in a very traditional, almost nineteenth-century fashion. Every year the borders are planted with hundreds of thousands of spring and summer bedding plants, and every summer the zoo shows tens of thousands of roses, their varieties all carefully labelled. The gardens are criss-crossed with waterways (water is a prominent feature of this zoo), and in the spring many of the canal banks and islands bloom with a Wordsworthian throng of daffodils. Every animal house seems to be bedecked with flowering plants, and there are flower beds around almost every corner.

Not everything in the garden is rosy however. Here and there are signs that parts of the zoo are becoming a little old, or rather overdue for improvement. Maintaining a huge zoo like Chester is an enormous logistical operation, and as visitor numbers have fallen since the mid 1960s, so the zoo has had difficulties in maintaining its essential fabric. The camel house, many of the aviaries and the old bear pits are all overdue for rebuilding or demolition. Nonetheless, the fact that the zoo has survived the turbulent decades of the seventies and eighties, with such a huge and diverse collection of animals, is a tribute to the two hundred staff and to the management of the zoo. In the decade and a half since Mottershead's death, they have taken his vision and carried it successfully through into the 1990's. Visitor numbers have risen somewhat in recent years, and this is excellent news for the zoo and for its visitors who will benefit from the further improvements that this will enable the zoo to afford. With continued firm and enlightened direction, Chester Zoo should be able to sustain its position as a first class zoo, and as one of Britain's finest.

COLCHESTER ZOO

Maldon Road, Colchester
Essex CO3 5SL
Telephone: 0206 330253

How to find it:
On the B1022 Tiptree to Colchester road,
3 miles south of Colchester

Open: All year from 9.30am

Prices: adult £4.50; child £2.50; OAP £4.00.

Area: 16 hectares / 40 acres

	Species	Animals
Mammals	83	194
Birds	62	192
Reptiles	30	130
Amphibians	5	15
Fish	21	186
Total	201	717
Conservation		★★
Enclosures		★★
Education		★★
Recreation		★★
Research		

Colchester Zoo is set in the grounds of the historic Stanway Hall in forty luxuriant acres of Constable country. There has been a manor house on the site since the time of King Harold, and the land was owned by the Crown until the time of King Henry II. The name 'Stanway' is thought to derive from the 'stone way', the original Roman road which ran from the garrison at Colchester to London. Today the zoo is just a few miles from the new A12 trunk road linking the two towns, and it is a splendid setting for a zoo. Cars park within the zoo grounds, and a tour of the zoo takes you on a languid figure of eight on a lightly wooded, hilly, walk.

Colchester Zoo has a large collection of animals, despite its size. There are around 180 species here and there is a lot to take in. This is a typical

Ocelot

'collector's' zoo, with most of the popular species represented; animals like lions, elephants, sealions, chimpanzees, and penguins. There is also a rather circus-like attitude here with daily performances by the sealions, parrots, elephants, and birds of prey.

Cats are perhaps the speciality with fifteen species including the rarer seen leopard cat of eastern Asia, and beautifully exhibited ocelots. Most of the cats are well housed, although possibly more space could be made available if fewer species were kept. There are jaguars, leopards and panthers, all beautifully housed in splendid good sized enclosures. A pair of snow leopards share an enclosure, well landscaped with a waterfall and high rocks. Snow leopards are secretive, and you may need patience to see them. Patience is also needed to spot the little fishing cats in a densely planted, interesting enclosure, and there is an excellent nocturnal exhibit featuring the rarely seen black-footed cat; and here, as elsewhere in the zoo, the information signs are very good.

The tigers occupy one of the newest developments – a carefully landscaped area of the zoo called 'tiger valley'. A taped commentary provides some background information about the tigers and the other animals that share the valley. The compounds are glass fronted, and the design motif is predominantly Indian, which is attractive, although slightly inappropriate for the pair of Siberian tigers. Nevertheless, tiger valley is well designed, and bodes well for future developments within the zoo. The same area houses a pair of maned wolves in a new and imaginative enclosure, the jaguars, and a little group of coatis. There are wooden walkways which provide good vantage points for seeing the animals.

Perhaps the first animals to catch the eye at the zoo are two young African elephants, both female. A signboard explains how they were rescued from a Southern African cull – a justification for several baby elephants within British zoos. The enclosure, and the elephant house, already look much too small for the growing elephants, especially the doors, and for a while the zoo was worryingly reluctant to answer enquiries about how they expected to cope as the elephants grew to adulthood. Such a tendency towards secrecy was quite unnecessary, and now the zoo has openly launched an appeal to raise money for a brand new elephant house; but this may not be started much before 1994. Rather boldly, the elephants are being trained, an uncommon idea with African elephants, and they perform a popular, regular show in the centre of the zoo.

There is a children's farm area, an amusement arcade, a miniature scenic railway, and a wonderful adventure playground. The animals in the children's area are labelled 'Familiar Friends', and are fenced off with very effective ranch-rodeo corral-style fencing. Among the more unfamiliar of the familiar friends are 'zeedonks' – the strange hybrid offspring of a zebra and a black Arabian ass. Colchester claims to have the only zeedonks in the world, and there is little reason to doubt it.

Some new accommodation for primates houses an interesting group of silver leaf langurs, and there is a well designed marmoset house with high, interesting enclosures. There are golden lion tamarins here, among others.

There are white rhinos with a generous outside pen with a pond, tree trunks, and muddy wallows. A wooden walkway provides a good view of these splendid animals. There are condors, and bateleur eagles, in rather cramped aviaries, and there is an effective wolf-wood with Canadian timber wolves; a satisfactory aquarium, a small reptile house, improved accommodation for bears, an attractive birdcage walk, good waterfowl and flamingo ponds, and a small penguin pool. There are also sealions in a fairly small pool, and they put on performances at regular times.

There is a mood of change and rebuilding that is currently possessing this zoo, and many of the unsatisfactory enclosures that characterised the zoo in the 1980s have been rebuilt or replaced. Most notable among these is the new £250,000 chimpanzee house which covers an impressive 6,000 square feet, and which provides the chimps with very good day and night accommodation, allowing them plenty of climbing, with ropes and trees, and access to a large outdoor area that will open in 1992, including an artificial termite mound, and more features for climbing. The outdoor compound is walled, with viewing through glass.

Another new development has been 'Out of Africa', a walk-through area featuring mangabeys and colobus monkeys, and the zoo now keeps endangered lion-tailed maqaques in impressive new enclosures.

Through all the changes, Colchester looks set to remain a traditional, and very varied collection. It would be good to think that the visitors would welcome more specialisation –perhaps with the cats that the zoo keeps so well. However, there is still a place for generalist zoos like this, and with innovative direction, the New Colchester Zoo, as the signs recently called it, could well become The New and Improved Colchester Zoo. The omens look good.

THE COTSWOLD WILDLIFE PARK

Burford
Oxon OX18 4JW
Telephone: 0993 823006

How to find it:
Off the A361 Lechlade to Burford road, just
south of Burford.

Open: All year from 10.00 am

Prices: adult £3.80; child £2.20; OAP £2.20.

Area: 50 hectares / 120 acres

	Species	Animals
Mammals	42	246
Birds	125	532
Reptiles	64	208
Amphibians	11	24
Fish	32	134
Total	274	1144
Conservation		★★
Enclosures		★★
Education		★★
Recreation		★★★
Research		

The Cotswold Wildlife Park is set in the grounds of a nineteenth century
manor house in the lush countryside of Oxfordshire. One hundred and
twenty acres of the Bradwell Grove Estate has been set aside by its owner,
John Heyworth, as a fascinating and extremely beautiful setting for a
zoological collection.

A long straight drive leads from the park gates to a car park right in the
heart of the zoo. At once there is the impression of a great country estate,
given emphasis by the huge trees which dominate the park. One enormous
old oak that stands outside the manor is said to be six hundred years old,
and a massive wellingtonia behind the house is 130 years old and stands
almost 120 feet high. Equally impressive are several huge yews, and giant
Californian redwoods which rise high above the park.

The park is flat, and the walk around is pleasant and undemanding despite its size. Most paths are tarmac, and there are plenty of benches for the
weary to stop and rest. The zoo is, in a sense, divided into two: there is the
park with its huge open paddocks, aviaries, cats, and primates, and then
there is the walled garden-almost a zoo in itself.

The tour around the park begins with aviaries for owls and griffon vultures, and a big cage for those acrobats of the monkey family, the spider
monkeys. There is a children's farmyard which has an assortment of farm
animals. Then the path weaves away through dense woodland, past a neat
tapir house with Brazilian tapirs underneath a dark avenue of overhanging
oaks. Here too you might be rewarded with a glimpse of wallabies or of
capybaras – the world's largest rodents – hiding among the trees, and a
graceful flock of flamingos wading in a picturesque lake.

The major feature of the park is a magnificent five-acre African exhibit
where white rhinos, and zebras graze peacefully together. In front of the
manor is a second major attraction, red pandas in a circular moated compound; look out for the delightful little pandas high in the trees.

Nearby there are giant tortoises from Aldabara Atoll, and from the 'Tortoise Terminus' alongside, a miniature railway offers one of the best train rides in any zoo (Whipsnade excepted), providing an excellent view of the park.

Despite all the available space, the tigers look rather cramped with no platform or vantage point, but nearby the ostriches have a large wild field where they have successfully bred.

The Gothic style manor was built in 1804, and parts are now open to visitors as a brass-rubbing centre, and a bar.

In the courtyard of the manor buildings are the lar gibbons whose whoops can be heard all around the park, an aquarium, a small reptile house, an insect house with some vivid butterflies, and a splendid new exhibit for Indian and Egyptian fruit bats. Here too is a tremendous adventure playground where the remains of a huge Cedar of Lebanon carries a high tree house and slide.

The walled garden at the Cotswold Wildlife Park is a delight. It combines the quaint old-world charm of a kitchen garden with a whole collection of animals in among meticulously laid gardens. Little suricate meerkats stand motionless on little hind legs underneath an open sun lamp; clearly not lovers of the English weather. Here in the walled garden are pink-backed pelicans, Humboldt's penguins which breed regularly, coatis, otters, and many more smaller mammals and birds. Among the birds are scarlet ibis, kookaburras, and several parrots. A tropical house built in 1982 is the home to Mississippi alligators, a whole variety of birds like tanagers from America, and white eyes from Africa. The building was opened in 1982 and now has a rich luxuriant tropical foliage, hibiscus, bougainvillea, and banana trees, among others. There are primates too in the walled garden – ring-tailed lemurs, squirrel monkeys, and various tamarins, all pleasantly housed, and doing well.

There was once a time when the Cotswold Wildlife Park rather resembled a small zoo that had found itself a home in a big country estate. Huge fields that could well accommodate species of some conservation value instead grazed those ubiquitous domestic creatures llamas, Ankole cattle, and Bactrian camels; but things are changing for the better. The wide paddocks alongside the driveway now graze splendid scimitar horned oryx, and animals that were once kept only in pairs now seem to be building up encouraging groups. The Cotswold Wildlife Park would do well to resist the temptation to grow the collection to resemble yet another non-specialist zoo, but to use their space wisely with endangered hoofed mammals, and with primates that seem to do well here. Visitors will always come to the Cotswold Wildlife Park, it is a refreshing and pleasant place to spend a day among some very beautiful animals, and it has the potential to become a valuable conservation zoo.

CRICKET ST THOMAS

Chard
Somerset
Telephone: 0460 30755

How to find it:
Between Chard and Crewkerne on the A30

Open: All year from 10.00 am

Prices: adult £5.50; child £3.00; OAP £4.50.

Area: 16 hectares / 40 acres

	Species	Animals
Mammals	34	173
Birds	70	354
Reptiles	7	42
Amphibians		
Fish	9	51
Total	122	630
Conservation		★
Enclosures		★★
Education		★
Recreation		★★★★
Research		

It would be difficult to imagine a more beautiful setting for a wildlife collection than the country estate of Cricket St Thomas in the spectacular green rolling countryside of Somerset. We are not the first generation to recognise the splendid natural beauty of this valley. There has been a country house here since the time of the Domesday Book of 1086, and the estate particulars in 1896 describe Cricket as 'one of the healthiest places in the United Kingdom'. The present house was built by Sir John Soane in 1804, and both the house and the grounds were used as settings in the BBC TV series 'To the Manor Born'.

Cricket St Thomas first opened to the public in 1967 as 'The West Country Wildlife Park'. In those days the animals and the scenery were the sole attractions; but in recent years the park has diversified and now provides craft workshops, fairground rides, a scenic railway, a children's fort, and adventure trails as well as the growing wildlife collection. Perhaps for this reason the estate is now called simply 'Cricket St Thomas'.

As soon as you drive into the estate, the beauty of the place begins to work its charm. The long driveway is flanked with enormous beech trees, and the fields roll away revealing magnificent views down the valley. You park in the estate, not far from the house, and close to a little nineteenth century church. The walk around the park would be well worth taking, even if there were no animals present at all, just to relax and absorb the tranquillity of the countryside, and the beauty of the gardens. The park is spacious, but the paths are easy and well defined. You can even take your dog (if you have one), although understandably certain parts of the zoo will be out of bounds for him.

Like several other 'estate zoos', Cricket uses its walled garden to very good effect, and within it there is a major part of the collection. Among the many animals you will find here are Asian short clawed otters in a brand new enclosure with a flowing river, leopards in an interesting new enclosure featuring a huge tree trunk, wallabies, raccoons, lynx, coatis, and several attractive aviaries with eagle owls, boobook owls from New Zealand, and African fish eagles.

There are gibbons in an enclosure with lots of ropes, where they brachiate well. There is also a row of well kept monkey cages that are simple, but look well designed for breeding, with spacious off show nesting boxes. They hold cotton top tamarins, emperor tamarins, and a family of common marmosets. In the middle of the walled garden is a lemur house where several species of lemur breed successfully. They include the endangered black lemur, the Mayotte lemur and mongoose lemurs. Along one wall of the garden is a large tropical aviary, richly planted with lush vegetation. It is home to several species of free flying birds.

Outside the walled garden there is also a great deal to see. There are three Asiatic cow elephants, and they are exercised around the park by a mahout. This was originally intended to compensate for the lack of space in the old, small, elephant compound. A spacious new elephant house and a long half acre paddock have greatly improved the accommodation for elephants at the zoo, and they now have a bull elephant, Sahib.

Look out for the entrance to the aquarium down a dark grotto-like tunnel that opens out into an artificial cave with fish tanks in the walls. The fish are not spectacular, but children will love the dungeon like atmosphere of the place.

Outside once more, and the real delight of Cricket is the walk around the park. The river is fairly wide, and is flanked with rich pasture where Chapman's zebra, camels, wapiti, guanaco, and geese graze contentedly. The pathway leads along the river to the rare breeds farm, and across to the heavy horse centre: hardly traditional zoo animals these, but well worth seeing nonetheless, they are splendidly groomed, their hooves are spotless, and they look quite magnificent. The size of the heavy horses is always a surprise, and here the contrast is emphasised by a miniature Fallabella horse in the very next stall.

Flamingos wade in an idyllic setting on the river, and there are plenty of water birds, black swans, ducks, and geese. There are pelicans too, in a walk through enclosure. Near the flamingos is a spectacular new lemur enclosure, home to black and white ruffed lemurs and ring-tailed lemurs, and close by is a big new aviary for blue and gold macaws.

The animals at Cricket are well cared for, most of them breed well, their accommodation is, for the most part, spacious, and where the enclosure is less than satisfactory, such as the rather bare sealion pool, then a new and better one is being built. If zoos are to succeed then they must be rewarding to visit, and they must encourage you to come back. Cricket St Thomas is exactly the sort of place you will want to return to, often.

DRUSILLAS ZOO PARK

Alfriston
East Sussex
Telephone: 0323 870234

How to find it:
At the junction of the A27 LewesPolegate
road, and the B2108 to Alfriston

Open: All year from 10.30 am

Prices: adult £4.10; child £3.85; OAP £2.80.

Area: 5 hectares / 12 acres

	Species	Animals
Mammals	39	150
Birds	48	143
Reptiles	10	56
Amphibians	4	17
Fish	1	1
Total	102	367
Conservation		★
Enclosures		★★
Education		★★★
Recreation		★★
Research		

Drusillas Zoo Park is the smallest Good Zoo in this guide. With a reported area of 5 hectares (about 12 acres) it should be the same size as Bristol Zoo, but this includes the 'zoo village' as well, and the space occupied by the animal collection is really no more than five acres. Smallness, however, is almost a virtue here, and Drusillas has progressed from promoting itself as 'The Best Small Zoo in the South' to claiming now to be 'Probably the Best Small Zoo in the Country'. Drusillas is also one of the oldest Good Zoos in this guide. It was opened as a Tea Cottage and Pet's Corner by Captain Ann in 1923 which makes it the same age as Paignton Zoo, and older than Chester, Whipsnade, and just about all of the estate zoos in the country. Today the zoo is run by the founder's son Michael Ann, and while it is now a Zoo Park with a whole collection of exotic animals, yet it still retains the ambience of the Tea Cottage and Pet's Corner it once was.

'We want Drusillas to be a child's first zoo,' says Michael Ann, and with that aim in mind the whole emphasis of the zoo is upon learning, and the target audience is quite clearly not the adult visitor, but the child. The scale of the zoo is small, not simply in land area, but also in the size of animals in the collection. There are no large cats, but there are small cats (serval); there are no large primates, but there are small ones – lemurs, marmosets, tamarins, capuchins, and vervet monkeys. The space in the zoo has been used well, so that most enclosures are a fair size by comparison with other zoos that keep the same animals, but the pathways and public spaces have been proportionately reduced. Many of the enclosures have plainly been designed for best effect from a child's eye view, and there is plenty for young children to look at and do.

A walk around the zoo begins with an innovative 'Life on Earth' display, a combination of natural-history-museum type exhibits, and live animals that unfold the story of evolution. There is an ominously smoking volcano, and a collection of fish, amphibians and reptiles here, and behind the crocodiles looms the model head of a triceratops.

Other attractions for children include the children's farm with some very tame animals, a classroom and discovery centre inside an old double-decker bus, a rainforest display where children can write their feelings about forest destruction on a blackboard, and a superb adventure play-ground and train ride.

Many of the animal enclosures at Drusillas share a common design concept which is virtually unique to this zoo. Instead of a wire or glass barrier, they are constructed like enclosed stockades of pine, open to the sky, or roofed (where appropriate) with wire. Visitors look in through glass windows. This creates the curious impression of looking out upon the animals, almost as if it were the visitors who were enclosed, and the animals at liberty. It is a very effective technique, used at its best with the new monkey mountain sanctuary. Big shop-windows, set into pine walls, look into a carefully landscaped compound, home to perhaps a dozen little squirrel monkeys. It is a fine example of the way that Drusillas has taken a group of animals that might elsewhere have been housed in a dull wire cage, and presented them in an interesting and naturalistic setting. Another, still more imaginative enclosure, is the meerkat mound. Meerkats are delight-ful little dark eyed burrowing mongooses from the Kalahari, notable for their unique social structure, and the selfless, apparently altruistic way in which senior members of the group will stand on guard duty while the rest of the group digs for grubs. Drusillas have turned their meerkat exhibit into a total educational experience. The Meet-the-Meerkat display has push-button information explaining the social group, and children can squirm through a rubber tube and emerge in a perspex dome in the middle of the meerkat mound to look at the meerkats from the perspective of their own world.

Imagination has played its part in the creation of the World of Owls, designed like an ancient wooden barn complete with old farm tools, and home to a well housed collection of owls. There is a new penguin pool (Penguin Bay) with good underwater viewing, and a rocky beach for Humboldt's penguins, a flamingo pool (Flamingo Lagoon) complete with an imitation hippo, and an excellent beaver compound, home to Canadian beavers. The enclosure won a UFAW (University Federation for Animal Welfare) award in 1987. Unfortunately, perhaps, great patience may be needed to spot the beavers who contrive to spend much of the time hidden.

Another new feature of the zoo, aimed almost exclusively at children, is the highly educational farmyard which features themed displays show-ing how much our daily lives depend upon cattle and pigs and sheep and hens. The farmyard includes, among the animals and a host of other attrac-tions, a full size (but artificial) milking cow named Matilda, that children can 'milk' into a pail.

Otters are well displayed in a new and well landscaped otter enclosure, and the path winds out through an Australian Outback exhibit with wal-labies and emus.

On the whole, Drusillas succeeds very well in in doing what it aims to do – providing a place where children can be educated and entertained, and introduced to animals.

DUDLEY AND WEST MIDLANDS ZOOLOGICAL SOCIETY

2 The Broadway, Dudley
West Midlands
Telephone: 0384 252401

How to find it:
Follow signs to Dudley Town Centre. The zoo is signposted just to the north of the town.

Open: From 9.00 am Mon Sat. From 10.00 am Sunday. All year.

Prices: adult £3.60; child £1.60; OAP £1.80.

Area: 19 hectares / 47 acres

	Species	Animals
Mammals	63	179
Birds	75	300
Reptiles	28	84
Amphibians	1	3
Fish	10	300
Total	177	866
Conservation		★★
Enclosures		★★
Education		★★
Recreation		★★
Research		

The town of Dudley lies to the West of Birmingham and to the South of Wolverhampton in the heart of the 'Black Country', once the industrial heartland of Britain. In the centre of town rises a high round hill, topped by the ruins of a 13th century castle, and all around the castle on the slopes of the hill lies Dudley Zoo.

It is a strange and rather grandiose setting for a zoo; and unlike other hilly zoos, such as Edinburgh or Penscynor, Dudley Zoo occupies the entire hill. For the energetic visitor there is a recommended route that follows a long spiral right round the hill, climbing slowly upwards towards the castle. The less energetic visitor might choose to take advantage of a short chair-lift ride from the main entrance to a spot halfway up, after which most of the zoo is downhill. There is also a free land-train ride from the zoo gates to the castle so visitors can start their day at the centre (and at the top) of the zoo.

Stepping from the streets of Dudley onto the tarmac pathways of the zoo, you might be surprised how green the whole place is. Much of the zoo seems to be under a dense canopy of trees. The climb takes you up past a wide variety of animals, beginning with a beautiful group of salmon-pink flamingos in a crystal clear pool, and several well planted aviaries. Among the best exhibits at this part of the zoo are the spotted hyenas– in a very good large enclosure, but viewed unusually from above, and giraffe in a clean paddock with a light airy house. There is a lovely herd of Barbary sheep in a terraced paddock, a herd of delicate Arabian gazelle – an endangered species which Dudley Zoo was the first to keep – and fallow deer in a large, steep but treeless field.

There are two African elephants, with an adequate although not large outside paddock, and slightly small and dark inside accommodation.

One individual and novel idea at Dudley is a wildfowl walk, half way along the recommended route. This takes the visitor on a winding nature trail past open wildfowl enclosures that each exhibit birds from a different continent. The setting for this is heavily wooded; the trees are all old and well established, and the walk is criss-crossed with streams, and well provided with picnic tables. The view at one point across to a limestone cavern could make you believe you were in the peak district, instead of in the heart of an industrial city.

There is a children's corner with a few popular favourites, but with no contact area. The reptile house has several huge pythons and a few venomous snakes; there is a small invertebrate house, and a farmyard. Also, at the foot of the hill are a few fairground rides, and a trainride through the woods. On the walk around the zoo are penguins, lions in a big grassy enclosure, maras in a large hillside area, tapirs, peccaries, and zebras.

One impressive, and optimistic new, glass-fronted enclosure takes in a swathe of hillside with an artificial stream. It houses a delightful pair of Asian short clawed otters. This enclosure was the joint winner of the Universities Federation for Animal Welfare Award in 1991.

The monkey house is imaginative with good high outside enclosures, well branched, with patas monkeys, lar gibbons, cotton topped tamarins and grivet monkeys, among others. The house is attractively built, mainly of wood. But if one thing can be said to spoil Dudley Zoo, then perhaps it is that other building material, concrete. How marvellous this all-purpose building material must have seemed to the zoo designers of the forties and fifties, and now at so many zoos the result of their designs, the concrete edifices of yester-year, still stand like monumental follies, supremely unsuited to the accommodation of wild creatures. Old concrete has a habit of looking its age, of growing damp, crumbling, and shedding flakes of paint. Dudley Zoo has a sad case of excess concrete, and the problem is worse because many of the concrete houses are now listed buildings, and the zoo could not legally demolish them if it wanted. Sometimes the concrete does its job reasonably well. The bear pit is better than most, and the Himalayan bears that occupy it have a high sloping back wall that provides them with a vantage point from which to look out. The enclosure takes in the old polar bear pit, once one of the less attractive parts of Dudley Zoo, but now quite an acceptable annex for the black and white Himalayan bears. The Patagonian sealions have a large but boring concrete pool.

Rather worse is the accommodation for the apes – the chimpanzees, orang utans and a single male gorilla. Inside, the dens are small, basic, and functional; outside, the yards are disappointing. They are small and entirely concrete with a few token posts or rubber tyres, although some new climbing facilities have recently been added. It is, however, an inadequate exhibit, and the apes all look bored.

It would be a shame if the few rather disappointing enclosures threatened to spoil the reputation of this zoo, because otherwise the impression at Dudley is of animals well kept and well cared for. Certainly this must rank as one of the cleanest zoos that we visited. Every enclosure is kept spotlessly clean, raked, brushed, and washed.

The climax of the visit to Dudley Zoo is the castle and the ruins of the Tudor Manor. Fifty two spiral steps lead to the top of the keep from where there is an astonishing view across the industrial West Midlands to the East, and the rolling hills of Wales to the West. A lot of money is being spent renovating the buildings which represent a fascinating attraction to visitors in their own right. If this spending is matched by appropriate spending on the animal collection, sweeping away the worst excesses of the post-war designers, and if some money is spent upon improving the visitor facilities including the rather derelict car park and the drab entrance way, then Dudley will be well on the way towards becoming a very good zoo.

THE ROYAL ZOOLOGICAL SOCIETY OF SCOTLAND: EDINBURGH ZOO

Corstorphine Road, Murrayfield
Edinburgh
Telephone: 031 334 9171

How to find it:
On the A8 road signposted to the Airport, 2 miles from the City centre.

Open: Weekdays from 9.00 am, Sundays from 9.30 am incl Christmas.

Prices: adult £4.30; child £2.30; OAP £2.30; family (2a2c) £12.00

Area: 32 hectares / 79 acres

	Species	Animals
Mammals	64	319
Birds	79	382
Reptiles	25	179
Amphibians	7	491
Fish		
Total	175	1371
Conservation		★★★
Enclosures		★★
Education		★★★★
Recreation		★★
Research		★★

The first zoo ever established in Scotland was The Royal Edinburgh Zoological Gardens. It opened its gates to the public in 1839, and closed them again eighteen years later, after running into difficulties. For over half a century the Scots still had to travel south of the border to see the exotic creatures that had captured the imaginations of the English. Eventually it was not a naturalist or an animal collector who provided Scotland with a new zoo: it was a solicitor. He was Thomas Hailing Gillespie, a law agent from Dumfries, who despite his profession had no great love for the law. Instead he longed to establish a Zoological Park in Scotland's capital city. The advice he received was not encouraging. 'You'll never get animals to live in a climate like Edinburgh's', he was told; and he might have believed it had he not, in 1908, read of Carl Hagenback's new zoo at Hamburg where tropical animals were happily thriving in a winter climate more severe that any experienced in Scotland.

Gillespie determined that he would pursue his dream. He started by founding a Zoological Society, and then by searching for a suitable site. In 1912 he found it. The estate of Corstophine Hill House, close to the city centre, with a fine house and pleasant gardens, was offered to the Society for the sum of £17,000. The money proved difficult to raise, but on 4th February 1913 the Edinburgh City Council purchased the site for the Society, and with a further £8,000 provided by members, Gillespie set about building his zoo.

It took only fifteen weeks to prepare and stock the site – initially with borrowed animals, and the new Zoological Park opened its gate to visitors on 15th July 1913.

Two of the principal enclosures on the new site were to set the style for what was to become an exciting and innovative city zoo. These were the lion and bear enclosures, fashioned after Hagenback's open compounds. Both were quarried out of the hillside housing the animals behind ditches against a natural backdrop of whinstone rock.

Under Gillespie's direction the new Edinburgh Zoo grew and flourished. New buildings and enclosures were gradually added to the collection, and as adjoining land became available, this too became part of the zoo. In 1927 a grant enabled the building of the great Carnegie Aquarium, a new Ape House followed in 1929, and in 1933 the Wolf Wood was planted. Twice bombed in the second war, the zoo survived very lightly scathed, and in 1947, following a visit by King George VIth and Princess Margaret, the King granted the Society the honour of becoming 'The Royal Zoological Society of Scotland'.

During its early years, Edinburgh Zoo soon established a reputation for sound animal management. Its first sealion was born in 1934, the same year as the first of numerous beavers. In 1936 it reared its first chimpanzee, and in 1938 its first litter of wolves – a litter that three years later had to be destroyed for fear that bombing could lead to their escape. The war years saw the birth of Britain's first baby orang utan at Edinburgh. But despite these achievements, and others, the park made its most notable mark with a group of animals that were to become almost synonymous with Edinburgh Zoo – the penguins.

Edinburgh's long association with penguins owes its origins to the involvement of the Society's first president, Lord Salvesen, a law lord related to the family who owned the Leith whaling fleet of the South Georgia Whaling Company. Today a relationship between a conservation zoo and whalers would surely be unthinkable, but for the young zoo the whalers provided a rare supply of wildlife from the Southern oceans – among them a seemingly endless quantity of penguins. The first six arrived in 1914, and were met without any great enthusiasm from Gillespie, who was far more interested in the elephant seals that accompanied them. But as more penguins arrived every year, so it became clear that these animals thrived in the mild Scottish climate. Over eight hundred penguins were brought to the city by Salvesens over the years, for Edinburgh and for other zoos, and at one time or another the zoo has had representatives of almost every penguin species, including the first Adelie penguins ever seen in Europe and the first New Zealand 'fairy' blue. In the 1950s a came an incident now preserved in folklore. A keeper accidentally left open a gate to the penguin pool, and was followed by a parade of penguins all around the zoo. It was the start of Edinburgh's now famous 'Penguin Parade', an event still enjoyed not only by visitors every summer afternoon, but clearly also by the two thirds of the zoo's 120 or so penguins who choose to join in.

Today Edinburgh is very much a zoo in transition. The present director, Roger Wheater, is steering the zoo firmly in a direction where species management is paramount, and conservation has become the new objective. Within the zoo the number of species is falling steadily as the emphasis moves towards keeping species in larger numbers of each, and concentrating upon those that can be self-sustaining. A great deal of redevelopment is taking place with old enclosures being renovated and new enclosures created. There is a strong feeling that here at last is an urban zoo genuinely trying to outgrow its legacy, in an attempt to become a vigorous and successful modern collection.

Walking around Edinburgh Zoo can be hard work. The park rises steeply from the Corstophine Road, widening in the middle, and it is a stiff climb from the main entrance to the open paddocks and African Plains exhibit right at the top of the hill. Probably the best plan is to zig-zag gently upwards, and for this the guide book is well worth buying.

The old Carnegie Aquarium has now been closed. The salt water of the seawater tanks had corroded away the very frames of the building, and repair was simply too expensive. It has instead been converted into an impressive new entrance complex and a shop, 'Arkadia', and it will soon also house a new 'wildlife interpretive centre'.

Among the first animals to greet the visitor, from a huge aviary, are bald Waldrapp Ibis – Europe's rarest and most endangered bird, now being kept at Edinburgh in a cooperative project with Jersey Zoo.

Climbing slowly you pass sealions in a rocky pool, rheas and storks, and an important collection of pheasants, well illustrated on the signs, including Edward's Pheasant – a species decimated in the Vietnam War, Reeve's Pheasant, and the Cheer Pheasant – now the subject of a reintroduction programme into its former range in Pakistan where it became extinct in the 1970s.

Red pandas are popular, as always, housed in an enclosure with a tall fir where they hide effectively among the branches. A pair of polar bears occupy one of the zoo's main rocky enclosures where, like the brown bears, they are viewed at ' visitor eye level'. The polar bear enclosure is visually attractive, and the polar bears have recently produced two cubs, Edinburgh Zoo's well promoted 'Wee Sweetie', and another yet to be seen by visitors in 1992.

The monkey house, opened in 1972, has successful groups of Diana monkeys, spectacled langurs, and white-faced saki monkeys. It also holds the best collection of guenons in Britain, including Allen's swamp monkey. The monkey house uses natural trees for the animals and both indoor and outdoor runs have been recently greatly enriched with plenty of extra climbing facilities. New ape accommodation holds a new group of lowland gorillas, the first ever seen in Scotland. All the gorillas are on breeding loan at present, from Dublin, Bristol, Rotterdam, and Chicago. A new range for marmosets houses breeding groups of Geoffroy's marmosets, pygmy marmosets, and Goeldi's monkeys. A splendid and noisy group of siamang gibbons are kept in a suitable long cage and have twice bred, and close by is a redeveloped chimpanzee house holding a family group of chimps with a large well equipped play area and glass-fronted indoor dens. The play area is viewed across a green barrier at tree height from outside, and at ground level from inside. It looks across onto a children's playground so that chimpanzee and human can both watch each other at play.

The reptile house is a long hall with vivaria along both sides. It is an older style house, but well maintained. The reptiles kept include many important species, several the subject of inter-zoo management agreements. Beyond is the reptile breeding unit where windows afford visitors the view of incubating eggs and newly hatched young. Species propagated here include blue tongued skinks, rainbow boas and plumed basilisks.

Small cats are housed in redeveloped 'rock-dens' behind glass. They include leopard cats and margays. Large cats - the lions, tigers, leopards, and jaguars - are held in attractive compounds with a high background of rock; excellent for photographs, but perhaps rather small for the animals themselves.

The zoo's wolf wood still holds a small pack of Canadian timber wolves, although these no longer breed here, there are giraffe in a recently enlarged enclosure, pens for those rarely seen but delightful little antelopes – pudus and duikers – pygmy hippos that have bred here, beavers, and a pair of white rhino which breed well, unusually for this species which normally only breeds if kept in a herd.

Right at the top of the hill, with a panoramic view across the city, is one of the best features of the zoo, making it well worth the climb. It is an African Plains exhibit where zebra, red lechwe, and scimitar-horned oryx herd together. The latter two are important captive stock of what are both endangered species, and oryx from Edinburgh Zoo have already been sent back to Tunisia for reintroduction into the wild.

The zoo keeps a great many birds; waterfowl, cassowaries, which breed well, golden eagles, plenty of parrots, Chilean flamingos which breed here, several owls, and pelicans. But without a doubt it is the penguins that are still the highlight of the collection. The zoo now concentrates upon four species: the tall, yellow- collared king penguin, the striking rockhopper penguin with its startling red eyes and yellow plumes, and the more familiar and entertaining gentoo penguin. King penguins were among the first to be kept at Edinburgh, and when in 1919 the first chick was hatched its story was reported in almost every newspaper in the land. Many false alarms, accidents, infertile eggs, and premature deaths followed before the zoo really began to breed king penguins regularly, although the hatching rate is still not high, and the colony is not yet self perpetuating. The gentoos have a more impressive breeding record, nesting on artificial stone-filled nests, and between twenty and thirty chicks are reared every year, keeping the population of these birds at the zoo safely above ninety or more. The rockhoppers too are breeding, although in small numbers, and the zoo has now established them as a self sustaining group. Recently 25 macaroni penguins were added to the zoo population. They were all hatched from eggs collected in South Georgia. They join the rest of the zoo's penguins in in spectacular new £600,000 penguin enclosure, due to be opened by the Princess Royal in April 1992. It will be, without a doubt, the best penguin enclosure in Europe. It will house all of the zoo's king penguins, gentoo penguins, and macaroni penguins, providing them all with deep water for swimming, and with extensive beaches, as well as with a creche pool for the chicks. Two keepers have been trained as divers in order to look after the penguins effectively. For visitors there will be expansive underwater viewing, and a 20 metre suspension bridge over the whole area to allow 'over water viewing'. More than half the money for the new pool was raised from the public, members of the Zoological Society, and local businesses. The hope of the zoo is that the new pool will better suit the king penguins, reversing their decline.

If it is some time since you last visited Edinburgh Zoo, then expect some changes. There is a new mood about this zoo, a positive and enthusiastic mood, and if it continues then Edinburgh should continue to deserve its place among the most respected of British collections.

THE ZOOLOGICAL SOCIETY OF GLASGOW AND WEST OF SCOTLAND: GLASGOW ZOO

Calderpark, Uddingston
Glasgow
Telephone: 041 771 1185

How to find it:
Well signposted from the A74 and M74, 8
miles east of the city centre.

Open: All year from 10.00 am

Prices: adult £3.20; child £1.95; OAP £1.95.

Area: 15 hectares / 37 acres

	Species	Animals
Mammals	34	117
Birds	19	60
Reptiles	28	60
Amphibians	20	60
Fish		
Total	101	297
Conservation		★★
Enclosures		★★
Education		★★★
Recreation		★★
Research		★

Just south-east of Glasgow by the great road North (now the M74), Glasgow Zoo occupies an attractive rolling, parkland, site. This is despite the urban sprawl that lies to one side, and the industrial sprawl of Lanarkshire that spreads out to the other. Somehow there is a park here, Calderpark, on a heavily wooded hillside, by the banks of North Calder Water, with views looking out over tree tops and down the river valley.

The Calderpark Estate, once farmland worked by Cistercian monks, was bought by the Zoological Society of Glasgow and West of Scotland in 1939. The splendid nineteenth century mansion that once dominated the estate had been demolished almost a decade earlier, after subsidence from underground coal mines had made the building unsafe. It was a perfect setting for the zoo that the young Zoological Society planned to construct; and its aim would be to provide for the people of Glasgow a wildlife spectacle of the sort that had been available to the citizens of Edinburgh since 1909.

It took eight years to fund, design, build, and stock the new zoo. The first director was Sidney Benson, and he opened the zoo to the public in 1947. The scale of the zoo was never likely to be as ambitious as Edinburgh's, and like so many institutions on the West of Scotland it grew for many years in the shadow of its more prestigious Edinburgh counterpart. But grow it did, and the land it now occupies gives it room for even more growth, down into the valley and alongside the ox-bow loch.

Additional land, now being developed for the zoo, was formerly a rubbish tip and landfill site for demolished Glasgow tenements when the new director of the Society, Richard O'Grady, took up his post at Calderpark Zoo. For a while this led to a curious problem of infestation – curious for a zoo at least – with the most abundant mammal on Earth after man, the brown rat; the problem was solved by a capable posse of fox terriers, along with more conventional methods of pest control.

Today, according to the guidebook, Glasgow Zoo is a 'fast developing and forward-looking zoo', and it does seem as if the zoo in recent years has been virtually rebuilt, starting with basic services – drains, water, electricity and new tarmac pathways, and extending to large new paddock areas and new animal houses. The rebuilding is sorely needed in many places, where some rather old-fashioned cages no longer really represent the new mood of the zoo.

The highlight of the collection here are the bears, the cats, primates, and reptiles. The cat house, although small, has some beautiful and fascinating species, and has had good breeding successes with leopard and jaguar. Today there are margays, clouded leopards, caracals, and Geoffroy's cats here too. The cat dens are not large, but are carefully branched with wood chips on the floors. Grassy enclosures house the lions, tigers and cheetahs. The tiger fields are imaginatively landscaped, and the cheetah enclosure has an excellent high platform where the cheetah can sit, high above the wire netting, proudly surveying the whole zoo and looking superb.

The monkey house is one part of the zoo that clearly needs rebuilding. It holds white-throated capuchin monkeys from South America, and black macaques from the Pacific island of Celebes. The outside enclosures are adequate, but the inside accommodation is poor, and there is little use made of the dimension of height. From the monkey house the pathway leads down into the valley, past neat little paddocks with camels and geese, maras, rheas, and peacocks.

There is a spacious enclosure here for those most lovely of deer, the axis deer of India, but the paddock is heavily grazed, with very little grass. Barbary sheep are here too, in a sloping little enclosure quite suited to their capable climbing skills. There are mouflon, too, and collared peccaries in a good sized enclosure.

The reptile collection is housed in a large tropical house. It is a long, rectangular building, and the vivaria are built-in down each wall. The building is not a tropical house in the sense of a well planted free-flight hall, but it is the zoo's largest building, and also contains the zoo's offices. Nearby are some splendid giant tortoises from Aldabara, a remote little atoll in the Indian Ocean. They have one of the biggest giant tortoise enclosures in Britain.

Of the older sections of the zoo that still survives the new broom of Mr O'Grady and the army of job creation volunteers, the most notable is the thirty year old polar bear pit, now at last empty of polar bears. It is a very deep pit with high rockwork, but like polar bear pits around the country it attracted vociferous criticism, and when the last bear died in 1990, it was decided that no new bears would be brought in.

Much better, in fact the undoubted highlight of Glasgow Zoo, is the new Himalayan black bear enclosure. This is an outstanding zoo exhibit, the culmination of a long and productive cooperation between the zoo authorities, several animal welfare societies, and Alloa Brewery, who pro-

Cheetah

vided some of the funding. The enclosure opened on 1st August 1988, and it won the Zoo Animal Welfare Award from the Universities Federation for Animal Welfare in 1989. It consists of a three-acre tract of woodland with well established trees, and some younger fir trees planted around. The whole area is terraced, and you may have to be patient and watchful to spot the bears if they have chosen to stay hidden. The compound is carefully landscaped; there are great pipes to hide in, huge rocks, mountains of sticks and branches, and a towering observation platform in the middle (similar to the cheetah pen), where the bears can look out over the zoo.

A second new enclosure that deserves mention is the big white rhino field, with its great muddy wallow, and its grassy, landscaped terrain. The pair of rhinos look well here, and there are high hopes that they might soon breed. The rhino house has extended into the elephant house, vacated while Glasgow's only elephant, Kirsty, spends a long but hopefully productive vacation with Jubilee at Chester Zoo.

Overall, Glasgow Zoo has succeeded rather well in maintaining its mixed collection of animals during a period of major rebuilding and extension. The new bear enclosure must be one of the finest in Europe, and there seems to be a positive mood of regeneration about the place. To date, the conservation objectives of the zoo have been fairly low key, but as more of the land is developed, and more species are added, there is a real hope that some significant Red Data Book species will arrive here. All things considered, it looks as if the Glasgow and West of Scotland Zoological Society are at last providing for the people of Glasgow an exciting and developing zoological garden.

THE ROYAL ZOOLOGICAL SOCIETY OF SCOTLAND: HIGHLAND WILDLIFE PARK

Kincraig, Kingussie, Nr Aviemore
Invernessshire
Telephone: 054 04 270

How to find it:
Well signposted off the A9 at Kingussie

Open:
Telephone for details

Prices: car driver only £4.00; driver + 1
£6.00; driver + up to 6 £9.00; walkers £4.50.

Area: 105 hectares / 259 acres

	Species	Animals
Mammals	29	177
Birds	30	139
Reptiles		
Amphibians		
Fish		
Total	59	316
Conservation		★
Enclosures		★★
Education		★★
Recreation		★★★
Research		

Twelve thousand years ago, when the great glaciers that created the Scottish valleys began to retreat, they were followed by a wealth of wildlife. Herds of reindeer, musk oxen, and saiga antelope followed the melting ice northwards. They in turn were followed by wolves and arctic foxes, lemmings and hares, brown bears, lynx, and bison. The early broadleafed forests that hugged the Scottish Highlands were rich with living creatures. Eagles and buzzards soared high over the rugged landscape. Beavers dammed the streams. Roe deer and wild cattle grazed in the clearings.

Then came man to farm the valleys, with wheat and barley, cattle and pigs and sheep. The stage was set for another slow change in the landscape and wildlife of Scotland. Roman and Vikings burned and cleared the forests. The auroches, the lynx and the bear were hunted to extinction; the beaver was trapped for its fur; and in the centuries that followed hardy breeds of sheep spread across the hills, and the forests became moorlands. The bountiful wildlife paradise that Scotland had been was gone forever.

Forever? Well, perhaps not quite. There is one small corner of Scotland that serves as a reminder of what was, and what might have been. It is the Highland Wildlife Park, two hundred and sixty acres of heath and hillside set aside to keep and breed and show animals of Northern Europe, cousins of the creatures that stalked the same highlands in the dying centuries of the last ice age.

The man responsible for this simple and quite natural idea was a chartered surveyor named Neil Macpherson. He leased the land from a local landowner, persuaded the Highlands and Islands Development Board to fund the project, and in 1972 he opened the park to the public. For most visitors, and even for most Scots, the park is a long drive north on the A9 to Aviemore and Inverness. It is part drive-around 'safari' park, and part walk-around zoo. The two halves of the park complement each other, and perhaps provide the best of both worlds for visitors and for the animals. For many, the drive through area may be just the opportunity to stop and admire the magnificent highland scenery. Be patient in this part of the park. Stop in a layby, and turn off the engine. Wind down the windows, and just watch the animals. Be sure to bring binoculars and zoom lenses if you have them. There is a great deal to see, and you will need time to take it all in. You can often find deer lying up in the natural vegetation, and a guide book may help you identify the different species that graze the park. As well as deer you will find European bison, Przewalski's wild horses, and a variety of highland sheep and cattle. There is something awe inspiring about coming accross a bison grazing on a Scottish hillside; and where else can you see such a magnificent herd of red deer where the back-drop is so perfect?

Drive through the park and eventually you reach the zoo, where your walking tour begins. Here you will find a scattering of well-sized pens, well planted for Scottish wildcat, lynx, polecat, arctic fox, red fox, otters, and badger, just to name a few. The last two on that list have indoor dens with viewing inside or out. Most enclosures are rustic, chicken-wire and rough-pine posts, but they are effective nonetheless. Small aviaries house capercaillie, black and red grouse and some pheasants, and there is a waterfowl area alongside the beaver lake with a variety of European geese and ducks.

The other side of the zoo has an attractive, rocky, reindeer pen (what superb animals they are, when you see them in profile on a crag); and a row of aviaries, tall and built into the cliff face, with golden eagles (that every visitor wants to see), white-tailed eagles, buzzards, ravens, snowy owls and eagle owls.

Very few zoos seem to know what to do with bears. The Highland Wildlife Park has two rather traditional bear pits. They are fortunate to have natural rock and trees as an alternative to concrete, but the pits are pits all the same. They house European brown bears.

Close by are pens for wild boar, and there is a wolf compound which you can see walking or driving, but you cannot yet drive through in the way you can at some safari parks. It is an irony, perhaps, in the zoo world that it is often easier to get exotic species than it is to get native Europeans. Thus it is that the wolves are Canadian, rather than, say, Pyrennean, or Italian wolves, which are both particularly rare.

In January 1986 the Highland Wildlife Park was taken over by the Royal Zoological Society of Scotland, which also operates and develops Edinburgh Zoo. The merger looks as if it may benefit both collections. In particular, the Highland Wildlife Park will now fall under the direction of a society whose objectives are becoming rigorously conservationist. Already the park has introduced an education service, and has begun to outline its plans for future development. The otters will be moving to a larger enclosure; small mammals like hedgehogs, mice, stoats and shrews will be exhibited, as will some reptiles. The adder, after all, is not uncommon in these Highland pastures, but is not yet kept in the park. An education centre, with classroom facilities for sixty children was opened by the Princess Royal in 1991. More interpretational signs are planned, and the collection may even be rearranged around the habitat zones in the park. Imagine roe deer and lynx in adjoining broadleafed woodland paddocks, to represent the predator and its prey; or bison and wolves in mixed pine forest.

Finally, be sure not to leave the Highland Wildlfe Park without climbing to the hill-top for the magnificent views, east over the valley to the Cairngorms, north towards Aviemore and Loch Insh, west to the Monadhliath range, and south down the River Feshie valley. Imagine how it must been as the melt waters of the great glacier swept down the valley, and the land belonged to the animals. The animals must be protected for the future. One day much of the land may belong to them once more. That is the sustaining image that we hope you bring away from this optimistic and attractive wildlife park.

HOWLETTS ZOO PARK

Bekesbourne, nr Canterbury
Kent
Telephone: 0227 1721286

How to find it:
Signposted from A2 (Canterbury to Dover road) or the A257 Canterbury Wingham road. 1 mile from Bekesbourne station.

Open: All year from 10.00 am

Prices: adult £6.50; child £4.50; OAP £4.50. Includes half-price entry to Port Lympne Zoo.

Area: 27 hectares / 70 acres

	Species	Animals
Mammals	49	411
Birds	5	17
Reptiles	3	20
Amphibians		
Fish		
Total	57	448
Conservation		★★★★
Enclosures		★★★★
Education		★★★
Recreation		★★★★
Research		★★

What sort of man could singlehandedly change the entire genre of zoo-keeping in Britain, despite over a century and a half of experience that tells us what sort of places zoos ought to be? What sort of man could turn his back upon the zoo community, and yet could still build up within two decades one of the most self-sustaining collections of endangered species in the world? What sort of man could turn zoo-keeping literally on its head, spoiling his animals, spending far more on each animal than any other zoo in the world, achieving the grudging admiration of even the anti-zoo lobby? He would need to be a notably singleminded pioneer; and to have a very great deal of money as well as a passion for animals.

The man who achieved this is John Aspinall. He has conceived, built and financed two of the most outstanding zoos in the world (his other zoo is twenty miles further south at Port Lympne). A series of accidents at them brought some early notoriety, but they should not divert attention from what may justly be presented as landmarks in the history of zoos, and probably in the history of a fair number of animals as well.

Howletts *is* John Aspinall, and there are not many people in the world quite like him. As a gambler, dilettante and socialite, he made and lost fortunes. He missed his final exams at Oxford because they clashed with Royal Ascot and he fancied a horse (which won). But even while he was earning a reputation as first a card player then casino operator in London, an unexpected side of his personality was beginning to emerge: Aspinall the high-roller was becoming Aspinall the animal-lover. In 1956 he bought a capuchin monkey, his first animal, as a present for his wife. He followed it with a tigress, 'Tara', and a pair of Himalayan bears, 'Esau' and 'Ayesha'. The strange collection shared their flat in Eaton Place. He began paying regular visits to London Zoo, particularly to see 'Guy', London's famous silver-back gorilla. In time Guy came to recognise him among the crowd, and so began a friendship and a fascination with gorillas, that would eventually lead Aspinall to establishing the largest and most successful captive colony of gorillas in the world, at Howletts Zoo.

Howletts began when the little collection moved out to the country home that Aspinall bought in 1957. The mansion at the centre of the estate was practically derelict, but the grounds seemed exactly right for his purpose – to provide the right home for the animals he thought of as friends. The zoo would not open to the public for almost two decades when bankruptcy forced the move; but in that time an extraordinary thing had happened at Howletts: the 'zoo' had been reinvented.

One essential thing sets Howletts (and by association, Port Lympne) apart from every other zoo. It is the simple maxim that keepers are encouraged to develop close emotional bonds with their animals. That bond tends to involve playing with the animals, as well as cleaning up after them and feeding them. In this respect Aspinall is either a pioneer, a prophet, or a pariah, depending upon your point of view. Certainly other zoos and many lofty voices have reacted sternly against this idea. After all, it runs counter to the most modern dictums in zoo keeping – that animals are essentially *wild*, and that they need to develop a distance between themselves and human beings. Yet Aspinall dares to challenge this most closely held dogma with almost religious fervour. He rough-and-tumbles regularly with tigers and gorillas, often on a Sunday when visitors can watch, and his family join in with, it seems, equal enthusiasm. The zoo guide shows his wife Sally in with the tigers, and describes how their youngest son Bassa was 'shoved in with adult gorillas when he was only six months old'. This is more than simply a technique in animal husbandry: it is a doctrine that places animals and man on the same level and urges us to love and understand animals in the same way as we do each other, through close physical contact, communication, and respect.

Treating animals as friends manifests itself particularly in the way that animals are fed at Howletts. Most zoos settle upon a scientifically formulated diet for each species – often a dull form of 'cattle cake'. Aspinall believes in feeding with variety and quality. The gorillas at Howletts have a diet that consists of more than 150 different things, including the freshest and finest tropical fruits, mangoes, paw paws, celery, strawberries, sugar cane, even roast pork; and what is true for the gorillas is equally true elsewhere – the elephants receive maize, herbal hay, mangold, lucerne, and a whole variety of fruits and vegetables.

Good or bad, right or wrong, one thing is certain about the Aspinall approach: it seems to work. Even his critics will admit that the animals at Howletts breed well, perhaps better than any other zoo. Ninety percent of the species kept here breed successfully; and while many zoos will claim only to keep animals that they confidently expect to breed, at Howletts you can believe it. Many of the animals here are rare both in the wild and within zoos, and yet they breed; bongos, for example, are elusive, lovely, striped forest antelopes, and have bred here; (Howletts founded the only captive herd in the world, now kept at Port Lympne). Howletts was the first zoo in the world to breed the secretive honey badger, and was the first British zoo to breed clouded leopards, Siberian tigers, African elephants, Przewalski's horse, fishing cats, snow leopards, Javan brown langurs, and chousingha (little four-horned antelope). Douc langurs from Cambodia and Vietnam, one of the most beautiful of all monkeys, with white and yellow faces, were almost wiped off the planet in a war they had no part in. Nowadays you will hardly ever see them, but Howletts keeps and breeds them.

Every enclosure, and every group of animals at Howletts is so special, and so out of the ordinary, that if you were to visit and see only one species each time it should be reward enough. The park itself is also a delight. It has been a park since the time of Henry VIII, and many of the great trees are still believed to date back this far. Prominent among them is the 'Howletts chestnut', probably one of the oldest in Britain, and the path around the zoo takes in a woodland walk beneath some quite magnificent cedars, oaks, sweet chestnut and beech. Many ancient trees came down on the night of the hurricane in 1987, including two mighty Huntingdon elms, and the zoo closed for several months as repairs to enclosures were undertaken. Now the gardeners are busy replanting, and although our generation will not see Howletts again as it was, perhaps our great-grandchildren will.

Tigers and their prey species are a dominant theme at Howletts. Tigers were Aspinall's first love among the animal kingdom, and this zoo breeds more tigers than any other zoo in the world, around twenty a year. In true

Aspinall fashion no animal will ever be 'put down' as surplus to require-
ments, so the tiger population here is burgeoning. Perhaps this is a problem because the tiger compounds are starting to look rather full, and many
will soon be due for rebuilding. The traditional prey species of the tigers at
Howletts include blackbuck, chousingha, sambar deer, nilghai (the largest
Asian antelope), axis deer (beautiful, lightly spotted deer), water buffalo, and
hog deer (which are tiny by comparison with the rest). Many of these animals
inhabit the walk-through deer park, and others require patience to spot in the
huge wooded paddocks in which they roam.

There are ten African elephants at Howletts at present, including one
adult bull and an infant bull. They look magnificent, and are usually seen
browsing their way through a mountain of branches. For several years they
occupied a single, long concrete stockade, fenced with railway girders.
This accommodation, although satisfactory, never seemed quite sufficient, especially as the group of elephants grew. Negotiations were held
with a neighbouring landowner, and finally an agreement was struck for
the zoo to buy twelve additional acres of an adjoining orchard. In 1991 the
elephants were introduced into the first few acres –the sand paddock –a
circular, sandy field which at a stroke more than quadrupled their space.
But more is to come. Fencing work on the long, sloping orchard should be
complete in 1992, and the elephants are then to be admitted. Quite how
long it will take them to dispose of all the trees (and there are dozens) is any-
body's guess. But it should be a sight worth seeing.

Apart from the tigers there are a great number of cats at Howletts, but
do not expect to see many of them. Their enclosures, in general, do not
invite close inspection; the barriers are well back, and most, like the
clouded leopard, the marbled cat, the ocelot, and the rusty spotted cat from
Sri Lanka are either nocturnal, or highly secretive, or both, and Aspinall's
zoos do not oblige many creatures to display themselves unless they particularly chose to do so. Visit early in the morning, or late into the evening,
however, and be patient, and you may be rewarded; the experience should
mean more than any number of cats seen elsewhere behind glass on a tiled
floor.

Primates, including the famous Howletts gorillas, are the crowning glory
of this zoo. Siamangs are the largest of the gibbons; they are black and bushy,
and have balloon-like inflatable necks that amplify their whooping calls so
that their duets can be heard not just around the zoo, but all around Bekesbourne as well. They are master acrobats, and no other British zoo gives them
such opportunity to show it, with great, tall, intensively roped cages. There
are similar homes for capuchins, and few visitors will fail to be moved by the
family groups of three of the rarest monkeys in the world, the Douc langur,
the Javan brown langur, and the banded langur. They are all leaf-eating monkeys, and none have been well served by zoos in the past. If Howletts succeeds
with just one of these most precious creatures, then future generations will
have much to thank them for.

It would take more space than is available here to describe the full riches of Howletts. It is the Louvre of zoos. The late Dian Fossey, famous for her pioneering work with mountain gorillas in Rwanda, hated all zoos with a passion; but she made an exception for Howletts when she visited the zoo in 1984. What convinced her was the colony of gorillas. Many other zoologists also consider what she saw at Howletts to be the single best zoo 'exhibit' of any kind anywhere in the world. What is special about Aspinall's gorillas at Howletts is the sheer nerve of it. At present there are thirty five gorillas in the 10,000 square yard gorillarium. The numbers have been as high as forty, but five gorillas departed to Port Lympne in 1991. At the time of writing another baby is expected soon, but then gorilla births are practically routine here now, and all but ten of the gorillas were born at Howletts. They are formed into three social groups (a fourth is planned), each with a huge silver back male. Djoum, the largest of Aspinall's gorillas, came to Howletts as a starving infant in 1970. Today he weighs over 450 lbs (33 stone), and has fathered four youngsters. John Aspinall calls Djoum (who is now at Port Lympne Zoo) one of the 'greatest successes of his life', and counts him as one of his closest friends; and despite their size, their enormous latent power and the mistaken reputation of the gorilla for brute savagery, there are few visitors who could stand and watch the gorillas playing in the great playground at Howletts who would not wish to have one as a friend as well.

The gorillarium, consists simply of two huge wire cages, and a row of bedrooms connected by overhead tunnels. The complex is reported to have cost only £20,000 to build (in the 1960's), a fraction of the cost of many grossly more elaborate, but far less suitable gorilla houses elsewhere in the country. The ceiling of the cages is rimmed with struts, along which the apes can swing, and hung with ropes and playthings. The floor is more than four feet deep with oat straw, which is changed only every two to three years. The idea horrifies many zoo directors who favour white tile and concrete, and despite the example of Howletts, so many zoo gorillas are still kept in what look like mortuaries. The straw serves several functions. As it slowly rots down it generates warmth, right through the year; it mimics the soft forest floor that gorillas would find in their wild habitat, protecting them in their boisterous play; and it gives them the opportunity to forage all through the day for the fruit and nuts which the keepers scatter daily, and for the grubs and beetles that find a natural home in the straw. This means that the gorillas here never seem bored; as you walk into the kitchen garden and first encounter the gorillas, the impression is one of great activity, movement, and play. The effect is magnetic, and visitors find themselves rooted here, spellbound by the sight of so many great apes at play.

In less than three decades this small zoo near Canterbury has entirely raised the horizons of zoo keeping. There are places where the zoo is beginning to show its age, but this is trivial when you consider the achievements that have been made, and still are being made. Aspinall is still treated as something of an interloper by many zoo people, resented perhaps for his idiosyncratic ideas, for his lack of professional training, and for the way he openly shuns organisations like the National Federation of Zoological Gardens, to which most other Good Zoos in this guide (apart of course from Port Lympne) belong. In time, perhaps, Howletts will have to face up to the role it must play in the wider community of zoos; but other zoos too will need to watch Howletts – it is an ideas factory that is setting the standards that they will have to follow sooner or later. In the end, that may prove to be the most valuable legacy of this zoo.

JERSEY WILDLIFE PRESERVATION TRUST: JERSEY ZOO

Les Augres Manor, Trinity
Jersey, Channel Islands
Telephone: 0534 864666

How to find it:
Five miles north of St Helier well signposted.

Open: All year from 10.00 am

Prices: adult £4.00; child £2.00; OAP £2.00.

Area: 9 hectares / 22 acres

	Species	Animals
Mammals	28	325
Birds	37	538
Reptiles	25	414
Amphibians	4	81
Fish		
Total	94	1358
Conservation		★★★★
Enclosures		★★
Education		★★★★
Recreation		★★
Research		★★★★

No other British zoo has a reputation quite like Jersey Zoo. In the zoo world it stands almost alone. Visitors from all around the world, who might never think to visit Alderney or Skye or the Isle of Wight, make a special pilgrimage to this little Channel Island just to drive from one corner to the other and visit a modest manor estate whose name has almost become a synonym for conservation in zoos: ' The Jersey Wildlife Preservation Trust'. No other zoo devotes such a high proportion of its resources towards conservation projects overseas; no other zoo in the world (it would seem fair to guess) attracts such a high proportion of its visitors from other countries; and no other zoo has had a character quite so eminent as Gerald Durrell as director.

It might so easily have been 'Bournemouth Zoo', or 'Poole Zoo'. Those were the first two places that Gerald Durrell tried when he decided that the time had come, in 1956, to start his own zoological collection. Durrell was himself a former zookeeper. He worked as a student at Whipsnade with a whole variety of animals, and in 1947 he set off for the British Cameroons, on a privately financed six month trip to collect animals for British zoos

– angwantibos for London, guenons for Chester, mongooses and drills for Paignton, and a treasure hoard of other creatures for Manchester and Bristol. The journey, the first of many, was a turning point in Durrell's life. For a start it embarked him upon a literary career – his book, 'The Overloaded Ark', chronicled the trials and tribulations the of trip; but more importantly, some would say, the journey to the Cameroons began what he would later describe as 'an ever growing sense of disquiet'. He began to grow unhappy about the attitude of zoos towards their animals – as essentially disposable and replaceable commodities. He grew impatient with what he saw as hopeless ignorance of wildlife among zoo owners and directors, and he began to develop a concern for what he described as 'the low ebb species', animals that mankind had a duty to sustain as a precaution against their disappearance in the wild.

The only resolution to the unease was to start his own zoo; but it would be a different zoo. In 1956 it was difficult, almost impossible, to get anyone to believe that a zoo could have a serious purpose beyond mere entertainment. Durrell believed that it was possible. Bournemouth and Poole resisted his approaches, but their loss was Jersey's gain. Armed with a £25,000 loan from his publishers, Durrell flew to Jersey in 1959, and rented the fifteenth century Les Augres Manor and its surrounding twenty acres with an option to buy if his venture succeeded. The early days were a hand-to-mouth existence. Durrell wrote furiously to maintain a steady income from his books to support the fledgling collection; and then at last, what began as a fairly traditional resort zoo began to take on a unique new identity. Jersey's conservation work had begun.

At the entrance to the zoo stands a pottery model of a dodo. It has become Jersey Zoo's symbol, and its stark warning of extinction is an everyday concern within the park. The list of the zoo's occupants reads like a roll call of creatures whose futures hang literally in the balance: animals like the parma wallaby which was thought for many years to be extinct until a small group was found on the Island of Kawau; the Rodrigues fruit bat which may number fewer than a hundred wild individuals; the bald (or 'waldrapp') ibis now restricted to only two perilous breeding sites: Edward's pheasant and white-eared pheasant whose wild populations are quite unknown. These and many other creatures, familiar and unfamiliar, may owe their very existence to the Jersey Wildlife Preservation Trust; and what the trust does (if only every other zoo would copy them) is to seek to provide holistic support for every species that it cares for. So it is that Jersey has managed or been involved with such a list of projects that it would take a booklet to cover them all. They have cooperated in releasing golden lion tamarins back into the wild in Brazil, have repatriated literally dozens of hutias to Jamaica, have reared and released nearly extinct native kestrels and pink pigeons in Mauritius, and thick-billed parrots into Arizona, where they had been considered extinct for fifty years. They have cooperated with the Indonesian government in an attempt to save the white Bali starling, with the Philippines government to save the Palawan pheasant, with the government of St Lucia to save the St Lucia parrot, with the government of Madagascar to provide lemur breeding facilities at Parc Tsimbazaza, and with the United States National Zoo in Washington to breed Goeldi's monkeys (over sixty have been born here). The US National Wildlife Service decided the black-footed ferret was extinct, but when one turned up alive the trust became involved and a few wild ferrets were found with financial help from the Trust, and bought into captivity in Wyoming where they are now breeding. Recent projects involve the volcano rabbit (a creature found only on the slopes of four Mexican volcanos), and the hog-like tusked babirusa from Sulawesi and Tonga. And one highly imaginative project involves the little Mauritian island, Round Island, whose native fauna and flora was practically eradicated by introduced rabbits and goats. Durrell and his team have helped to manage a showcase rescue of the island. The offending mammals have been removed, the vegetation is regenerating, and three Round Island reptiles, a skink, a gecko, and a boa (probably the rarest snake in the world) are breeding well at Jersey Zoo.

Most zoos offer up the palliative that their animals are being bred for reintroduction into the wild. Jersey Zoo has proved that with dedication it can be done.

It is not a large zoo. At only twenty-two acres it is one of the smallest zoos in this guide. Space has never been one of Durrell's primary concerns; indeed in 'The Stationary Ark' he roundly refutes the zoogoer's demands for more space for animals, which he claims they do not need. The outcome is an unusual collection of some of the world's rarest animals, with many in rather unnoteworthy enclosures. The impression at Jersey is of tidy, park-like grounds, with grassy open spaces, neat pathways, well tended shrubberies, and a swampy valley that snakes into the park and provides a home for the splendid colonies of water fowl and rare cranes. The manor house is a beautiful example of French-style Jersey architecture. Its oldest parts date back to the fourteenth century, and the rough granite outbuildings and kitchen gardens are now an integral part of the new zoo.

Probably Jersey's most celebrated residents are the gorillas. Gorillas have a long association with the zoo, and the new 'gorilla breeding centre', opened in 1981, is astounding. It consists of glass-fronted indoor dens with plenty of space, leading outside to a rolling grassy field. The field is landscaped with a shallow pool, sand pit, climbing trees, nets and ropes. Much of the grass is left to grow long and provides an excellent foraging area. The whole enclosure is surrounded by a high wall overlooked by visitors. The dominant male of this group is a huge silver-backed gorilla named Jambo, himself captive born and parent reared, and he is now the father of numerous young gorillas, and has proved to be an excellent parent. There are nine gorillas at the time of writing, but the zoo has been unselfish in sending its gorilla offspring far afield where they are needed. Seven of the twelve gorillas reared at Jersey are away on breeding loans.

Alongside this enclosure is a 'gorilla walk' that mirrors the climbing facilities within, allowing children to exercise in true ape fashion while being quizzically observed by a family group of Western lowland gorillas.

Such is the dedication towards species conservation at Jersey, that the zoo thinks nothing of filling an entire house or a whole row of aviaries with a single species. In many other zoos this idea would be unthinkable, but far from being boring, this specialisation can encourage you to look more closely. The sole species within the nocturnal house are little Jamaican hutias (a primitive ground living rodent), and the volcano rabbits. They are hardly the sort of animals that will be familiar to any but the regular zoo-visitor, and yet the experience of visiting this one house is unique. On a slightly elevated site by the gorillas a double row of cages contains endangered black lion tamarins, the only ones outside Brazil. There may be less than fifty of these lovely creatures left in the wild. Even rarer is the rotund and delightful Mauritius pink pigeon which was rescued from the very brink of extinction when perhaps only ten birds remained in the wild and six in captivity. ('Don't miss the rarest bird in the zoo' reads the sign).

Most visitors should enjoy the twin marmoset houses with their heavily planted outdoor pens where several species of little marmosets and tamarins are kept. Infant silvery marmosets might be seen here, playing next door to a family of beautiful golden lion tamarins. The cages are perhaps a little small, but no zoo has been so successful in breeding tamarins as Jersey. More than thirty golden lion tamarins have been born here

Most of Jersey's birds are extremely rare in the wild. One of the best known successes has been the white-eared pheasant, a native of China. When Jersey received its first two pairs the species was down to fewer than twenty known birds. Several hundred have since been bred at the zoo, and a great many have been sent to other conservation zoos and bird gardens.

The reptile house (actually called the Gaherty Reptile Breeding Centre) holds several rare or endangered lizards, snakes and tortoises. Outside are little corrals for more terrapins and tortoises. Most zoo reptile houses do not take the idea of breeding particularly seriously; but here there are more off-show breeding units than there are vivaria on display, and signs give an indication of the very high level of breeding success. Over a hundred red-footed tortoise have been bred here, and a trust programme is underway to repeat this success in Madagascar with ploughshare tortoise, one of the rarest animals in the world.

Despite its deserved reputation as the world's first conservation zoo, Jersey Zoo does not entirely escape criticism. Durrell makes a point of inviting it; and there are areas of the zoo which do not fairly represent the mood of the collection. The Bornean orang utans are disappointingly housed in grim bunkers. The Sumatran orangs fare little better in a hard concrete den with more reasonable, but nonetheless uninspiring facilities for climbing. Disaffection with these enclosures has led the Trust to reconsider their keeping of orangs. A substantial new enclosure is on the drawing-board for the Sumatran orangs, which will borrow ideas from the gorilla compound, and the zoo will relinquish their Bornean orangs to another zoo in 1992. Some primate enclosures look designed primarily for ease of cleaning, and the monkey and lemur accommodation around the manor is boring and unattractive. The spectacled bears have a pit with a difference; it has a tangle of fallen trees, a grassy mound, and a pool, and bears have twice bred here; but it is small. It may seem niggardly to pick upon points like this, but expectations of this zoo run so high, that it might be a shame to have them spoilt for the sake of a handful of disappointing exhibits.

Still the zoo is continuing to develop. One new addition is an innovative landscaped field for the growing colony of Celebes macaques, where they are contained by a simple electric fence. There are over twenty of these delightful, jet black monkeys in this enclosure now, and the enclosure won a zoo award in 1991. It is easy to see why. The fence is astonishingly low so that the impression for the visitor is virtually of unconfined monkeys on a sort of playground-lawn. The monkeys apparently like it too, and the group is fascinating to watch. The lemur wood which holds three groups of lemurs around the banks of a little lake, contained only by a shallow polythene overhang on the fence, is superb. The Rodrigues fruit bats (the rarest bat in the world) are magnificent in two separate colonies; and there are snow leopards, parrots, serval, and some beautiful Chilean flamingos. A short run of cages displays several rare lemurs, a pair of cheetah occupy an impressively planted compound, and there are dozens of aviaries with Congo peacocks, Rothschild's mynah, various parrots, and some extremely rare ducks.

In 1991 Jersey Zoo announced another sensational coup which will undoubtedly help to reinforce its international reputation. Drawing on their long association with the government of Madagascar, they negotiated permission to import six aye-ayes. The aye-aye has long been considered one of the rarest primates on earth. A curious relative of the lemurs, it occupies a zoological family all of its own. It has wild black fur, a slightly pinched face, large rolling eyes, and an absurdly long middle finger which is used to extract termites from holes in the trees. Sightings of aye-ayes in the wild are rare, and they have been virtually unrepresented in zoos (although London Zoo had one earlier this century). For almost a decade it was assumed that the only viable population was a protected group on the offshore island of Nosy Mangabe, at the north eastern corner of Madagascar. Then reports began to come in of other aye-ayes, and it became clear that there were still active groups of aye- ayes scattered around Madagascar. The status of these, however, looked perilous. In places the aye-aye may have been protected by local superstition, but farmers are increasingly driven to kill them as potential pests, and the six animals at Jersey come from an area where, according to John Hartley of the Trust, they could not have survived for long. The six animals (two adult males, two adult females, and two infant males) will be kept off show until the spring of 1992, awaiting the completion of a new nocturnal enclosure alongside the manor. To date the animals are thriving. They are fed on imported green coconuts, sugar cane, and fruit (although their sugar cane has now been rationed on the advice of a dentist). If any zoo can succeed in breeding aye-ayes, Jersey can. And if they do, then these six animals (and those now also in America and France) may become the progenitors of a whole zoo population for our grandchildren to visit and appreciate and wonder at the bizarre design concept of this unlikely little primate.

Madagascar has also provided two other species which will go on show for the first time anywhere in the world, in Jersey in 1992. The Alaotran hapalemur (or gentle lemur) comes from a very small area of reedbeds around Lake Alaotra in Western Madagascar. It is a highly endangered subspecies, and will be the first of the gentle lemurs to be brought into captive management. Jersey have complemented their capture of ten of these delicate lemurs with an effective poster campaign in the area of Lake Alaotra, drawing the attention of local people to the plight of the hapalemurs, and of the gravely endangered Madagascar Pochard, which has not been seen for a number of years. The other Malagasy newcomers are five giant jumping rats, looking like chunky jerboas (or even small wallabies). They come from a very small area of West Coast forest and their status is extremely uncertain. But of the group at the zoo, all three females have already bred, and there is optimism that they could rapidly become the nucleus of a self-sustaining captive population.

Jersey has complemented its remarkable conservation work with record keeping of the highest standards, and well documented research work that has parallelled every project. There are comprehensive education facilities, and the information displays alongside every enclosure are excellent. One scheme which illustrates the commitment of the trust towards conservation is an overseas training scheme for keepers who will eventually manage captive breeding units for endangered species in their own countries. Students from over fifty countries have completed the residential course here. This is not the sort of endeavour that is visible to the average zoo visitor, but it is indicative of the responsible attitude taken at Jersey towards the whole issue of wildlife conservation, and of the seriousness with which the role of the zoo is seen.

'Of the 500 or so zoological collections in the world,' wrote Durrell in 'The Stationary Ark', 'a few are excellent, some are inferior, and the rest are appalling.' Here on this unlikely holiday island, Durrell and his team have tried to redefine the concepts of the modern zoo, and have thrown down the gauntlet to those inferior and appalling zoos. The Jersey Wildlife

Preservation Trust now has sister organisations in the United States and Canada, and has probably done more than any other zoo in the world to draw attention to the urgent plight of the disappearing animals of our planet. The world is a big place, and the problems that its wildlife faces are too extensive for any one organisation, or any one zoo. But through its example, Jersey Zoo has started a movement that may one day draw upon the support of hundreds of zoos. The history books of the 21st century or beyond will tell if they have succeeded; and if they have, they will surely keep a place for Jersey Zoo.

KNOWSLEY SAFARI PARK

Prescot
Merseyside
Telephone: 051 430 9009

How to find it:
Leave the M57 at Exit 6 Follow the A68 to Prescot.

Open: Late February-early October 10.00 am

Prices: adult £8 car (not including entrance to Sealion show).

Area: 160 hectares / 395 acres

	Species	Animals
Mammals	19	227
Birds		
Reptiles		
Amphibians		
Fish		
Total	19	227
Conservation		★
Enclosures		★★★★
Education		★
Recreation		★★★
Research		

Wild animals are nothing new to Knowsley. Over a hundred and fifty years ago Edward Lord Stanley, the thirteenth Earl of Derby kept a huge private zoo here – one of the largest in the world at the time. It covered almost 100 acres of Knowsley estate and it included 94 species of mammals and 318 species of birds, which even today would make it the largest bird collection in Britain, and the third largest mammal collection (after London and Chester). Lord Derby was an avid collector of animals, and a President of the Zoological Society. He employed agents all over the world to send him new animals, and his estate must have been a fascinating one to visit – matched only perhaps by the Duke of Bedford's collection at Woburn, and the fledgling zoos at Regent's Park and Clifton (now Bristol Zoo). A regular visitor was the landscape artist Edward Lear, and in the 1830s he stayed at Knowsley for five years, painting many of the animals in the menagerie. The animals may have provided literary inspiration too, for it was here that Lear entertained the thirteenth Earl's grandchildren with nonsense verses and limericks, later to be published as 'The Book of Nonsense' for which Lear is now best remembered.

In comparison to the thirteenth Earl's incredible zoo, today's safari park is a much more modest affair with no more than 22 different mammal species on display, and no birds at all (but for a few pheasants and wild-fowl). It was the eighteenth Earl who made the decision to bring animals back to Knowsley, and when the safari park opened in 1971 it was the fifth to be opened in Britain in five years, and the fourth to benefit from the close involvement of Jimmy Chipperfield, who partnered Lord Derby in the enterprise. The three and a half mile original route has been extended to five miles, but despite the fact that the road snakes languidly back and forth, the rolling nature of the landscape here creates the impression of a longer and more varied journey than many similar parks. Even without the animals it would be an interesting drive – past swampy waterfowl ponds, through shady oak woodlands, up onto the windy grassland, down past White Man's Lake. The animals look well here. There are tigers (in sep-arate zoo-style cages), a splendid pride of lions, magnificent baboons, a proud herd of Père David's deer, and groups of zebra, gnus, guanacos (wild llamas), bison, camels, and eland. There is also a quartet of hand-some white rhino (which have bred here), and four African elephant. The elephants have a large area to graze, and are kept safely away from cars by an electric fence. Here there are also expanding herds of lechwe, black-bock and African buffalo, and the park will soon add scimitar-horned oryx to that list.

In addition to the drive round park there is a very good children's zoo, for which an extra admission charge is made, but where children can feed and stroke farmyard animals. Extra tickets also have to be bought for the small reptile house, which has a few impressively large snakes, and for the sealion show which takes place in the old dolphinarium. There is also a fairground, and a train ride out along the lake.

Knowsley is hardly the great innovator it once was, nor is it a critical conservation resource; but for countless families in and around Mersey-side it is the closest and best place to come face to face with some magni-ficent wild animals in an impressively realistic setting. Edward Lear, seeing all these 'Beasticles, Birdlings and Boys', would surely have ap-proved.

THE ZOOLOGICAL SOCIETY OF LONDON: LONDON ZOO

Regent's Park
London
Telephone: 071 722 3333

How to find it:
Nearest Underground station: Camden Town on the Northern Line (about ten minutes walk). Regent's Park station is further but the walk is more pleasant. Various busses.

Open: All year from 10.00 am

Prices: adult £5.60; child £3.50; OAP £4.50.

Area: 15 hectares / 36 acres

	Species	Animals
Mammals	142	1255
Birds	279	955
Reptiles	101	446
Amphibians	30	138
Fish	240	3600
Total	792	6394
Conservation		★★★
Enclosures		★★
Education		★★★★
Recreation		★★★
Research		★★★★

The London Zoo is our best known zoo, our National zoo, and one of the most famous and prestigious collections in the world. It is the primary home of the Zoological Society of London, and it occupies thirty six acres of a Royal Park, less than two miles from the centre of the city of London.

The Zoological Society of London was founded in 1826 at the instigation of its first president, Sir Stamford Raffles (who is rather better known as the founder of Singapore). Raffles obtained the land, and saw the first plans for the zoo, but in the same year that the Zoological Society was founded, he died, reportedly of apoplexy; so he never saw the scientific establishment that he had envisaged, for 'teaching and elucidating zoology.' That was left to his successor, the third Marquis of Lansdowne, who obtained a parcel of land from the Crown at Regent's Park at a nominal rent, and who supervised the building of the first animal houses.

The gardens opened in April 1828 to members of the Zoological Society. The public were not to be admitted for almost two decades, but among the animals they might have seen before the turn of the century were such rarities as Arabian oryx, greater kudus, Indian and Sumatran rhinoceros, aye aye, the now extinct quagga (a species of zebra), and the equally extinct thylacine (a marsupial wolf). Among the zoo's regular visitors was Charles Darwin, a fellow of the Zoological Society, from 1831. His particular fascination was the orang utan, the first ever seen in Europe.

One of the great popular characters of the nineteenth century was Jumbo, an African bull elephant who came to the zoo as a baby and ended up as a six-ton cantankerous beast. Jumbo was so loved by Londoners of the time that there was a national outcry when the Zoo Council and Abraham Dee Bartlett, the zoo's superintendent, sold him to Mr Barnum of Barnum and Bailey's Circus. Jumbo sailed to the United States where he drew huge crowds until his death in a train accident two years later. London Zoo benefitted from the sale to the tune of two thousand pounds.

One of the first architects at the zoo was Decimus Burton, an ambitious young man already famous for his designs of the Colosseum theatre and Marble Arch in London. Over the generations since, new buildings have come and gone, and today very little of Burton's original zoo remains. The East Tunnel which links the north and south halves of the zoo under Prince Albert Road dates back to 1829, and the clock tower building, was Burton's llama house in the 1830s.

For the first sixty-five years, every tropical animal in Regent's Park was kept indoors in the belief that they would not survive in the cold, fresh air of London. This was to change with the new century when Dr Peter Chalmers Mitchell, who was appointed secretary of the Society in 1902, set about a major reorganisation of the zoo's buildings. Many of the animals came out into the open, and most of them thrived. This was a revolutionary new idea inspired by Hagenbeck of Hamburg Zoo, and it led to a new era of building and design which has firmly left its mark upon the park. Today there is still a great feeling of history about London Zoo, lending the whole park a special ambiance quite fitting for this, the birthplace of British zoos.

For decades the London Zoo has had no real equal in this country. Other zoos have opened, and flourished, but for generations there have been at least twice as many species here in the heart of London as there have been at any other British zoo. At the beginning of the 1990s there were almost 7,000 animals in the Royal Park. The nearest any other collection came to matching that figure was Chester Zoo with just under 3,500 animals; and despite the fact that 4,000 or so of London Zoo's animals were fish or invertebrates (and most of those were ants), there was still a superabundance of wildlife that you would see in no other zoo: the wombat for example, or the Tasmanian devil, the long nosed potoroo, the grey ground cuscus, or the four eyed opossum – and these were only the marsupials. Altogether on a day at London Zoo you might have seen representatives of nearly half the mammal species kept in British Zoos. The sheer size of the collection at London was part of the zoo's appeal, but may also have been the root cause of the zoo's financial problems. There may never be a collection of this size in Britain again.

There is a recommended route to take you economically around the zoo, but it is worth buying and using the excellent guide book; otherwise you may soon find that the zoo seems much larger than you might expect, and it is difficult not to miss whole sections out.

Most tours around London Zoo begin with the primates. The Sobell Pavilions, built for the apes and monkeys in 1972, are right in front of you as you come through the gates. This will also be your first introduction to the signs – another feature of the London Zoo that has no equal. Perhaps it is the influence of the great museums nearby; perhaps it is a spin-off from the education department that plays host to sixty thousand children every year; or perhaps there is just a greater commitment to educate the public here than at any other zoo. Whatever the reason, Regent's Park seems to have a policy of putting a sign upon every available blank space, and you could easily spend a day simply reading your way around the zoo. Some zoo directors are sceptical about the value of interpretational signs. They doubt whether the average visitor will ever read more than a fraction of the information that a zoo could display. Maybe there is a danger of this when every sign is a monotonous litany of gestation times, litter sizes, and diets – and that surely applies to the signs at many zoos; but not at London. Here imagination has taken over, and nowhere are there two sets of signs the same, even in format. The signwriters have decided that we want to know what is interesting about the occupants of each enclosure, and that is what they have given us. So our tour around the Sobell Pavilions begins with a huge evolutionary tree showing our own relationship to the old and new world monkeys. Then, as we proceed around, each section has a sign that announces its residents: 'Spider Monkeys – The tail hangers', reads one; 'Squirrel Monkeys – sociable and chirpy', 'Gorillas – vegetarian gentle giants', and 'Macaques – the all-rounders'. The enclosures are all grass floored and well branched with a ceiling of girders to provide more climbing space. They are a little low, but seem well suited to the needs of most of the monkeys, which are kept here in large social groups. Indoors the dens are brick-built and fairly roomy with glass viewing windows. Nearly all the primates breed well here, and you may see several parents carrying young. The chimpanzees ('Like us – noisy and showy') spend more time swinging arm to arm than in many zoos which provide less three-dimensional space, but perhaps they would be noisier and showier if they had a little more room to rush around.

The gorillas have the same outside pen and climbing roof as the monkeys; and maybe here the pavilion suffers from a slight uniformity of design – these huge apes looking rather uncomfortable in what is quite clearly a monkey cage.

A statue of Guy the gorilla stands alongside, climbed upon by countless children. It is a permanent reminder of the zoo's best loved resident since Jumbo.

All the apes are identified by photographs and names. Chimp faces vary almost as much as humans, and the photographs remind us that every animal is an individual, each with his, or her, own unique personality.

The aquarium at London Zoo was built in 1924, and it is still the largest in the country. Two hundred thousand gallons of fresh water and sea water circulate through its hundred exhibition tanks. Twice a year sea water from the Bay of Biscay is brought in the ballast tanks of ships to top up the water in circulation. The hall is long, with most of the light coming from the tanks themselves. Perhaps the best feature is the seawater hall where a three thousand gallon display tank holds a whole variety of tropical marine fish and invertebrates.

Next door is the reptile house, with a huge collection of snakes and lizards on display. Many of the signs there feature venom as their point of interest, and one of the many snakes on display is the carpet viper, responsible (so the sign tells us) for several thousand deaths a year in Africa.

Outside again, the elephant and rhino pavilion is good from the visitor's point of view, but maybe somewhat lacking in space for the animals. To make up for this the elephants are widely exercised out and about in the zoo, to the clear delight of visitors, and one hopes of the elephants too.

One recent resident of this building was Ben, a northern white rhino who was flown in 1986 to join the only other captive rhinos of his race at Dvur Kralove in Czechoslovakia, a move that looks likely to be helpful in saving this subspecies from extinction. The newest residents (at the time of writing) are Rosie, an adorable black rhino who was born at the zoo in 1989, and Jos, a young male black rhino who arrived from Dvur Kralove in November 1990.

The jackass penguins have a famous and fascinating pool, dating back to 1934 and designed by the architect Lubetkin, with a network of concrete ramps and bridges.

So often the children's corner in a zoo is no more than an afterthought where a few rabbits and a few goats supposedly represent animals with a special appeal to children; but at few zoos will you see children enjoying a children's zoo so much as at London, where they are offered a whole range of animals to stroke, including calves, piglets, lambs, rabbits and donkeys.

The nineteenth-century reptile house was converted into a tropical bird house in 1927, and it now houses a whole variety of birds in aviaries around the walls. One inhabitant is the bell bird, which makes the loudest of all bird calls, like a hammer striking on an anvil. When the male is in full throat it is quite deafening to stand too close.

The essential Victorian flavour of this building is captured in the interpretational signs. For these the zoo has drawn from its archives of nineteenth century drawings, prints and paintings, and has combined them with up to date information in the style of a Victorian naturalist's notebook.

The cats at Regent's Park are housed at the East corner of the zoo in well planted enclosures, faced with tent-like erections of steel square fencing. Signs here educate us on the fur trade, teeth and claws, spots, cubs and kittens, and invite us to compare our physical skills with those of the cat family. Did you know, for instance, that a leopard can leap twice as high as an Olympic high jumper?

In the open parkland of the southern side of the zoo are open wildfowl ponds, parrots, sealions and gibbons, camel rides, and a meet-the animal show under a big open-air tarpaulin.

Two tunnels lead under the road to the north side of the zoo. Here you will find the high, walk-through, Snowdon Aviary, the giraffe, zebras, deer and cattle house where you might also see vicuna, kudu and okapi, the insect house, and finally the one building which most visitors remember more than any other – the Charles Clore Pavilion.

Known by keepers simply as 'The Clore', this building houses the society's small mammal collection – one of the most impressive in the world. The ground floor is home to daylight creatures like marmosets and tamarins; but it is the basement where the real magic lies. Here is the 'moonlight world' where large eyed nocturnal creatures like the Tasmanian devil, jerboas, douroucoulis, casiraguas, and fruit bats abound in enclosures that are skilful recreations of their natural wild surroundings. The Clore is a fascinating place indeed, and once your eyes have become used to the dim artificial moonlight you can spend a long time in this mysterious world among the rarely seen creatures of the night.

A new attraction at the zoo in 1991 were a pair of koalas, Mije and Billi, the first seen in Britain for almost 80 years. They were housed in a large but rather stark circular room in what used to be the old orang house, and here they would climb contentedly on a wooden climbing frame against the painted backdrop of a eucalyptus forest. Sadly Mije died in November 1991, but Billi is still at the zoo. Koalas are notoriously difficult to keep in zoos, primarily because they rely on just a single food source, the leaves of eucalyptus. The original koalas of London, almost a century ago, were fed on eucalyptus cough pastilles, but today the zoo buys regular quantities of fresh branches from a supplier in Cornwall. The branches are inserted into holes in the climbing frame, to make browsing a more natural process. For many years it has been the policy of successive Australian governments not to allow wildlife exports of any kind, although an exception was made in 1990 for some endangered Leadbetter's opossums sent to London Zoo. London's koalas therefore came from San Diego Zoo, where they were born.

Pandas have been a feature of London Zoo for more than five decades. The first London Zoo panda this century was Ming, one of four pandas who arrived in 1938 and who featured in propaganda to boost morale during the war. Twenty years later, in 1958, came Chi-Chi. She was originally destined for an American zoo, but at the time Washington had banned all trade with Communist China. Chi-Chi was branded 'communist goods' and was refused entry to the United States. The Zoological Society of London had previously ruled that they would not encourage the collection of wild pandas, in the interests of conservation. But since it was pointed out that Chi-Chi had already been collected, her purchase (with assistance from Granada TV) was approved. She at once became the scene-stealing, star attraction of London Zoo, and remained the best loved zoo animal in Britain until her death. As the only giant panda in the west, she was the inspiration behind Peter Scott's design for a symbol for the World Wildlife Fund. She was greatly pampered, and often indulged with chocolates by visitors. In the late 1960s her fruitless liaison with Moscow Zoo's An-An made regular front page news.

When she died in July 1972 she was widely mourned, but the vacuum at the zoo was soon filled by Ching-Ching and Chia-Chia who arrived in

September 1974, a gift to Edward Heath from the Government of China. Once again, however, all of the technology and best intentions of the zoo failed to persuade the pandas to produce any offspring. Ching-Ching needed almost constant medical attention, and after her death, Chia-Chia departed, in 1988, on a breeding loan to Mexico City Zoo, which has a good record of panda breeding. Once again London Zoo was without a panda, and it felt the absence profoundly. For the first time in decades the zoo had no real star. There was hope that the arrival of the koalas would fill the void, but somehow they failed to do so. So negotiations that had begun with the Chinese in 1988 for the loan of another panda grew more urgent. At about the time that the future of the zoo began to be questioned, the imminent arrival of Ming-Ming was announced. She arrived in the autumn of 1991 and was followed by a male, Bao Bao, from Berlin Zoo. They occupy the original panda cages in the Sobell pavilions. It is not perhaps the most imaginative home for a panda. The panda cages were originally designed for monkeys. But they will offer the zoo the opportunity to create a star once more, if the public still has affection for the very lovable, and still rarely seen, giant panda. And if they do succeed in mating, during the few days in the spring when Ming-Ming will be on heat, then who can guess what effect the arrival of a baby panda might have upon the future and the financial fortunes of London Zoo.

Throughout its 165 year history, London Zoo has rarely been out of the news. In 1991 the zoo once again dominated the front pages after reports that the Department of the Environment was to order its closure. 'Animals face slaughter' read the headlines, and leader columns were drawn into debating what has become the perennial controversy of the rights and wrongs of zoos as places of entertainment. Not for the first time in its history, London Zoo was faced with the dilemma of hugely mounting costs against a background of fairly stagnant visitor numbers.

The reason behind the threat of closure seemed to be the simple failure of the zoo to balance its books. This was never going to be an easy exercise. London Zoo is a zoo of enormous variety and complexity. As well as its huge collection of animals it also houses the Institute of Zoology, a body of around 100 research scientists, funded in part through the Universities Finance Council. Their work currently covers seventy or more projects from the examination of rhino urine, to the insemination of pandas. But to run such a large and diverse zoo has its cost. In this case the cost was the £40 million required to cover the zoo's backlog of repairs, and to secure its financial future.

An early indication that a threat might be looming for London Zoo had come in 1990 when the Zoological Society announced its plans for some major changes in the collection. These were expected to include a huge reduction in the number of species along with the departure of many of the larger animals to Whipsnade. For a while it looked as if these changes could prove to be sufficient to bring running costs down to manageable proportions. But the plans were clearly not enough to stave off a crisis. The fact is that, apart from a government endowment of £10 million made to the zoo in 1988, London Zoo is expected to be self financing, unlike, for example, Kew Gardens or the national museums and galleries. This may have been a realistic attitude in the 1950s and 60s but not, it would seem, in the 1990s.

In May 1991 a new plan emerged. This time the cash required would be £12 million and the zoo would be restructured, using existing buildings, into a themed collection, with exhibits highlighting emotive issues – the destruction of rainforests, the crisis in Africa, and the plight of endangered species. The plan was accompanied by a promotion to 'Save Our Zoo', and in response the gate receipts rallied.

Quite simply, there seems to be a straightforward decision to make. If London Zoo is to continue in its present form, as a huge National collection of seven hundred or more species, then more money will have to be found – and essentially this may mean that the taxpayer will have to contribute in some form or another. Other countries, it can be argued, support their prominent collections with money from the National purse.

However, for the present at least it would seem that the government lacks any intention to bail the zoo out of its crisis; and the zoo itself seems to be reconciled to the fact that it cannot continue in its present form. But perhaps that might be no bad thing. If public (or private) money is not forthcoming, and if London Zoo could come to terms with redefining the collection into a smaller, simpler, cheaper zoo, then it could surely continue to survive on the gate receipts of the million and a quarter visitors who come every year. After all there are several good zoos that occupy no more land, with far smaller gates, that seem to do quite nicely thank you. Jersey Zoo (with less than a quarter of the number of visitors) is perhaps the best example. It could represent a rather attractive model for a future role for London Zoo. Imagine London becoming associated with the type of international species rescue that Gerald Durrell has shown to be possible. This great and popular zoo would have a platform second to none for capturing the public imagination with the tasks it would undertake. That great reptile house could devote its efforts to the dozens of island reptiles on the edge of extinction. Most of the birds, so many of them non-breeders would go; but perhaps the much criticised (and in need of repair) Snowdon Aviary could house colonies of endangered primates – maybe douc langurs or lion tailed macaques, or drills. The Clore could specialise in half a dozen or so of the most critically endangered bats and small mammals; there would be schemes to link conservation work in the countries of origin with captive breeding at the zoo – plenty here to keep the Institute of Zoology busy well into the next century.

So what will happen? Will London Zoo be transformed into a highly commercial animal theme park, or will it slim right down and continue as a conservation zoo on a more modest scale? At present there seem to be few further options; apart, that is, from closure. Of all the available choices, this would surely be the saddest. London Zoo will have to change. That much does seem certain. Some fundamental new ideas will be needed, and they could be very welcome. The zoo will need to reflect the changing expectations of visitors, providing more space for the animals they have, and shedding off the residual Victorian menagerie image and infrastructure that sometimes still haunts the place. But for generations there has been a zoo here in the centre of our capital city. It has become the place where countless children have first been introduced to wild creatures, where families have shared the experience of discovering animals they never dreamed existed, where our knowledge and understanding of the animal kingdom has been progressively advanced. It would be a great loss to our cultural heritage if London Zoo were to finally close its gates.

The City of London is full of venues for an exciting day out. There are galleries, museums, waxworks, and the Tower. But consider: a baby Arabian oryx is rarer than a da Vinci painting or a Henry Moore sculpture; and what creation of man can compare with nature's artistry in the face of a mandrill or the plumage of a flamingo? One word of warning however: don't plan too full an itinerary on the day you visit the zoo. You may find it takes up much of your day, leaving you too footsore for very much else.

LONGLEAT

Longleat Park, Warminster
Wiltshire
Telephone: 0985 844328

How to find it:
Between Warminster and Frome Signposted from the A362 or the B3092.

Open: All year from 10.00 am

Prices: adult £4.50; child £3.00; OAP £3.00.

Area: 81 hectares / 200 acres

	Species	Animals
Mammals	40	233
Birds	6	39
Reptiles	3	6
Amphibians		
Fish		
Total	49	278
Conservation		★★
Enclosures		★★★★
Education		★
Recreation		★★★
Research		

Longleat is surely Britain's most famous safari park, and justly so. It was, after all, the first park in the world, outside Africa, where visitors could admire the splendour of a pride of lions from the security and comfort of their own cars. Today the idea of the drive-through safari park is so common-place that it is hard to appreciate the huge controversy that Henry Thynne, the sixth Marquess of Bath aroused in 1964 when he announced his intentions to construct a 100 acre reserve for fifty lions in the grounds of his estate. Expert opinion was divided about whether the venture could ever succeed. The lions would fight, they would escape, visitors would be hauled from their cars and eaten. 'No amount of soothing assurance,' *The Times* leader proclaimed, '... can persuade sensible people that a quite gratuitous and unnecessary risk to life is not contemplated.'

In the end, of course, the scaremongering publicity was the best thing that could have happened to Longleat. 'The Lions of Longleat', as the park became known for its first twenty years, opened in 1966 and the queue of cars waiting to drive through the park stretched for miles. No lions escaped, no children were eaten, and eventually the furore died down and Lord Bath was seen as an astute innovator instead of a danger to the population of Wiltshire.

The real motive for the Lions of Longleat was of course to make money. The upkeep of the four hundred year old Longleat House was hugely expensive, and although Lord Bath had been the first peer to open his home to the public in 1949, the hundred thousand visitors or so who came to the house each year were not sufficient to cover the burgeoning costs. But the man behind 'The Lions' was not Lord Bath himself, but an inveterate animal trainer, circus owner, and showman, Jimmy Chipperfield. It was Chipperfield who had noticed how cars in African game-parks would always congregate around the lions, and he felt convinced that with secure fencing, the same thing could happen in the English countryside. It was some time before he found a man with the land, and the enterprise to put the ideas into action, but not surprisingly, what was true for Kenya became equally true for Wiltshire, and today the visitors still flock to see the lions – perhaps not in the colossal numbers they did in the early years, but still numbering over half a million people every year.

Today it is simply called 'Longleat', and the lions are just one of a host of attractions. There are probably more than forty lions at any time, and they occupy a huge area of woodland ('Lion Country'), living quite contentedly in large prides. There are tigers too (in 'Tiger Territory'), and they include a white Bengal tiger, 'Mayura', and several tigresses that carry white-tiger genes. The group are well accommodated in a spacious tract of woodland, and undoubtedly there will soon be white tiger cubs to attract still more visitors.

The first animal reserve at Longleat is a massive sixty acre rolling pasture where visitors are encouraged to leave their cars and walk or picnic among the animals. A magnificent herd of Rothschild's giraffe graze here, and Longleat has been consistently the most successful collection with giraffe in Britain. Over a hundred have been bred and reared here, and it is easy to see why – the giraffe are kept in a large, healthy group, and they have abundant space in which to exercise. There are zebra too in this reserve, and camels which give rides during the holiday periods.

The monkey jungle at Longleat was, like the lions, the first in the country. Originally it housed baboons, but today these have been replaced by altogether more docile rhesus monkeys which can usually be relied upon to climb all over your car without doing any real damage. A herd of Père David's deer graze in the monkey jungle, looking splendid beneath the huge 300-year old oaks.

In the 'Big Game' reserve there are white rhinos, and a small group of African elephant. There are plans to build a secure corral for a bull elephant, but for the time being only cow elephants are present, kept safely at bay by the simple expedient of a movable electric fence.

The final animals in the drive-round park are a splendid pack of over forty Canadian timber wolves, a healthy breeding group.

Beyond the Safari-Park itself there is a pet's corner, a small reptile house, and a 'Water Safari', which offers the opportunity of a river boat ride down half-mile lake alongside Longleat House. Hippos graze a generous ten-acre field next to the lake, and wallow contentedly in the murky water. Behind the boat swim California sealions, and the group here breed regularly. More sealions have been bred here than at any other British Zoo. The climax to the boat ride is Gorilla Island, which houses a small group of three gorillas on a spacious, grassy island.

Many zoos, and conservationists were highly critical of Longleat when it opened. It was seen as little more than a outdoor circus, and Chipperfield was seen as an opponent of the new ideals that zoos were seeking to achieve, a reversion to a crude commercial exploitation of animals. True, no safari park can contain the same variety of species as a traditional zoo, but Longleat's success with its giraffes, wolves, and sealions has made its critics think twice.

A question mark seems to hang over Longleat's future. Will it or won't it continue under the seventh Marquess of Bath? If it continues with what it does so well, and starts to put conservation well above commerce, then let us hope it will.

Timber wolf

MARWELL ZOOLOGICAL PARK

Colden Common, nr Winchester
Hampshire
Telephone: 0962 777406

How to find it:
Well signposted from the A33 Winchester
Southampton road 8 miles South West of
Winchester

Open: All year from 10.00 am

Prices: adult £4.80; child £3.70; OAP £4.20.

Area: 40 hectares / 99 acres

	Species	Animals
Mammals	70	469
Birds	55	192
Reptiles		
Amphibians		
Fish		
Total	125	661
Conservation		★★★★
Enclosures		★★★
Education		★★★
Recreation		★★★
Research 3		

The village of Colden Common, seven miles from Winchester, is the sort
of place that barely merits inclusion in the map books, but when you find
your way there to Marwell Zoological Park you will be very well rewarded.
Here is what writer Anthony Smith wrote about Marwell in his book
'Animals on View': 'Marwell is a tonic. It can restore faith in those who
are wondering whether animals should ever be kept captive for our
satisfaction. It shows that conservation need not be just a platitude...but a
guideline for policy and endeavour.'

To those who know Marwell Zoo, it is indeed a tonic; and yet it is one
of Britain's newest zoos. Like so many of the best conservation zoos it
owes its existence to a man of vision, an animal lover who came from
outside the zoo community, without too much luggage of preconceived
ideas. John Knowles was a successful poultry breeder, and when he started
Marwell Zoo brought with him a valuable insight into animal genetics. He
is a stoic, but determined man, and he has a passion for the great opportunity presented to humankind through an understanding of genetics: to
manage small zoo populations of endangered animals, away from the de-
predations that other humans are wreaking upon the last remaining wilderness. His animal keepers will tell you how, when he first began his zoo
in 1972, he used to drive a Rolls Royce, but this was speedily sold to pay
for the zoo's foundation group of Grevy's zebra. 'Zoos are a wonderful
way to lose money,' he has said. And yet no one who knows him could
ever imagine him doing anything except running Marwell Zoo. Perhaps
this is one reason why the zoo and its work have so quickly become well-
known in the international community of good zoos. In March 1978 the
ownership of Marwell in its entirety was passed to a registered charity, the
Marwell Preservation Trust. 'As a philosophical point' Knowles has said,
'I do not feel comfortable with the concept of an individual owning endangered species'.

Knowles' greatest passion are a small group of antelope, the 'hippo-traginae', better known as oryx. This group includes some of the rarest and most endangered grazing animals on earth, the Arabian oryx (once extinct in the wild), the gemsbok, the beisa oryx, the addax, and the animal that has always been the symbol of Marwell Zoo, the scimitar-horned oryx. This is a striking ivory-white antelope with sandstone-red flanks and neck, and magnificent long sweeping horns. Not long after the herd was first established at Marwell, it became clear that the wild population was in grave danger. The small population in Chad was threatened by the civil war, and no other individuals had been spotted for some years. Marwell was perhaps the first zoo to identify the threat, and was swift to act. The herd they established in the 1970s bred so well that their descendants have now been sent to other zoos in Britain, Australia, and New Zealand, and have also been reintroduced into the wild in a specially gazetted reserve in Tunisia.

Marwell Zoo occupies a wide swathe of rolling pastureland surrounded by dense woodland, and the zoo seems in places like a large clearing in the woods. The walk around the zoo is not at all demanding, covering a winding figure-eight. Visitors may bring their cars into the zoo for an extra fee which is waived in the case of cars bearing a disabled sticker, but other-wise the admission of cars is discouraged.

Anyone who expects a traditional zoo, with the usual compulsory col-lection of species, may be disappointed by Marwell. There are no ele-phants here, no penguins, no sealions; for this is a zoo that specialises in keeping rare and endangered animals, and there is no room and not enough money to keep anything just because it happens to be popular. Many of Marwell's animals are may seem unfamiliar at first; the kulan (or Turk-menian wild ass), Malayan tapirs, Przewalski's horse, okapi, sitatunga, barasingha, vicuna, and pudu. These are not animals we learn about at nursery school, they do not advertise petrol, and they rarely, if ever, appear in anyone's list of favourite animals. Yet they are all beautiful, rare and precious creatures, and here at Marwell you will see them in plenty. Many zoos keep zebras, and to most visitors a zebra is a zebra; but Marwell keeps the rarer species, the endangered Hartmann's mountain zebra, the thin striped Grevy's zebra, and Chapman's zebra which is a cousin of the com-mon plains zebra, recognisable by the faint shadow lines between its broad black stripes.

Lions are popular animals everywhere, although the conservation argu-ment for keeping so many in captivity is thin. Marwell, however, keeps the Asiatic lion, members of a race whose ancestors, as recently as Roman times, roamed right across Asia and Southern Europe. Today there is only a relict population of around two hundred in a single forest in India, and the case for a reservoir population in zoos is compellingly strong. Yes, you would need to be an expert to distinguish an Asiatic lion from an African lion. But the distinction is there nonetheless, and here is a zoo that takes account of it. The same concern is reflected in all the cats at Marwell. The tigers, in long grassy enclosures, are Siberian tigers – the wild population of which is estimated as less than four hundred; the several leopards which have bred here include Persian leopards, members of a race that is now extinct in the wild ; the endearingly beautiful, but highly endangered snow leopard (which is not a leopard, but whose soft white and black fur is in demand by the so-called 'civilized world') has bred here, despite slightly disappointing enclosures; and now even the cheetahs, notorious for their reluctance to breed in zoos, have produced and reared cubs. Black jaguars too have bred here, and they look superb.

While many zoos, especially the older ones, pride themselves on their buildings, Marwell, curiously, seems to have no buildings to speak of at all. Of course there are buildings, but they are all neat, wooden, unobtrusive, and functional. There are no grandiose architectural designs here, very little brick or concrete, very few iron railings or bars. This is a zoo of wire fences, open fields, and wooden stables. The idea is a challenging one, and it does seem to illustrate something fundamental about this zoo: while other zoos are busy planning their next new building, Marwell is busy planning its animal management programme.

The one building that does dominate the park is Marwell Hall, a Tudor mansion that sits at the centre of the estate looking down across the scimitar horned oryx herd, the showpiece of the zoo. The gardens of the Hall are now home to a variety of smaller creatures like tamarins, mara, owls and parrots. Alongside the Hall golden lion tamarins now occupy a grassy island with plenty of space to show off and be photographed, and delicate dama gazelle, and the endangered Arabian gazelle have a small but attractive pen where they can be closely managed to help ensure breeding successes.

Most estate zoos are pleasant places to walk around. After all, the reason they became estates in the first place was because they were beautiful places to live. Marwell is no exception. The landscape is green and tranquil, and the animals seem somehow to belong here. Perhaps that is a side-effect of the low profile buildings – the zoo doesn't look as if it has been engineered to look after its occupants. The scale is always human, comfortable, non threatening. And there seems to be always something new and unusual around every corner. For example, African wild dogs (no relation to the domestic dog), or secretary birds (named for the pen-like quills that stick out from around their ears). If you're lucky you might glimpse the maned wolf, a long legged carnivore from South America (not a true wolf), which Marwell was the first British zoo to breed, or the pygmy hippo, no larger than a pig, grazing at the bottom of its field. Then there are, of course, some familiar animals; giraffes (remember when the plight of Victor the giraffe so captured the imagination of the nation that the Winchester telephone exchange was jammed by concerned callers?), white rhinos, camels, flamingos, siamang gibbons, and ostriches. The wallabies live in a small parcel of woodland, and you can walk among them, and for children there is a farmyard, a short train ride, a road trailer trip, an excellent playground, and plenty to do all around the zoo. In 1991 Marwell won the Holiday Care Service Best Attraction Award for its positive attitude and excellent service to all people irrespective of disability or special need.

A new feature for 1992 is the 'World of Lemurs' which is in an attractively landscaped area within the former kitchen garden of Marwell Hall. Visitors see the lemurs in their outdoor enclosures from a glass covered walkway. The exhibit includes beautiful red- ruffed lemurs, and black and white lemurs.

It is hard to avoid the feeling at Marwell that this zoo represents exactly what all zoos should be, need to be, if all our platitudes about conserving wildlife are ever to be anything more than hot air. It proves that conservation zoos need not be dull, they can be exciting, attractive, entertaining places. Marwell, like Jersey, like Howletts and Port Lympne represents a whole rethinking of British zoos. Its influence will last for a very long time.

THE NORFOLK WILDLIFE PARK

Great Witchingham, Norwich
Norfolk
Telephone: 0603 872 274

How to find it:
12 miles north of Norwich on the A1067

Open: 1st April-31st October 10.30 am

Prices: adult £3.00; child £2.00; OAP £2.75.
Two children free with each adult on
Saturdays only.

Area: 16 hectares / 40 acres

	Species	Animals
Mammals	28	192
Birds	64	465
Reptiles		
Amphibians		
Fish		
Total	92	657
Conservation		★★★
Enclosures		★★
Education		★
Recreation		★★
Research		★

When Philip Wayre founded the Norfolk Wildlife Park in 1961, it was with the bold claim that this was a 'wildlife park' as distinct from a 'zoo', and was therefore the 'first of its kind'. However much other zoo keepers may have disputed this, the Norfolk Wildlife Park very soon did become the first of a kind when it made the decision to eschew exotic animals, and to concentrate instead upon the animals of Britain and Europe. To this day there is only one other good zoo (the Highland Wildlfe Park) that has made the same decision; and for Philip Wayre it has been a particularly good decision. The Norfolk Wildlife Park now holds the largest collection of European mammals in Britain, has achieved considerable breeding successes with a whole range of species, and has taken part in several reintroduction projects where zoo-bred animals have been released back into the wild. These projects have included badgers, otters (in cooperation with Philip Wayre's Otter Trust at Bungay), yellow-billed bean geese reintroduced into Sweden, European eagle owls which are regularly bred in the park and released into the wild in Sweden and Germany, and little owls which have bred here and which now help to bolster the local Norfolk population.

The zoo occupies a rectangle of around 40 acres of rolling grassland surrounded by arable farmland. There are few defined pathways – it was always the intention that visitors should walk around the grassy fields and lawns – and this idea works fairly well, conveying the idea that you can explore at will, without being restricted to any official routes. The downside of this idea is that a lot of the zoo's acres are devoted to people rather than animals, and some of the enclosures that may have seemed huge in 1961 now seem quite ordinary.

The animals to look out for at Great Witchingham include Barbary macaques (really a North African species with a relict European population in Gibraltar), European lynx in an excellent enclosure about an acre in size, a small herd of impressive European bison (one of the first animals to be rescued by captive breeding) in a large paddock, fallow deer in a large field, and badgers in interesting pens that allow you to watch them asleep in their burrows (although there is no cover for them outside).

Other animals, not all European, include muntjac (from China), the rarely seen pine marten, and the little known European suslisk – a little squirrel-like burrowing mammal, maras (from South America), and red necked wallabies (from Tasmania).

Other animals to see include the Artic foxes – snow white in the winter, and scraggy brown in the summer, in a large new enclosure, mouflon –Europe's only true wild sheep from Corsica and Sardinia, wild boar, and polecats.

Otters have always been a passion of Philip Wayre's, and at Great Witchingham you can see British otters (most zoos keep the more readily available Asiatic short-clawed otter). The British otters breed well here, and the cubs are sent to the Otter Trust for their reintroduction programme. There are short-clawed otters here too, three groups, and they occupy good sized enclosures. There is a splendid collection of waterfowl, and there are owls, including the impressive European eagle owl, the world's largest owl, which regularly breeds here, snowy owls, barn owls, tawny owls, and little owls, all of which also breed regularly in the park.

For bird watchers, the park has a particular treat. On the island pool, in among the waterfowl, is a wild heronry. It began with a small collection of injured and pinioned herons that bred there successfully, and their young that returned in subsequent years to build new nests, not only on the Island Pool, but in the surrounding trees. There are now twenty five nests, and the herons appear to have become sufficiently used to visitors to incubate their eggs, and to feed their chicks, in full public view; a rare sight indeed.

There is a turtle pool with a number of fresh water turtles, including the only European freshwater species – the pond tortoise, and there is a trout pool where visitors can throw handfuls of feed to the fish. A small children's area includes trained reindeer which can be stroked, and which offer a real reindeer sleigh ride, and there is a model farm where children can encounter angora goats, pot bellied pigs, and other favourites.

There is a small children's area, where reindeer can be stroked, among others, and the park also offers a reindeer 'sleigh' ride.

The Norfolk Wildlife Park is a very representative and important collection of European mammals and birds, displayed in pleasant rural surroundings.

PAIGNTON ZOOLOGICAL AND BOTANICAL GARDENS

Totnes Road, Paignton
Devon
Telephone: 0803 557479

How to find it:
On the A385 Totnes to Paignton Road. Half a mile from Paignton Town Centre.

Open: All year from 10.00 am

Prices: adult £5.40; child £3.00; OAP £4.20.

Area: 40 hectares / 99 acres

	Species	Animals
Mammals	65	253
Birds	153	592
Reptiles	50	189
Amphibians	12	80
Fish	36	136
Total	316	1250
Conservation		★★
Enclosures		★★
Education		★★★
Recreation		★★
Research		

Once there was a time when some sort of zoo at the seaside was a standard attraction, like the pier and donkey rides and funny hats. But like the pier, and like the hats, fashions have changed and all around the British coastline zoos have been languishing or closing down. There are still several small collections that survive, like Newquay and Southport, and Sandown, but of the survivors, Paignton is almost certainly the oldest, and most emphatically the largest. Paignton Zoo opened in 1923, and predates all but London, Bristol and Edinburgh zoos. It was founded by Mr Herbert Whitley, a naturalist who had kept a private botanical and zoological collection for several years, and who welcomed the opportunity to share it with the public. He was, however, a stubborn and eccentric man, and twice during the zoo's history he closed it down as a protest against the entertainment tax he was forced to pay. Zoos, he believed, were educational and not for entertainment. Paignton was the first British zoo to be constituted solely as an educational charity, after Whitley's death in 1955, and to this day it manages a busy education department among all of its other functions.

Today Paignton Zoo promotes itself as England's third largest. This, of course, depends upon how you measure size. In terms of the number of vertebrate species they hold (316), Paignton does indeed come third, after Chester (488) and London (792). The first impression of the zoo is rather like a municipal park. The grounds are tidy but the buildings themselves seem rather barrack-like and slightly dilapidated. Many of the gardens are well tended, but other beds seem strangely neglected. There are, as the figures prove, a very large number of species, yet the design of the place is rather dull and unimaginative, and perhaps too overcrowded.

The zoo was designed from the outset as a botanical collection as well as a zoo, and many exhibits are just plants. In the main these work well, like the wonderful collection of bromeliads, and it is good to see plants given some status among all of the animal species. Still, it is the animals that most people come to see, and you will see plenty at Paignton. There are a great many birds, and a host of aviaries with various birds of prey, parrots and owls, scarlet ibis, egrets, and pigeons, among many others. There is a tropical house and aquarium with lizards and snakes, featuring Nile crocodiles and dwarf cayman; and a sub-tropical house with some smaller birds, displaying a wonderful variety of shrubs and a tall banana tree.

Baboons are busy, active social animals, and Paignton shows them well on a large rocky mountain surrounded by a wide moat and a border of flowers. The baboons have plenty of room to rush around, and are fascinating to watch. Nearby is the giraffe enclosure, a gritty paddock with a concrete house, and a monkey house with good spacious glass-fronted cages inside, but the outside pens are small and rather metallic. The house holds the acrobatic black spider monkeys, and diana monkeys, both of which are vulnerable in the wild.

There is a chimpanzee house, with a small outdoor climbing area, cheetah, lions and tigers (of course), and kangaroos, but probably the best part of the zoo are the open rolling paddocks at the eastern end where there are a wide variety of creatures in much more spacious surroundings. Among the paddock animals are grey kangaroos, zebra, eland, bison, and a lovely herd of red lechwe. There are maned wolves too; these are South American carnivores and are not true wolves at all, but look something like a large long-legged fox. Their field at Paignton is a generous size, is well signed, and has plenty of cover for these secretive creatures to hide.

Of all the exhibits at Paignton, one stands out above all the rest. This is a whole area of the zoo that has been custom built for the white rhinos. It is an outstanding exhibit, and gives the impression that considerable thought and expense has gone into its design and construction. The area has been flanked with heavy timber fencing, and has been partitioned by imaginative landscaping. There is a backdrop of well established trees, and the heavy timber continues into the design of the house. The information here is especially good, with photographs and a carving of all five rhinoceros species.

The education centre at Paignton is called 'The Ark'. It is well staffed, and imaginative, with activities for all ages.

Next to the Ark are the elephants, with an interesting landscaped compound, and a small pool. There are two cow elephants on display.

One of the showpieces of Paignton are the gibbon islands. Gibbons ought to be one of the most spectacular animals in any zoo, but so often their cages are unimaginative and unattractive, and gibbons have a very human habit of looking just plain bored. Paignton has countered this with islands which goes a long way towards keeping the gibbons satisfied, and providing the spectacle that visitors ought to have. The islands stand in the middle of a wildfowl lake, and the gibbons swing confidently in the trees while ducks and geese nest below. A good way to see them is from the miniature railway which travels right around the lake.

In a strange way Paignton Zoo is a zoo caught between two decrees; on the one hand there is the seaside zoo, anxious to entertain, trapped by the dreadful seasonality of the visitors; on the other there is the serious educational zoo, trying with sparse resources to slough off the heritage of nearly seventy years of antiquated ideas, to create a modern, exciting, conservation zoo. In the 1990s Paignton hopes to spend over £2 million trying to realise some of these dreams. It will make the next decade an interesting one for friends of the zoo. If it results in a slimmed down zoo that can no longer claim to be England's number three, but instead concentrates upon the species it can keep well, and develops more enclosures like those for the rhinos, then that may be no bad thing.

PENSCYNOR WILDLIFE PARK

Cilfrew, nr Neath
South Wales
Telephone: 0639 642189

How to find it:
Signposted off the A465 Swansea to Merthyr
Tydfil road 2 miles NW of Neath.

Open: All year from 10.00 am

Prices: adult £2.75; child £1.50; OAP £1.50;

Area: 6 hectares / 15 acres

	Species	Animals
Mammals	34	164
Birds	104	373
Reptiles	4	19
Amphibians	2	6
Fish	34	5000
Total	**178**	**5562**
Conservation		★★
Enclosures		★★
Education		★★
Recreation		★★
Research		

Penscynor Wildlife Park occupies sixteen acres of heavily wooded hillside
in the Aberdulais Basin, a short drive north of Swansea. Described rather
boldly by its owners as 'one of Wales's foremost tourist attractions',
Penscynor is clearly trying to carve itself a niche among the holiday
attractions of South Wales. Emphasis is given to two of the Park's most
elaborate features: a scenic chairlift ride to the rocky hilltop, and an
'Alpine-Slide' – a sort of bobsleigh with wheels, to bring you hurtling back
down again.

But it must be the animals that draw the visitors to any zoo and Penscynor is as remarkable for the animals it does not keep as for those it does.
For a start there are no cats here; so absent are the traditional favourites,
the lions, tigers and spotted cats. Absent too are any of the 'big' mammals;
there are no elephants, rhinos, giraffe, bison or bears. Instead, Mr Idris
Hale, owner of the park and former wildlife film-maker, has chosen to
concentrate upon smaller animals that can be relied upon to convey almost
the same sense of wonder and entertainment. It is a formula well suited to
a park of this size, and it succeeds extremely well. Indeed the park seems
much more than its fifteen acres as you wind back and forth along its twist-
ing pathways. Here and there the zoo seems almost wild, like a densely
wooded glade from which you emerge to the almost surreal discovery of
Cuban flamingos gently preening themselves on an open lawn.

Parrots seem to be everywhere, and the zoo has specialised very successfully with these birds. Two new parrot house also display a large number of species to very good effect. Altogether there are as many as forty
five different species of parrots here, lories, lorikeets, cockatoos, parakeets, parrots, macaws, and lovebirds, they are around every corner,
bright, often noisy, and always beautiful. Particularly notable are the
hawk-headed and eclectus parrots.

There is a small tropical house with free-flying birds that could be very
easy to miss, a children's zoo, and a small aquarium and reptile house.

One prominent feature of the park is a striking natural waterfall that cascades down the hillside into a 'trout lake' with glass viewing windows. Vending machines dispense handfuls of fish food, and the trout swarm obligingly for the scattered pellets.

There are Humboldt's penguins, in a natural valley overlooked by tall trees, and they breed successfully here. Penguin feeding time is often a time for children to be allowed in to pat the more friendly penguins, and for Mr Hale to discourse on the importance of captive breeding.

A walled garden is home to monkeys, talking mynah birds and a children's area, and across the zoo there are hilly paddocks for attractive herds of guanacos and sika deer, a reasonable sealion pool with Patagonian sealions, and a small gibbon island. The new chimpanzee house, opened in 1977, is disappointing, with rather unimaginative outside yards, but there is a good little house next door, with golden lion tamarins, cotton topped tamarins, and several other delightful little tamarins and marmosets. A splendid group of high monkey cages overlooks the cafe, and is home to good families of ring-tailed lemurs, and crab eating macaques. Overhead wire tunnels connect the monkey cages to their indoor accommodation, and they scuttle back and forward through these above the heads of visitors. Nearby are otters in a hilly wild wood, with underwater viewing in their pool.

Penscynor is a well intentioned place, an attractive place, and should always be popular with children. The zoo manager, Rob Colley, is proud to emphasize the active part that the zoo plays in co- operative management schemes, and the zoo also contributes directly to a variety of conversation organisations. On the whole Penscynor does well with the species it has chosen to keep. It certainly deserves to be the tourist attraction it claims to be.

PORT LYMPNE ZOO PARK

Lympne, nr Hythe
Kent
Telephone: 0303 264646

How to find it:
Leave the A20 Ashford to Folkestone road
and follow the B2067 to Lympne. Exit 11 off
the M 20

Open: All year from 10.00 am

Prices: adult £6.50; child £4.50; OAP £4.50.
Includes half price entrance to Howletts Zoo.

Area: 121 hectares / 300 acres

	Species	Animals
Mammals	47	395
Birds	1	1
Reptiles		
Amphibians		
Fish		
Total	**48**	**396**
Conservation		★★★★
Enclosures		★★★★
Education		★★★
Recreation		★★★★
Research		★★

Port Lympne Zoo Park is the second, and more ambitious, of John Aspinall's zoos. (See also Howletts Zoo for some of Aspinall's other achievements.) In 1973 very few conservationists had ever heard of Aspinall. They might have known of him as a millionaire gambler, and an unorthodox keeper of animals, but his extraordinary achievements with endangered species had scarcely been reported. Howletts Zoo was not yet open to the public, and he had yet to see his first gorilla birth.

In 1973 however, John Aspinall was no longer a gambler, and was far from being a millionaire. He was, in fact, nearly penniless after a massive loss on Wall Street. What remained was barely enough to pay the wages of the dozen or more staff that worked at Howletts, or to feed the animals. There could not have been a worse time to start a completely new zoo. Yet on the cold February morning that he first saw the estate of Port Lympne with its 300 rolling acres of dense woodland and pasture, and its breathtaking views out across the Romney Marshes and the English Channel, Aspinall knew that his seven-year search for a new home for his growing collection of endangered animals was over, and straightaway he bought the entire estate, for £360,000.

It is hard to imagine that any visitor could come to Port Lympne without being deeply affected by the place. It is without a doubt one of England's most beautiful estates, and it is arguably England's finest zoo. That it survived the early years of penury is due in no small part to the investment and guarantees of the financier Sir James Goldsmith, and the support of many of Aspinall's friends and associates; but survive it did. The estate is not an ancient one like Howletts. It dates back little earlier than the first world war, having been commissioned by the young millionaire Philip Sassoon exclusively for his use during the month of August, when the famous and the fashionable were lavishly entertained here. The Prince of

Wales and the Duke of York (Edward VIII and George VI) stayed here; so too did Bernard Shaw, T. E. Lawrence, Lloyd George, and Charlie Chaplin. Winston Churchill, a regular house guest, painted several views of the house, three of which are here on display. The painter Rex Whistler painted decorative murals on an entire room, the tent room, and visitors to the zoo will almost certainly appreciate this. To complement the Whistler Room, John Aspinall commissioned the wildlife artist Arthur Spencer Roberts to paint another drawing room in the house. The resulting mural took three and a half years to complete, and is quite magnificent, featuring more than 220 species of South East Asian animals.

The park at Port Lympne is a huge natural amphitheatre, and the complete walk around the zoo (the zoo trek) is a gentle endurance test of probably more than three miles. If you add to this the great many splendid animals to see, the views to admire, and of course the house to visit, you should really allow a whole day to get the best from a visit. Arrive early, and do not expect to leave until late. There is a 'Safari Trailer Ride' that for most of the year provides the less nimble with a more leisurely tour of much of the zoo, driving directly through several of the larger paddocks, and lasting about an hour.

The animal collection at Port Lympne reads like a roll call of some of the rarest and most endangered mammals on the planet; animals like the Barbary lion (extinct in the wild), the African golden cat, swamp deer, Siberian tigers, Indian elephants, Malayan tapirs, black rhinos, and most remarkable of all a pair of Sumatran 'woolly' rhinos. Just as at Howletts, the Aspinall philosophy applies here: the animals are treated as friends, they are pampered, their food is the finest quality, the most varied, and without a doubt the most expensive in the world; and the emphasis is upon keeping animals in large numbers, as many as possible of each species, with as much space as possible. Like Howletts the final adjudicator of the technique is success. The animals at Port Lymne are vigorously healthy, and every species has either bred here, or can confidently be expected to breed here soon. The optimism of the place is heady, and the affection lavished upon the animals is evident from the signs providing us with the names and dates of birth of all but some of the herd animals.

There is no zoo quite like Port Lympne for walking around. At various times the path weaves through dense woodland, then across open grasslands, then through exquisite ornamental gardens, then along a splendid avenue of horse chestnut trees. It is a farm and a stately home and a forest bound into one. The car park is in an adjoining farm, one of several where the zoo grows much of the fresh produce for feeding the animals, mangold, lucerne, maize, red clover and kale. 150 tons of mangold alone are grown here between January and May for the elephants, the rhinos, and the grazing animals. Thirty acres are committed to growing red clover for the water buffalo and the bisons.

From the car park you cross the road into the zoo. You are at the top of the amphitheatre in some light broadleafed woodland. There are some small cat enclosures set so far back from the pathway that you are unlikely to see the cats. But don't be disappointed, there are more accessible cat enclosures later on. There are timber wolves in this part of the zoo, a breeding pack in a spacious tract of beautiful woodland. There are magnificent Siberian tigers too, in big new enclosures.

From the tigers you reach the top of a great stairway of York stone. One hundred and twenty five steps lead down through terraced gardens to Port Lympne Mansion, and the view from the top of the stairway looks out across the Romney Marshes to the English Channel, and on a clear day you can see Cap Griz Nez and the distant hills of France.

The zoo continues after the gardens with the woodland walk, and here there are monkeys – Sakis and de Brazza monkeys, diana monkeys and colobus monkeys in tall, spacious, richly branched cages, built of rough wooden posts, and covered with tennis wire. There are fields with hyenas and hunting dogs. You may have to search for the animals in the dense undergrowth, but they are there, and they look superb. Down at the bottom of the hill are more small cats, several cages of fishing cats, Temminck's cats, African golden cats (this is one of only two zoos in the world to keep these cats), and rusty spotted cats. Here also are the Barbary lions. This animal is the largest of all the lions, and is distinguished by its huge, shaggy mane which virtually covers half of the male lion's body. Barbary lions used to live in the forests of North Africa, but the forests disappeared and the lions were hunted to extinction. The last wild Barbary lion was reported killed in the Atlas mountains in 1922. Attempts were made to recreate the species with hybrid lions from Rabat Zoo, but then some presumed pure lions were rediscovered in the King of Morocco's private zoo, and an international programme was set up to breed them. The group at Port Lympne is splendid. They are housed in large, densely planted fields, enclosed only by chainlink fencing. It is a large group, and they interact well.

Much of the rest of the zoo consists of enormous open fields with splendid herds of grazing mammals. They include a huge herd of those most beautiful of all deer, the axis deer from India, and large herds of barasingha (also called swamp deer) which have become endangered in their native India where fewer than 3,000 animals still remain. The herd of more than sixty-five Przewalski's horses is the largest in the world and their paddock takes up about twenty percent of the whole zoo. To avoid interbreeding of these wild horses (which are probably now extinct in the wild), Aspinall has imported key animals from other important bloodlines all around the world. The herd is simply magnificent. Other herds in this part of the zoo include sambar deer (also from India), water buffalo and American bison. There are more cats too, caracals, servals, and Siberian lynx. Look out for Malayan tapirs (recognisable by their distinct black and white coats), and Brazilian tapirs with an appropriately swampy compound with plenty of

water to swim in. One unusual species here is the babirusa, a pig like animal with enormous curving teeth which come through the roof of the
mouth and curl around in a circle. There are chimpanzees too, but only a
small group, in a tall but otherwise unremarkable enclosure.

The group of Indian elephants at Port Lympne is the largest in the
country. At the time of writing there are six cow elephants, and two bulls.
One huge bull elephant is a most awe-inspiring tusker named Assam.
Three of the cows are believed to be pregnant.

The original elephant complex of around five acres has recently seen
the addition of a new twelve acre paddock so that the elephants now occupy an area larger than the whole of Bristol Zoo. The zoo provides a
raised spectator platform beside the elephants where you can simply sit
and watch them. It is well worth taking the time to do so. The new field,
fenced with huge red railway girders, is set away from public view so that
at times the only view of the herd is across the hillside from the viewing
platform. Bring binoculars if you can.The elephants occupy themselves
by feeding from mountains of fresh branches, by playing with huge tree
trunks in the compound, by wallowing in mud, or by dust bathing. They
are magnificent, and they look extremely well compared to so many zoo
elephants elsewhere.

Gorillas are newcomers to Port Lympne. The group of five here came
from Howletts Zoo, since that group, forty gorillas in 1990, had grown too
large for their accommodation. A new £600,000 gorillarium was opened
in 1991, after a public appeal had helped to raise funds for the building,
and the gorillas, a bachelor group including the silver back Djoum, moved
in. The building is sited in a circular clearing in the densest part of the
woodland. It is a curiously hi-tech structure – a high conical edifice of
concrete and stone and green painted steel and glass and wire. The primary
feature is a circular ring, several metres in width, wire fronted, which the
gorillas inhabit. Inside this doughnut is a tall stone-built cylindrical oast
house which presumably houses some off-show accommodation. The ring
shaped cage provides the gorillas with the opportunity to rush all the way
around in a virtually endless pursuit, which from time to time they seem
to do. But it also allows for a variation in the furniture, for considerable
exploration and play, and for gorillas to relax out of sight of the others,
should they wish. The floor of the loop is heavily packed with oat straw,
very much in the Howletts style, the ceilings are a complex lattice of
climbable girders, and ceilings and walls are hung with ropes and swings
and balls and objects of play. Rising up, here and there from the main
concourse are wire tunnels that lead the gorillas to another room, two
stories up at the peak of the cone. From here they can look down on the
visitors who congregate around, at an enforced distance. The whole structure is a magnificent piece of zoo engineering, and is unquestioningly
superb for the gorillas. Strangely it is a less comfortable place to sit and
watch gorillas at play than Howletts or Jersey; this is partly because the

design does not allow the gorilla-watcher to get particularly close, and partly the result of all that wire and glass. Nevertheless, this is part of the Aspinall style – enclosures are designed for the animals, not for the people – and again, if you bring binoculars, they will help.

John Aspinall's great passion for animals has lead to some outstanding zoo achievements, both here and at Howletts. Tigers were his first great love, and nowhere is there a collection of tigers quite like these two zoos. Then came gorillas, and the Howletts gorillas are universally acknow-ledged to be the best captive group in the world And finally there came rhinos. They may seem an unlikely group of animals to arouse great passion, but Aspinall admits that his favourite animals of all are the Su-matran rhinos. More about them in a moment. But there is an interesting connection between the three groups of animals that Aspinall has cham-pioned, tigers, gorillas, and rhinos (and, incidentally, wolves too); they are all animals that have suffered from an undeserved fiercesome reputation. They are animals badly in need of some good public relations. Perhaps Aspinall identifies with this. Whatever the cause (and perhaps the connec-tion is purely coincidental), Port Lympne and Howletts Zoos do every-thing to restore the natural gentility and dignity back to these animals.

So to the rhinos: there are five living species of rhinos, four may be found in zoos, and two of the most endangered species are kept at Port Lympne. There are ten black rhino here, more than there are at any other zoo in the world, and they occupy a spectacular fifteen acre field. Five of the group were born here, which is an achievement of note since so few of these precious rhinos breed successfully in the world's zoos. And there is every hope that they will breed again. Then finally there are the 'woolly rhinos', or Sumatran rhinos, Torgamba and Meranti. This pair are more than a simple zoo exhibit, to stroll past and casually admire. They repre-sent an extraordinary achievement, one which a decade ago few zoologists would have considered possible. It began when Francesco Nardelli, the curator at Howletts Zoo, alerted Aspinall to the plight of the world's smal-lest rhino. Fewer than five hundred, and possibly fewer than two hundred of these animals still survive in their native Indonesia, and most of these now occupy isolated pockets of forest – possibly often supporting no more than a single rhino. So little was known about the Sumatran rhino in 1984 that not a single photograph existed of a wild individual. But one thing was known: the creature was doomed. Forests were, and still are, being cleared at an alarming rate, and the commercial value of rhino products are inestimable to the local peasant farmers. But plans to bring Sumatran rhinos into captivity had always foundered because of the sheer costs, and the overwhelming political bureaucracy involved. Aspinall saw it as a challenge. His proposals to the International Union for the Conservation of Nature, to the Species Survival Commission, and to the government of Indonesia met with great approval. They coincided with similar proposals from a consortium of five large American zoos, but the American plan collapsed, and the future of the Sumatran rhino seemed to rest with Aspinall.

On 24th May 1985 a historic agreement was signed in Jakarta by Francesco Nardelli and the Indonesian Minister of Forestry, witnessed by the British Ambassador. It set in train a complex and ambitious project to rescue 'doomed rhinos' from forests earmarked for agriculture, and to establish captive breeding colonies both in Indonesia and in the UK. The project would cost almost £2 million, and success was far from guaranteed. It was a spectacular gamble. Equipment was air-freighted to Sumatra, living accommodation was built in the damp submontane forest, local people were employed, and in 1986 the first rhino, a male named Torgamba was caught. A road had to be laid into the forest to transport him, and back at Port Lympne a whole farm was prepared for his arrival with heated swimming pools, sun lamps, deep forest litter, and purpose-built pens. When Torgamba arrived the excitement at Port Lympne was so great that Aspinall threw a huge, extravagant party to celebrate.

The pair of rhinos occupy an expansive, purpose built house, and browse a hilly, roughly wooded ten acre field. The field is well provided with a swamp in which they wallow, and from which they emerge caked in mud. Alongside this field is a still larger tract of dense woodland into which the rhinos are also released from time to time. The pair have proved inseparable, and the woodland has been prepared so that they can be kept apart when needed. Be patient if they are not by the paddock fence. They often lie up for hours out of sight. If you find them that way, then be sure to come back an hour or so later. Eventually they will reward you with a walkabout. But beware of Meranti –her sudden sprays of urine often catch visitors unawares.

Despite the successes of Port Lympne, many zoo people still express reservations about the place. What these criticisms usually boil down to is an objection to the singlehanded way in which Aspinall approaches his collections and his reluctance to join the National Federation of Zoological Gardens. Undoubtedly there seems to be a real rift here, and quite clearly Aspinall's contribution to international conservation efforts would be even greater if his zoos were to seek closer co-operation with other zoos. But his attitude is understandable. He believes, with some justification, that no other zoo can offer his animals the quality of life that his zoos can; so he can be unwilling to share them. There must be some room for movement on both sides of this divide, because in the end the animals will benefit if organisations like the Zoo Federation can accord Aspinall's zoos a special status that will allow him to contribute more to species management programmes without compromising too many of his own ideals.

In the meantime, we recommend a visit to Port Lympne Zoo Park. However far you have to travel, it will be worth the experience.

EAST MIDLANDS ZOOLOGICAL SOCIETY: TWYCROSS ZOO

Twycross, Atherton
Warwickshire
Telephone: 0827 880250

How to find it:
6 miles north of Atherstone on the A444.

Open: All year from 10.00 am

Prices: adult £3.80; child £2.00; OAP £2.60.

Area: 10 hectares / 25 acres

	Species	Animals
Mammals	55	298
Birds	45	168
Reptiles	24	153
Amphibians	1	11
Fish		
Total	125	630
Conservation		★★★
Enclosures		★★
Education		★★★
Recreation		★★
Research		★

Like many Good Zoos all around the world, Twycross Zoo began simply as the private collection of an animal enthusiast. She is Miss Molly Badham, and her passion for keeping animals began in the 1940s when she used to run a little pet shop in Sutton Coldfield, just a few miles north of Birmingham. One day in 1949, into her shop was brought a woolly monkey named Sambo. He was the first monkey to come to the pet store, and Molly Badham could not bring herself to sell him. It was the modest beginning of what was to become a lifetime's obsession with primates. Within a year she had a collection of monkeys that threatened to overrun the shop, and in 1954 she moved along with all her animals to Stafford-shire, and opened a small zoo, Hints Zoological Gardens.

At Hints the collection grew rapidly, and in 1963 Molly Badham was ready to move again. This time the move was to Twycross, to the present, larger site on the A444 Tamworth to Hinkley road.

In the early 1950's, most monkeys had a pitifully short life in captivity. As Molly Badham relates in her book 'Chimps with Everything', many primates that are now considered endangered could be bought for a few pounds in the pet shops of Pimlico. Collectors and zoos found them so easy to obtain that the poor survival record was rarely a problem. Veteri-nary care and husbandry of primates was in its infancy, and captive breed-ing almost unheard of. It was against this background that Molly Badham started her zoo and set about learning almost from scratch how to care for her animals.

Many of the zoo's early charges arrived as weak and pathetic specimens from dealers who imported them under appalling conditions. Others were pets that had outgrown the ability of their owners to look after them. This was the way that many of Twycross's original chimpanzees entered the collection, and for many years the zoo was best known for its chimps and their television advertisements for Brooke-Bond Tea. This association has now ended, and chimps from European zoos now take the starring roles, but in the early days the royalties provided valuable revenue which paid for many developments within the zoo.

The site at Twycross is a broad rectangle of around fifty acres. About half the space is taken up with car parks, which are conveniently within the zoo. The rest of the zoo is flat, relatively unlandscaped, and grassy. The paths are good, and there are plenty of young trees, and some tall, well established trees, particularly on the Eastern side. The zoo is largely conventional in the design of most of its buildings which are fairly spaced out around the park, and unlike many country zoos it devotes very few of its acres to grazing herds.

Today Twycross Zoo is an internationally important centre for the breeding of primates. Very few zoos anywhere in the world have the experience that Twycross has with so many monkeys and apes. There are several groups of siamangs (the largest of the gibbons), pileated gibbons, Kloss's gibbons, lar gibbons, agile gibbons, and black gibbons, and most of these are breeding. There are chimpanzees, gorillas, orang utans, rare leaf-eating monkeys, spider monkeys, howler monkeys (lots of them), marmosets, and tamarins. There is even the startling skull-face of a red uakari (a little known monkey from Amazonia), and there are woolly monkeys, squirrel monkeys, and sakis. Several monkey houses occur all around the zoo, and they are all broadly similar in design; they consist of a central corridor into which visitors can wander, flanked by glass fronted indoor rooms which house the monkeys. The animals are free to move indoors or out, into long, well branched, and grassy aviary-style runs. The designs are clearly effective, and they allow successful management of the animals, although they somehow lack imagination, and the indoor accommodation often seems slightly bleak.

But the monkeys and apes themselves are wonderful. Most are now kept in generous family groups, and like all primates they are endlessly entertaining. The gibbons in particular are breathtaking, as gibbons always are, and they are made more so by the numbers of baby gibbons you will see, clutching confidently onto the adults as they swing the branches.

The great apes – the chimps, gorillas, and orang utans, all have essentially similar accommodation – outside a peninsula of grassland with some good climbing facilities, surrounded by a wall of armoured glass, and inside a collection of clean, tiled and rather sterile rooms, backed again by glass. They all afford excellent viewing, and are soundly and solidly built, although they lack the 'Jersey-esque' landscaping outdoors. The chimps are particularly noteworthy here – they have a splendid, large group.

At a zoo like this there is always a danger that the specialist collection might overshadow the rest of the zoo. But Twycross complements the primates with a fine general collection of exotic species. Here you can see all the regular zoo animals, and more. Big cats are represented by lions, tigers, and cheetahs in modest but well planted enclosures; there is a splendid new sealion pool featuring a high rocky backdrop with a cascading waterfall, and caves in the rocks for the sealions to hide away. There are giraffes in a large gravel enclosure, camels, alpacas and otters. Of special note are the Malayan tapirs in an attractive shaded field, tree kangaroos, bush dogs, meerkats, and 'marmot city' – a compound dotted with burrows, and richly populated with a host of quite delightful little prairie marmots.

Humboldt's penguins have an attractive large pool with underwater viewing. There is also a group of eight rare and beautiful Baikal seals from one of the worlds most threatened lakes, Lake Baikal in Russia. Birds of prey, waterfowl, and of course flamingos, adorn the grounds. All the birds are well housed in large, generously planted aviaries, or in waterfowl ponds along the northern perimeter of the zoo. There are groups of cassowaries which have bred, there is an attractive cluster of owl aviaries, and there is an aviary full of beautiful scarlet ibis.

There are Asiatic elephants in a good new elephant house which includes showers and a scratching rock. Outside they have a three-quarter acre compound with a deep pool and a mud wallow. The old, and now vacated elephant house is being converted into accommodation for bonobos – pygmy chimpanzees. It will be the first time that this endangered species will have been seen in Britain.

Education is taken seriously here, and every parent should be impressed by the imagination expressed in the interpretational signs which abound throughout the zoo. They are the work of 'the ZIP Squad' (the Zoo Interpretation Programme), and they involve signs that turn and lift and move to reveal their message. One building, the excellent 'Enchanted Forest' makes especial use of the signs to educate us about the richness of the rainforests. There are bats in this building, and signs invite you to open little doors and plunge your hands through into the darkness to discover fruits that are pollinated by bats (peaches, avocados, and cashew nuts, among others).

There is a good reptile house, with alligators, a variety of snakes and lizards, and close by is a purpose-built pet's corner with a variety of rabbits, goats, and other farm animals. The South West corner of the zoo houses an adventure playground and a few small fairground rides, and donkey rides.

But Twycross is really all about primates; the macabre looking red uakaris, the groups of colobus, the noisy and acrobatic gibbons and siamangs, the lovely ruffed lemurs, the cacophonous howler monkeys, the long limbed black spider monkeys, the striking saki monkeys, the beautiful and endangered golden lion tamarins, and the delightful pygmy marmosets. Twycross takes its role as a conservation zoo very seriously and is prepared to commit resources towards keeping surplus males and juveniles. It is an admirable commitment, and visitors may find it difficult to think of Twycross without remembering all the young animals there.

There is a quotation at the end of the Twycross Zoo guide, itself taken and altered from the Senegalese conservationist Baba Dioum, which sums up the philosophy of this zoo. It is this:

'In the end we will conserve only what we love and respect.

We will love and respect only what we understand.

We will understand only what we are taught, or allowed to experience.'

It is love, respect, and understanding that has led to the creation of this unlikely zoo, hidden as it is in the leafy backwaters of Leicestershire. The fact that well over a third of a million visitors make the journey every year to visit Twycross is testimony to the success that love, respect, and understanding can bring.

THE WELSH MOUNTAIN ZOO AND BOTANIC GARDENS

Colwyn Bay
Clwyd
Telephone: 0492 532938

How to find it:
Signposted from the centre of Colwyn Bay off the A55.

Open: Summer from 9.30 am Winter from 10.00 am

Prices: adult £4.30; child £2.15; OAP £2.15.

Area: 15 hectares / 37 acres

	Species	Animals
Mammals	30	229
Birds	48	240
Reptiles	21	121
Amphibians	3	7
Fish	5	32
Total	107	629
Conservation		★★
Enclosures		★★
Education		★★★
Recreation		★★
Research		★

The Welsh Mountain Zoo occupies 37 acres of a wooded hilltop overlooking the Irish Sea and the popular North Wales holiday resort of Colwyn Bay. It was the creation of a lifelong wildlife enthusiast, Robert Jackson, and it opened to the public on 18th May 1963. The site of the zoo, Flagstaff Gardens, had previously been open to the public, but Jackson had the vision to see that it could become an attractive, and even spectacular site for keeping animals. Tragically, in 1969, Jackson was killed in a fishing accident, and the management and direction of the zoo passed to his wife Margaret, and their three sons, Tony, Chris, and Nick. Since 1983 the zoo has been owned by the Zoological Society of Wales, a Registered Educational and Scientific Charity, but management has stayed with the three brothers.

Not all the zoo's acres are used for animals, and about half of the area has been left as wild woodland through which visitors can stroll, and which is kept as a habitat for native wildlife, like grey herons, grass snakes, and badgers. Do not be deceived by the 'Mountain' in the name. Admittedly the road up to the zoo winds and climbs a fair bit, but the zoo itself sits quite comfortably on the top of the hill, and the walk around is far from strenuous. The zoo is clean and attractive, with hundreds of tall trees, some open fields, and small but neat gardens.

The Welsh Mountain Zoo makes fairly conventional use of its small size to accommodate quite a wide range of familiar creatures. There are lions in a green, hilly, enclosure, a pair of African cow elephants in a small but adequate elephant house, Chilean flamingos in an attractive pool shrouded by trees and bushes, and a small group of Humboldt's penguins in a very good new pool with underwater viewing, and with breeding burrows in the grassy bank.

At the west end of the zoo are some splendid open paddocks with panoramic views over the Welsh hills. They make an ideal setting for Przewalski's horses, ostriches, llamas, kulan, and a lovely herd of fallow deer.

Sealions are considered a major attraction here, and they put on an entertaining display several times a day. They have bred successfully on more than one occasion, but their pool is circular, rather small, and earmarked for improvement. There are also daily falconry displays, and there can be few backdrops quite so suited to watching hawks, falcons, and even eagles flying.

The zoo claims to have been the first place in Britain to mount public falconry displays. But the displays are just one face of the raptors at this zoo, and several difficult and unusual species have bred here, including American bald eagles, and Australian wedge tailed eagles.

There is an impressive new enclosure for the chimpanzees, which for many years suffered rather cramped accommodation here. Chimpanzee World, as it is named, is a walled compound where the chimps can roam, and it affords good public viewing. Combined with the chimps is a conservation-education show 'Chimp Encounter' which helps to raise money for a chimp habitat project in West Africa. Close by are Persian leopards in a high hooped cage full of a tree. There are black panthers, and several beautiful green winged scarlet macaws. There are lar gibbons too in a long, but fairly simple enclosure, brown bears in a rather depressing pit, a good reptile house, and a new children's zoo, and tortoise lawn.

One new enclosure that demonstrates some sensitive and imaginative design is a hilly compound for European otters. It is extraordinarily spacious with a river, a waterfall and dozens of trees, and it provides both indoor viewing so that you can tip-toe inside and see the otters asleep in the semi darkness, and a viewing hide up a chestnut tree to watch the otters at play.

Like many zoos, the Welsh Mountain Zoo is a zoo in transition. It began life as a small, diverse, seaside collection. Now it has become a serious zoo with real conservation intentions. Zoological Director, Nick Jackson, chairs the Federation of Zoo's Conservation and Animal Management Committee, and during 1991 the zoo's offices were the centre of a radical reorganisation of all zoo-based breeding programmes in Britain. The new developments, especially the new chimp house, and the otter enclosure, demonstrate the way that the zoo is moving. A new facility for marmosets and tamarins will open in 1992, and the zoo is currently designing an ambitious new bear enclosure which will occupy some of the woodland. At the same time the Welsh Mountain Zoo remains a gently attractive and undemanding afternoon out for holiday makers to the North Wales resorts. Somehow it is managing to address all of its objectives remarkably well.

WEST MIDLANDS SAFARI AND LEISURE PARK

Bewdley
Worcestershire
Telephone: 0299 402114

How to find it:
Off the A456 between Kidderminster and Bewdley.

Open: April October from 10 am

Prices: adult £3.75; child £3.75.

Area: 81 hectares / 200 acres

	Species	Animals
Mammals	35	400
Birds	1	5
Reptiles	23	60
Amphibians	3	15
Fish	2	20
Total	64	500
Conservation		★
Enclosures		★★★
Education		★
Recreation		★★★
Research		

One man has been responsible, more than any other, for introducing the 'safari park' concept to Britain. He was the late Jimmy Chipperfield. Chipperfield came from a family of itinerant entertainers. He was born in the back of a circus caravan outside the Wiltshire village of Corsham in 1912, and he grew up among performing bears, monkeys, clowns and acrobats, as his family travelled the highways and byways of Britain. His colourful career took him from being a tight rope walker and a clown, to becoming a fighter pilot, a farmer, a circus owner, and an impresario. Many zoo people regarded him, and still do, as a gypsy, a man to whom animals were commodities, a man who must have grown up with the cruel excesses employed by many circuses to train their animals; and Chipperfield's own early attempts to open zoos in Southampton and Plymouth did not prove to be a success. But that was before he met the Marquess of Bath, and before their joint cooperation had led to the opening of The Lions of Longleat, Britain's first drive through animal park.

Longleat had been Chipperfield's brainchild, and he followed it with similar ventures at Woburn, Knowsley, Blair Drummond, Lambton near Newcastle, Loch Lomond, and in several estates in Holland, France, Spain, Germany, Canada, and Japan. But none of these belonged to Chipperfield himself. His involvement was that of an international safari park consultant, travelling the world, setting up for wealthy landowners the sort of park he would much prefer to have run for himself. The opportunity to do just that finally came in the early 1970s when he bought a 200 acre estate of rolling parkland at Bewdley, less than 20 miles from Birmingham, and set about landscaping his own new safari park.

The estate at Bewdley was founded by Samuel Skey, a Bewdley grocer who made his fortune manufacturing dye stuffs and sulphuric acid. He bought the land, a parcel of 270 acres from Lord Foley in 1775. A regular visitor was the artist John Constable, who courted his wife here. The gently rolling Worcestershire fields may well have provided inspiration for Constable, just as they inspired Chipperfield two centuries later

But perhaps Chipperfield had been too successful with all his earlier ventures, and perhaps the public appetite for safari parks was not what it once had been; for, despite the huge population within only a short drive from the gates, the West Midlands Safari Park was not a runaway success. The early years were a struggle, and visitor numbers fell steadily after the optimistic opening of the park in 1973. The land was leased to an American company in 1976, and management changes were made. The park was renamed the 'West Midlands Safari and Leisure Park' to reflect the new emphasis upon the growing fringe attractions of the park, and slowly the people of Birmingham and the West Midlands were wooed back through the gates.

The safari park occupies around one hundred acres of the estate, just off the A456 between Kidderminster and Bewdley. The entrance is impressive, with bold signs and colourful pictures that recur throughout the park. So in the first reserve, the African Reserve, there is a large clear sign that tells you what to look for – lion, eland, giraffe, brindled gnu, zebra, ankole cattle, white rhino, and camels. For once the lion reserve is not a drive-through section of the park. Instead they have their own fenced stretch of pasture, from which they can look out at the potential prey species which graze alongside. This is a deliberate feature of the West Midlands Safari Park, and the three main reserves (the African, American, and Eurasian) each has a central compound that holds a predator native to the respective continent. There is some economic sense behind the policy too, because it means that no special gates have to be operated between the reserves, with the animals kept apart by simple fences and cattle grids. This saves staff from having to manage the gates, and it also saves the staff who would inevitably have to patrol the lion and tiger reserves.

The next section of the park is moor-like, a huge open space furnished with gorse. 'Look out' reads a sign, 'there's a Wallaby about'. There is a lot of shelter here and you may have to search for your wallaby. The first animal you see may well be nothing more than a native rabbit, incautiously grazing among rather exotic company. There are monkeys here too, plenty of them, in one of the best monkey jungles around, and there are deer and camels hidden among the gorse and the trees. The roll of the landscape is deceptive, a testimony to the understanding that Chipperfield had of how these things should be done, and there seems to be a great deal of space. The gorse gives the surroundings the appearance of wilderness, and the whole area seems to be flanked with deciduous woodlands.

The road winds back into the first paddock, and then over a cattle grid into a wide stretch of grassland with fallow deer, and bison. Like the lions, the tigers are also separately enclosed in this section, but there is plenty of opportunity to watch them from the car. Timber wolves too have a separate enclosure of their own, and they occupy perhaps two acres or more of field, with a few trees, and concrete tunnel-like caves. It is a good sized pack, and there is plenty of group activity to watch.

The next reserve is the Eurasian Reserve. There are tigers again (in their own cage), surrounded by species that may, in some circumstances have been their traditional prey; yak, for example, looking beautiful with their full, shaggy, coats. There are Barbary sheep, Przewalski's horses, and deer.

Finally, back into the African Reserve, the road winds past the rhino house – an interesting enclosure with tree stumps, sand, a pond, and some huge rocks. Some splendid white rhino occupy the compound.

It has been some decades since zoos began to drop the habit of allowing visitors to feed the animals. For many it was a difficult decision to take. Visitors had grown accustomed to feeding buns to the elephants and peanuts to the monkeys. When the no-feeding rule was introduced the health of the animals increased markedly, but it placed a distance between people and animals that has never really been eroded. The West Midlands Safari and Leisure Park has taken a bold decision and reintroduced feeding by members of the public. To participate you have to buy bags of approved dietary pellets at the gate. This reduces any risk of animals being given inappropriate foods. With the dangerous animals (lions, tigers, and wolves) safely behind chain-link fences, you can feed all of the grazing animals directly; and of course the inevitable consequence is that the animals have learned to take full advantage of the idea, and they flock hungrily around the convoys of cars like Trafalgar Square's pigeons around a party of tourists. For visitors who have had the foresight to buy the food, this provides a greatly rewarding experience. In return for a few simple pellets you can stroke a Przewalski's horse or be nuzzled by a giraffe. Zebras will boldly nose their heads right through the car windows in search of food, while fallow deer delicately pluck the pellets from your outstretched hand. The price we pay for this humbling experience is something of the essence of the very animals that we reach out to feed – we lose their wildness, and their timidity. In return for being able to stroke their noses we turn them into beggars. But the experience of personal contact with the animals is a valid one nonetheless, and if one objective of modern zoos is to encourage a greater empathy and awareness of species other than ourselves, then here is a way of achieving it, and it seems to work.

The tour around the Safari Park brings you to the car park, where there is a small walk around zoo, and a pleasure park. There is a children's farmyard, with more opportunities for contact with animals, this time of a domestic variety. There is a reptile house with some attractive vivaria, and some monkeys and small mammals, and a sealion show. And of course there is the fairground with a host of theme park rides. The West Midland's Safari and Leisure Park is an unpretentious collection with a growing reputation. It offers a rare opportunity to see and touch a wide variety of species from three continents. Jimmy Chipperfield died in 1990 aged 78. The West Midlands Safari Park, like so many other parks he created, lives on.

THE ZOOLOGICAL SOCIETY OF LONDON: WHIPSNADE WILDLIFE PARK

Whipsnade
Bedfordshire LU6 2LF
Telephone: 0582 872171

How to find it:
Leave M1, Exit 9 or 12. Drive through
Dunstable and follow the signs.

Open: All year from 10.00 am

Prices: adult £6.95; child £4.95; OAP £5.60.

Area: 243 hectares / 547 acres

	Species	Animals
Mammals	65	1460
Birds	103	857
Reptiles	16	80
Amphibians		17
Fish	31	
Total	235	2414
Conservation		★★★
Enclosures		★★★★
Education		★★★
Recreation		★★★
Research		★★★

Whipsnade is Europe's biggest zoo. Compare its 547 acres with even our largest safari parks. Woburn and Windsor together don't amount to as much space as Whipsnade; and this is a zoo you can walk around. Many visitors do take the easy option and take their cars into the park, but even they will find that to get the best from Whipsnade they have to walk, at least some of the way around. Most still park outside, and take the really rather pleasant exercise of walking round the zoo.

Whipsnade is famous for being the world's first open zoo. Today the idea of keeping tropical animals in open fields seems perfectly natural. In the 1920s, however, it was revolutionary. Zoos at that time were city-centre affairs. They were invariably small and cramped, and most animals were kept indoors. Until 1902 virtually none of London Zoo's exotic species were allowed any fresh air, and whenever one died it was assumed that somehow it had been subjected to a fatal draught. It took developments in Germany at Carl Hagenbeck's zoo in Hamburg to convince informed opinion in Britain that perhaps animals could become used to a European climate, and perhaps even thrive in it. That was the view of Dr Peter Chalmers Mitchell, who in 1902 was appointed Secretary of the

Zoological Society of London. He proposed to London Zoo's Council that a farm in the country should be bought to house some of the surplus animals from Regent's Park Zoo. The Council repeatedly rejected the idea, but Chalmers Mitchell was stubborn. The idea began as a summer rest home for animals from London. Soon it became thought of as a 'breeding farm', and finally the idea emerged of a 'country zoo' to which visitors might travel by car or bus or train for a day of animal watching.

Under Chalmers Mitchell's repeated insistence the Council finally relented. They bought Hill Farm at the village of Whipsnade on the Dunstable Downs in 1927, and began to prepare it for the arrival of animals from London. Still there were problems; this time legal ones. It took a special Act of Parliament (The Zoological Society of London Act 1928) to be passed before the animals could be moved. But moved they were; and in May 1931 Whipsnade Zoo opened to the public for the first time.

Twenty six thousand people visited Whipsnade on that first Whit Monday. So great was public interest in the new zoo that railway bookings from London were cancelled by order of the police. Chalmers Mitchell must have been delighted. But no doubt he was more delighted by the success of his plans for the animals. Because they did thrive on the chalky downs of Bedfordshire.

Sixty years later Whipsnade remains a showpiece among British and European zoos. The zoo breeds successfully more large mammals within I.U.C.N. programmes than any other zoo in Europe. In places you may find that the relict ideas and constructions of the 1920s and 1930s sit rather uncomfortably in the 1990s, but in general the concept of specialising in herd animals in wide open spaces still works very well. The park today is broadly divided into five zones. The first three represent the Animals of Asia, the Animals of Africa, and the Animals of the North. The fourth is the 'Family Centre' where you will find the award winning children's farm, sealions, falconry displays, cafes and the excellent discovery centre: and the final zone is simply 'The Downs', an open area of hillside with the great white lion cut out of the turf, where you can picnic or stroll and admire the fabulous views out over the Vale of Aylesbury and beyond. The downs themselves have been designated a site of special scientific interest (SSSI), and are populated with hundreds of red necked wallabies, which effectively roam wild within the confines of the zoo. Visit in the early summer and you will see the little joeys popping in and out of their mothers pouches. Little muntjac (a tiny species of deer), and Chinese water deer, also roam free. So too do peafowl, jungle fowl, and mara. Look out for them all around the park, but especially on the downs.

The first animals you may see at Whipsnade are the Asian elephants, disappointingly housed in a rather pokey building with yards that seem small by today's standards. The building, however, is listed. It was built by Lubetkin and was presumably once seen as a model elephant house. The zoo has started 'Elephants at Work' demonstrations outside the enclosure to compensate for the shortage of space. Close by, however, are the cheetahs, and these are sure to raise your spirits. Whipsnade has become the world's leading zoo for breeding cheetahs, and over 130 have been born here. Considering the difficulties that most zoos have in encouraging cheetahs to breed, this is a tremendous achievement. On most visits to Whipsnade you should be rewarded by a endearing glimpse of cheetah cubs in the long grass of their simple wire enclosures.

The chimpanzees are housed in a chimp house based upon London Zoo's design, but in 1991 the zoo added a half acre outdoor enclosure to what had once been a disappointingly small cage. Now the chimps have plenty of space to rush about, as well as room to climb. They are held in by the simple, but effective, use of an electric fence.

The brown bears have a curious enclosure. It is a spacious dense wood of young hawthorns, with a small concrete pond in which they wallow. But the wood is surrounded by a wall topped by terrifying spiked bars which curve viciously inwards, making the enclosure a strange conflict between the open space of a country zoo and the ironwork of a Victorian one. Rather the same principle applies to the lions. Historically, perhaps, they might serve to remind us of the dreadful awe in which earlier generations held these great carnivores. As modern exhibits, however, they seem unnecessarily gruesome and anachronistic; this despite the relative spaciousness of the cages themselves. In 1993 the lions will be moving at last to a large open area.

Perhaps the real problem with the lions, bears and elephants, is that Whipsnade does not really feel comfortable about keeping them. Whipsnade exists for the great herd animals, and these it keeps extremely well. Most of the zoo is divided into huge grazing fields, each one tens of acres in size. Here is where the geographical 'zoning' of the park comes into its own. In 'Africa' you will find the giraffe, an exquisite herd of delicate Thompson's gazelle, the rare and beautiful Grevy's zebra recognisable by its fine stripes and its long upright mane, water buck, the 'bambi coloured' sitatunga antelope, and two great specialities of Whipsnade, the scimitar-horned oryx, and the white rhino. Scimitar-horned oryx are graceful fawn and white antelopes with sweeping curved horns. They are believed to have become extinct (or virtually extinct) in the wild over the past two decades. A joint operation by Whipsnade, Marwell, and Edinburgh Zoos recently succeeded in returning several oryx to a park in Tunisia, where they appear to be thriving: a good example, if you should ever need one, of real conservation in action. The white rhinos of Whipsnade were one of the first reserve herds established outside Africa. Dozens have been bred here, 15% of the white rhino world population in collections, and it is always a spellbinding sight to see a whole herd of these mighty lumbering creatures grazing so peacefully on the lush grass of Whipsnade. Hippos have bred here eighteen times.

The grazing animals of Asia include the rare barasingha (or swamp deer), blackbuck, mouflon, hog deer, fallow deer, nilgai, Przewalski's horse which has been breeding so well here, and Great Indian rhino which are guaranteed a place in the photograph albums of thousands of visitors. The Indian rhinos have twice bred here, and their first calf is now at Chester Zoo. A new idea to allow visitors closer to the animals is the 'Passage through Asia', a drive-through 80 acre field with no barriers and about 300 free roaming animals.

For many years the tigers at Whipsnade occupied the same sort of enclosures as the lions. But in 1991 the zoo opened 'Tiger Falls', described by the zoo's promoters as 'almost certainly the most ambitious and exciting project ever undertaken at Whipsnade'. The enclosure is home to endangered Siberian tigers, and is a large, richly landscaped and well wooded tract of hillside. It features a turbulent waterfall and a rock pool, and has a suspension bridge over which visitors can walk, creating the impression of a walk right through a tiger reserve. From all points of view it is a huge improvement upon the earlier cages.

'Animals of the North' are not really zoned, but are scattered around the zoo. They include quite a host of penguins (which are really animals of the South, but let us not quibble), musk oxen, European bison, and the bear; but perhaps the best displayed are the timber wolves in a splendid new wolf wood. 'The Timber Wolf' a sign informs us, were 'almost exterminated because of man's fear. Yet they have hardly ever been known to have attacked man.' All the wolves at Whipsnade are descendants of eight brought here in 1953.

The family area and children's farm here is one of the best in Britain. It is a real 'encounter' centre where children can meet and touch a variety of creatures, from hand-reared calves of the grazing herds, to domestic animals of all sorts. It houses a variety of rare breeds – redpoll cows, shire horses and Lincoln long wool sheep, among others. There is also the best railway ride in any zoo, the Umfolozi Express, a real steam train ride which winds right through the paddocks of the Animals of Asia. The 'Runwild' play centre offers children a fortress of an adventure playground. There is also a 'Woodland Bird Walk', a delightful pathway through an ancient tract of broadleafed woodland.

Finally there are sealions, which mount daily demonstrations, an excellent wildlife museum, and impressive displays of falconry.

Whipsnade Park Zoo was conceived by Chalmers Mitchell as a breeding farm for grazing herds. Today his vision stands, broadly unchanged after over half a century. Apart from the notable exception of the cheetah, that is where its success has been. The 'Whipsnade Experience' is the experience of those splendid herds. Long may it continue to be so.

WINDSOR SAFARI PARK

Winkfield Road, Windsor
Berkshire
Telephone: 0753 869841

How to find it:
Leave the M4 at Exit 6 Follow the B3022 to
Bracknell 2 miles from Windsor centre.
(M3 Exit 3. M25 Exit 13 – follow signs)

Open: All year from 10.00 am

Prices: adult £7.95; child £5.95; OAP £3.95.

Area: 57 hectares / 141 acres

	Species	Animals
Mammals	43	386
Birds	45	200
Reptiles	7	16
Amphibians	1	3
Fish	5	9
Total	101	614
Conservation		★
Enclosures		★★★
Education		★
Recreation		★★★
Research		

It isn't easy to make money out of wild animals. Plenty of people try, as
the long list of animal collections at the end of this book will confirm. But
just try to earn the commercial return on capital that big investors want to
see, and you can rapidly come unstuck. Animals are expensive; they
require a heavy commitment of paid staff to look after them; they need
veterinary care; they grow old and die; and, perhaps saddest of all, they go
out of fashion. All of this begins to explain the dramatic changes that have
occurred at Windsor Safari Park in recent years. The name of the game is
'diversification', – give the paying public what they want; and what the
paying public evidently wants in the 1990s are not simple safari parks or
zoos, they want 'Theme Parks'.

To be fair, Windsor has always been a Theme Park of sorts, even though
those two words may not have been common currency in 1969 when 'The
Royal Windsor Safari Park' (as it was then) was opened by the Smart
Brothers, owners of Billy Smart's Circus. It was the second drive-through
wild animal park in Britain, following hot on the heels of Longleat which
had opened it's gates to huge queues of cars only three years before. The
Smarts had the straightforward idea of combining a Longleat-style safari
tour with a walk through zoo, a few small children's amusements, a fort,
and some slides and swings. To add excitement they introduced a dolphin
show, and their biggest attraction in the early years was Ramu, a magnificent killer whale who so filled the small pool he eventually had to be sold
to a zoo in America.

In 1977 the Smart Brothers sold Windsor to Trident Television for £1.5
million, and the safari park was extended, with more attractions added. In
1984 Trident sold the park to Southbrook & City Holdings, then in De-
cember 1988 the park changed hands once again. This time the purchasers
were Themes International Plc, a holding company that operated in the
leisure sector in the UK, America, and Spain. They had hopes of becoming

the major leisure operator in the UK, and ultimately in the world. Grand ambitions, and their name said it all – Themes. Themes are big business, they are part of our developing cultural landscape, and the managing director of Themes International, Marc Etches, had big theme plans for the once humble Royal Windsor Safari Park. In January 1992, however, Themes International went into receivership. At the time of writing, the Park is being prepared by the receivers to be sold yet again.

Windsor is not the only Good Zoo in search of a theme. Chessington is equally obsessed. Both zoos are owned by larger holding companies, and their primary objective, in both cases, is profit. Of course the message of the market economy is that profit is the oxygen of conservation, and so perhaps we should be looking for these zoos to fund some high profile conservation projects, in the UK, or even overseas. Well, we shall see.

The theme at Windsor is 'The African Adventure'. Designers have been hard at work all around the park, and the result is an African motif that appears on almost every wall and every sign. Staff are all dressed as white hunters in the fashion of Stewart Grainger, the fairground is enclosed within the mud and wattle walls of an African village (Port Livingstone), and a new Arabian Knight's extravaganza is housed in a great Egyptian temple with a corridor of sphinxes. It is pure Hollywood of course, nothing more real than a film set, and even the Zulu dancers look a rather ethnic mix. But the illusion is an enticing one, and well maintained throughout the park. The park itself occupies 141 acres of a commanding hillside alongside the B3022 Bracknell to Windsor road. At the bottom and top of the hill are two great car parks. On either side are two halves of the drive through safari park; and in a stretch up the middle is a walk around area leading up from the fairground, past a splendid elephant compound, up to Sea World and the zoo. One ticket price covers all the attractions, and it is expensive, but arguably good value, especially for families with lively children.

The safari park is small, when compared to say Longleat, Knowsley, or Woburn. The road winds tightly past a magnificent group of lions in an oak wood, tigers that roam free past your car, and alongside a spacious enclosure with cheetah. Cheetah have bred at Windsor. There is a open plains area where you drive past camels, black buck, zebra, and some beautiful giraffe. There are crowned cranes in this area too, as well as Cape buffalo, zebras, and emus. There is also an enclosed wolf wood, bears, and a hippo lake. White rhinos occupy a 'Rhino Lodge', with a modest parade ground of a paddock, and housing some impressive rhinos. The rhibnos also roam free much of the time. The monkey jungle is small, with only a couple of reasonable sized trees, and on a busy day it isn't possible to spend too long within this part of the park without unfairly causing a traffic jam behind. But there are a large number of baboons in this area, in a fascinating troupe. In the height of the summer season the monkey jungle is closed to cars and access is by road train only.

The walk-around area of the zoo is not particularly large, and consists of a gentle uphill walk (or downhill, depending upon where you park). The new chimpanzee compound, alongside the fair in Port Livingstone, is home to about half a dozen chimps. It is aimed at providing much improved chimpanzee accommodation for Windsor. The enclosure owes a lot to the Twycross design, which is sensible, but wholly unexciting. It is a circular compound with a high wall that encloses a grassy mound. On the mound stands a hammock of ropes and logs and slides. Windows and a glass section of wall afford a view of the chimps within. On one face is the indoor accommodation through which visitors can see the chimps through toughened glass. By zoo standards it is among the best chimp enclosures in the country, but for a new enclosure in a wealthy zoo, it is, perhaps, a rather disappointing and unadventurous development.

The new elephant area is, by contrast, quite spectacular. It takes in about an acre or two of the hillside, a sandy landscaped slice of valley with river rapids churning through, and a backdrop of a great waterfall ('Victoria Falls'). The park used to keep Asian elephants, but now, in keeping with the theme, the seven elephants are all African. They are also all young. There is a large off-view elephant house, transformed to look like a huge cavern, and high above the compound is 'Treetops', a wooden pier that affords a perfect viewing post for watching the elephants beneath.

Undoubtedly the main attraction at Windsor during the seventies and eighties was Sea World, the dolphin and sealion show, which sits at the top of the hillside. It is an attraction that has earned both plaudits and stricture for Windsor. Supporters of the park have drawn attention to the dimensions of the pool, greater than any other in Britain. They have pointed out the breeding successes among the dolphins, and have emphasised the great pleasure that watching the show has given to millions of visitors. Critics, including the influential conservation pressure group Greenpeace, have made much of the limitations of the pool when compared to the dolphin's natural home in the open oceans. They have also cast doubt upon the ability of any zoo to breed dolphins in the long term, despite apparent short term successes. Over the years the zoo has learned to tread a cautious path between appearing overly defensive about the exhibit, while acknowledging some validity in the discontent of the conservationists.

Much of the attention, favourable and unfavourable, has focussed upon the killer whale, a splendid black and white dolphin with a wide, heavy body, and a high, shark-like dorsal fin. Killer whales are found in most of the world's oceans, and have suffered unnecessarily because of their name; in reality they are barely a threat to man. They are the largest of the dolphins, social predators that largely depend upon fish and squid for their diet. There has been a killer whale at Windsor for much of its history; originally the magnificent Ramu, and more recently Winnie who has spent more than a decade with only dolphins and humans for company. Intrinsically this must be unacceptable, however sensational a display the animal is trained to perform (and Winnie's performances are amazing indeed). At present Winnie is absent from Windsor, absent indeed from Britain, on a breeding loan at Sea World in Florida. This should go some way towards satisfying the critics. Indeed for a profit making concern to relinquish their leading attraction for an indefinite length of time hints at sincere motives; which is what Windsor has been claiming all along.

The killer whale may have gone, but there are still the Atlantic bottle-nosed dolphins. They occupy a relatively spacious and deep outside pool and viewing windows provide an opportunity to watch the dolphins underwater. Dolphins at Windsor have bred a number of times, and despite several early disappointments, they now seem to have solved most of the problems associated with rearing these wonderful sea mammals. The first dolphin to be born in captivity and reared to independence in Britain was born here on 6th June 1984. His name is Juno, and he now appears alongside the six other Windsor dolphins in the regular performances. Sealions perform too, and whatever your views may be about this type of display, there can be few people who will not be awed by the natural skills, and apparent intelligence of both groups of animals.

Back in the park, there are a small group of Humboldt's penguins in a traditional circular pool with a concrete island painted in swimming pool blue and white, with artificial burrows in the wall. The effect is supposed to evoke an Antarctic landscape, a little inappropriate perhaps for birds that live along the sandy beaches of South America. Elsewhere, flamingos stalk imperiously beneath a bank of willows, and there is a brick paved courtyard that features black-capped capuchins, ruffed lemurs, golden lion tamarins, love birds and macaws, in tall teepee- like enclosures. Tropical World is a humid hothouse of plants with butterflies and alligators, and there is a children's petting zoo, and a walk through deer forest. There is also a birds of prey show that features hawks, buzzards, falcons, owls, and an eagle. And there is a regular parrot show during which macaws perform such incongruous activities as roller skating and riding bicycles along a high wire.

The whole park is overlooked by 'The Old Colonial Mansion', once owned by Horace Dodge the motor car manufacturer. During the last war it was home to Joseph Kennedy, father of John, Bobby, and Edward. He was US Ambassador to Great Britain at the time, and the house was loaned to him by Mr Dodge. Neither man could surely have ever envisaged the way that this splendid estate would be transformed into such a varied assortment of animal attractions and fairground rides. The Kilimanjaro Toboggan run now sweeps beneath the house. The drum beat of the Zulu dancers sounds out over the park, and visitors cruise in little replicas of the African Queen on a Congo River ride past artificial elephants, hippos, and crocodiles. How curious that a place with so many live animals chooses to furnish one of its best rides with life-sized models. It blurs the

distinction between fantasy and reality in a slightly discomforting way.
Maybe one day when all the elephants in Africa are gone, visitors will still
cruise around Tsavo in their zebra-striped mini busses looking out for ro-
botised fibre glass elephant replicas who will squirt them with nice clean
water from their synthetic trunks. Of course this is only a theme park, and
the ride is fun. Does it betray a feckless attitude towards the real wild creatures, or is it harmless and educational? Alas, this is the dilemma of the
animal theme park. What is the park there for, the animals or the people?
And if the animals fail to interest the people any longer, can they be dis-
pensed with altogether and replaced with life-like imitations? Windsor
will probably always attract huge crowds, and since, despite the demise of
Themes International, this has always been a very profitable safari park,
it will probably grow and prosper. But it will always have a harder task
than most to convince the sceptics that it really means to be a serious conservation collection. The answer may be for it to spend even more on
worthy wildlife projects. If it does then it will deserve its popularity for its
contribution to wildlife conservation as well as for its undoubted entertainment value.

WOBURN WILD ANIMAL KINGDOM

Woburn Park, Milton Keynes
Bedfordshire
Telephone: 0525 290407

How to find it:
Leave the M1 at exit 13. The park is close to
the motorway and is well signposted.

Open: All year from 10.00 am

Prices: adult £7.00; child £4.50; OAP £4.50.

Area: 142 hectares / 351 acres

	Species	Animals
Mammals	23	197
Birds	8	48
Reptiles		
Amphibians	1	4
Fish		
Total	32	249
Conservation		★
Enclosures		★★★★
Education		★
Recreation		★★★
Research		

Whenever the history of zoos is related, the name 'Woburn' will always
appear. This huge private park has for many years been a sanctuary for
wildlife, and over a century ago there were zebra, giraffe, wildebeest,
moose, llama, and camels in the park. The Dukes of Bedford seemed to
have a passion for rare grazing animals, and during the latter part of the
last century there were also pampas deer from South America, swamp deer
and hog deer from India, alpine ibex, kudu, musk ox, European and
American bison, anoa (a dwarf forest buffalo), musk deer, goral (a Himalayan goat-antelope), and several rare wild asses among many others. But

it was in 1895 that the eleventh Duke of Bedford made the decision that was to earn Woburn its special place in the wildlife history books. In that year he made a special effort to collect together in the deer park every possible individual of a newly discovered species of deer from China, the Père David's deer. There were a dozen or so available, scattered among several European zoos; apart from these the only remaining animals were a semi-captive herd in the Imperial Hunting Park near Peking, and a possible small relict population in South East China. Within ten years of the eleventh Duke's prompt action, the last Père David's deer in China was killed in the Boxer Rebellion, and Woburn had the responsibility and the opportunity to be the first place in the world to consciously save from extinction, an animal from another country.

The story of the Père David's deer has become symbolic of all conservation work in zoos, and Woburn Deer Park has become the closest that conservationists might come to having a place of pilgrimage, where today several hundred Père David's deer graze on a seemingly endless pasture that rolls away to the horizon.

Today the great deer park and the stately home of Woburn Abbey are quite separate from the 'Wild Animal Kingdom' which is a traditional safari park, opened in 1970 following the success of Britain's first African-style park at Longleat four years before. As at Longleat, the animals were provided by Jimmy Chipperfield.

The half mile drive to the entrance takes you past two colossal lion statues, created for the 1924 British Empire Exhibition. They are a foretaste of what is to come, for the lion enclosure at Woburn is possibly the best in any British park. It is simple enormous, and you might have to drive for several minutes before you spot your first lion. If that sounds less than attractive, you need not fear, there are plenty of lion in the reserve, and when you come across them it is with almost the same thrill as encountering lions on a bend of a road in Africa. Tigers get the same treatment at Woburn. They will walk right alongside your car, wade in the murky water of a pond, or bask arrogantly on raised platforms, almost posing for the cameras. Many safari parks still keep tigers in cages, but Woburn has rejected this idea to excellent effect.

With the exception of the tigers, most of the Wild Animal Kingdom has a distinctly 'African feel' to it, heightened by the presence of hippos that wallow in a muddy lake and graze a large grassy paddock, the white rhino that stroll majestically around a huge field, zebra, eland, crowned crane and giraffe. Also, in a similar enclosure are a small group of bongos, a rarely seen African forest antelope, with a russet, almost red, coat broken with a few fine white stripes. Bongos have been resident at Woburn since 1972, and this was the first group ever to be shown in a British collection. Since then the group has bred well, and their progeny have found their way to other zoos all around the world. The bongos at Howletts and London Zoos originated from this group at Woburn.

There is the customary monkey jungle where a whole host of rhesus macaques share a large tract of woodland with several Canadian black bears and more than 300 tall and unprotected oak trees. Both the bears and the monkeys climb the trees, and you may spot a sleeping bear stretched out along a high branch, or propped in the crotch of two branches, oblivious to the gaze of visitors beneath.

After years of keeping African elephant, Woburn has now switched to Asian elephant, and they have plans to accommodate an adult bull and to breed elephant eventually.

After the five mile drive the day is not yet over; sealions give regular displays in what was once the dolphinarium, and there is a splendid amusement park. The leisure area includes fairground attractions. The cable-car ride ends up at the Pet's Corner where there are llamas, donkeys, parrots, and farmyard animals to be fed and stroked.

The deer park is a separate institution, surrounding Woburn Abbey, the ancestral home of the Dukes of Bedford. Here, in addition to the magnificent, unique herd of Père David's deer with their long tufted tails, and back-branching antlers, you will see large herds of red deer and fallow deer, as well as the smaller and more elusive muntjac and Chinese water deer.

Woburn Wild Animal Kingdom and the Deer Park claims to attract almost more visitors than any other British zoo, except for London. Whether its claims are true or not, it does provide a very good day out, and does keep the name of Woburn, however symbolic, as an important part of the international zoo community.

Part 5
Where To Find the Mammals

An Index to the Mammals in The Good Zoos

There are over 350 different mammal species and subspecies in British Zoos, and the enthusiast will have to visit almost every zoo to get a good chance of seeing them all. The following pages are a 'snapshot' of the species held by the Good Zoos, to our knowledge, at the time of writing. Since animals move frequently from zoo to zoo, and zoos aquire new species as old ones move or die, the index can be no more than a guide to the likely species on display.

The animals are listed in zoological groupings, and within each order the species are listed in alphabetical order of their generic and species names. The common names of species can vary (as can the latin names from time to time), and we have used our own preferences for the common names of mammals.

Where a species is displayed at a zoo, a record appears on the table.

[O = On Display] indicates simply that this species is kept and displayed.

[G = Good] indicates an exhibit of particular note. These are the animals that you might like to look out for when you visit this zoo. They may be simply animals that are endangered, or are rarely seen in captivity; they may be kept here in large numbers, and be breeding well; or the enclosure may be particularly well designed for its occupants.

[E = Excellent] is awarded to outstanding zoo exhibits. These are excellent examples of the best that British Zoos are doing to keep, breed, and display animals in conditions most appropriate to the animal's biology and behaviour, and in many cases allowing visitors the best opportunity to watch and to learn.

Naturally, with almost four hundred species to consider at thirty-one zoos, we hope you will be forgiving if our estimate of the relative worth of each exhibit does not match your own. These are opinions, and when you visit any of the zoos in this book you might like to contrast them with your own. Our greatest fear in these tables is one of omission. It may well be that there are excellent breeding groups at many zoos that have been churlishly awarded only an 'O': for these, our apologies.

* An asterisk after the common name indicates the wild status of the animal according to the IUCN Red List of Threatened Animals:

* E	Endangered
*V	Vulnerable
*R	Rare
*I	Indeterminate
*IK	Insufficiently Known

MONOTREMES

Species	Banham	Belfast	Blair Drummond	Blackpool	Bristol	Chester	Colchester	Cricket	Chessington	Costwold	Drusillas	Dudley	Edinburgh	Glasgow	Highland	Howletts	Jersey	Knowsley	Longleat	London	Marwell	Norfolk	Paignton	Pensynor	Port Lympne	Twycross	Whipsnade	Windsor	Welsh Midland	Woburn	Welsh Mountain
Australian echidna *Tachyglossus aculeatus*			O	O																O											
Bruijins echidna *V *Zaglossus brujini*																				G											

MARSUPIALS

Species	Banham	Belfast	Blair Drummond	Blackpool	Bristol	Chester	Colchester	Cricket	Chessington	Costwold	Drusillas	Dudley	Edinburgh	Glasgow	Highland	Howletts	Jersey	Knowsley	Longleat	London	Marwell	Norfolk	Paignton	Pensynor	Port Lympne	Twycross	Whipsnade	Windsor	Welsh Midland	Woburn	Welsh Mountain
Rufus rat kangaroo *Aepyprymnus rufescens*																															
Brush tailed bettong *Bettongia penicillata*																															
Byrnes pouched mouse *Dasyuroides brynei*																															
Dorias tree kangaroo *V *Dendrolagus dorianus*																								O							
Matschie's tree kangaroo *Dendrolagus matschiei*		O																													
Leadbeater's possum *V *Gymnobelideus leadbeateri*																				O											
Tamar wallaby *Macropus eugenii*				O																											
Western grey kangaroo *Macropus fuliginoseus*				G								G							G	G											
Parma wallaby *Macropus parma*	G		G						O	O		O		G	G				O				O								
Wallaroo *Macropus robustus*			G		O																										
Red-necked wallaby *Macropus rufogriseus*	G	G		O		G	O	O	O	O		O	O		G		O	E	O	O			O	O			E		E	E	O
Red kangaroo *Megaleia rufa*	G		O																												
Short-tailed opossum *Monodlphis domestica*									O																						
Sugar glider *Petaurus breviceps*																															
Koala *Phascolarctus cinerus*																				G											
Grey ground cuscus *Phalanger gymnotis*		G																		O											
Long nosed potoroo *Potorous tridactylus*			O	O	O																										
Quokka *Setonix brachyurus*		G																													

INSECTIVORES

Species	Banham	Belfast	Blair Drummond	Blackpool	Bristol	Chester	Colchester	Cricket	Chessington	Costwold	Drusillas	Dudley	Edinburgh	Glasgow	Highland	Howletts	Jersey	Knowsley	Longleat	London	Marwell	Norfolk	Paignton	Pensynor	Port Lympne	Twycross	Whipsnade	Windsor	Welsh Midland	Woburn	Welsh Mountain
Pygmy hedgehog tenrec *Echinops telfairi*															O																
European hedgehog *Erinaceus eurpaeus*																							O								

BATS

Species	Banham	Belfast	Blair Drummond	Blackpool	Bristol	Chester	Colchester	Cricket	Chessington	Costwold	Drusillas	Dudley	Edinburgh	Glasgow	Highland	Howletts	Jersey	Knowsley	Longleat	London	Marwell	Norfolk	Paignton	Pensynor	Port Lympne	Twycross	Whipsnade	Windsor	Welsh Midland	Woburn	Welsh Mountain
Sebas short tailed fruit bat *Carollia perspicallata*																				G											
Indian fruit bat *Pteropus giganteus*									G																						
Rodrigues fruit bat *E *Pteropus rodriguensis*				E													E	E					E								
Egyptian fruit bat *Roussetes aegyptiacus*	G		G	G					G																			G			

	Banham	Belfast	Blair Drummond	Blackpool	Bristol	Chester	Colchester	Cricket	Chessington	Cotswold	Drusillas	Dudley	Edinburgh	Glasgow	Highland	Howletts	Jersey	Knowsley	Longleat	London	Marwell	Norfolk	Paignton	Penscynor	Port Lympne	Twycross	Whipsnade	Windsor	West Midland	Welsh Mountain	Woburn
TREE SHREWS																															
Large tree shrew *Lyongale tana*																			O												
Common tree shrew *Tupaia glis*				O					O															O	O		O				
EDENTATES																															
Naked-tailed armadillo *Cabassous centralis*																															
Hairy armadillo *Chaetophractus villosus*			O	O															O												
Two-toed sloth *Choloepus didactylus*				G															G												
Hoffman's sloth *Choloepus hoffmani*																															
Nine-banded armadillo *Dasypus novemcintus*																															
Giant anteater *Myrmecophaga tridactyla*																															
RABBITS AND HARES																															
Common rabbit *Oryctolagus cuniculus*																				O											O
Volcano rabbit *Romerolagus diazi*																	G														
CETACEANS																															
Bottle-nosed dolphin *Tursiops truncatus*																													O		
Killer whale *Orcinus orca*																													O		
PRIMATES **Lemurs & Aye Ayes**																															
Alaotra gentle lemur *E *Hapalemur griseus alaotrensis*																	G														
Fat-tailed dwarf lemur *Cheiroglaeus medius*			G																O												
Ring-tailed lemur *V *Lemur catta*	G	G		O	O	E		O	O	O	O	O	O	O					O						O		O	O			
Brown lemur *R *Lemur fulvus*																			O												
White-fronted lemur *R *Lemur fulvus albifrons*			O	G	O																										
Mayotte brown lemur *R *Lemur fulvus mayottensis*																	G														
Black lemur *V *Lemur macaco*	G			G		G																									
Mayotte lemur *V *Lemur macaco mayottensis*						O			O						O								O								
Red-fronted lemur *R *Lemur macaco rufus*				G		G																									
Mongoose lemur *E *Lemur mongoz*				G																											
Ruffed lemur *E *Lemur variegatus*	O	G																	O												
Black-white-ruffed lemur *E *Lemur variegatus variegatus*				O	O	O	O									E	G											G			
Red-ruffed lemur *E *Lemur variegatus ruber*				O												E															
Grey mouse lemur *Microcebus murinus*	O																		O												

162

	Banham	Belfast	Blair Drummond	Blackpool	Bristol	Chester	Colchester	Cricket	Chessington	Cotswold	Drusillas	Dudley	Edinburgh	Glasgow	Highland	Howletts	Jersey	Knowsley	Longleat	London	Marwell	Norfolk	Paignton	Penscynor	Port Lympne	Twycross	Whipsnade	Windsor	West Midland	Woburn
Aye Aye *E *Paubentonia madagascarensis*													E																	

Lorises, Galagos, etc

	Banham	Belfast	Blair Drummond	Blackpool	Bristol	Chester	Colchester	Cricket	Chessington	Cotswold	Drusillas	Dudley	Edinburgh	Glasgow	Highland	Howletts	Jersey	Knowsley	Longleat	London	Marwell	Norfolk	Paignton	Penscynor	Port Lympne	Twycross	Whipsnade	Windsor	West Midland	Woburn
Slender loris *Loris tardigradus*				O																G										
Slow loris *Nycticebus cougang*				O	O															O										
Lesser slow loris *Nycticebus pygmaeus*	O			O																										
Thick-tailed bushbaby *Galago crassicaudatus*				O																										
Senegal bushbaby *Galago senagalensis*					O															O										
Dourocouli (owl monkey) *Aotus trivirgatus*				O	O					O										O					O	O				

Marmosets and Tamarins

	Banham	Belfast	Blair Drummond	Blackpool	Bristol	Chester	Colchester	Cricket	Chessington	Cotswold	Drusillas	Dudley	Edinburgh	Glasgow	Highland	Howletts	Jersey	Knowsley	Longleat	London	Marwell	Norfolk	Paignton	Penscynor	Port Lympne	Twycross	Whipsnade	Windsor	West Midland	Woburn
Goeldi's monkey *R *Callimico goeldii*	G	O		O						O		O		G	G					O	O		O	O	O					
Silvery marmoset *Callithrix argenta*						O																							G	
Silvery marmoset *Callithrix argentata argentata*	O															E													G	
Black-tailed sil. marmoset *Callithrix aargentata melanura*																										G				
Geoffroy's marmoset *Callithrix geoffroyi*	O	O														E														
Tassel-eared marmoset *Callithrix humeralifer*	O																													
Common marmoset *Callithrix jacchus*	O								O	O	O									O			O							
Black-eared marmoset *Callithrix pennicillata*									O															E						
Pygmy marmoset *Callithrix pygmaea*	G	O		O	O	O						O								G	O		O		O					
Golden lion tamarin *E *Leontopithecus rosalia*		G			O					G				G	E					G	E		O	G		G	O			
Golden-headed lion tamarin *E *Leontopithecus r. chrysomelas*		G														E				O	O									
Black lion tamarin *E *Leontopithecus r. chrysophygus*																G														
Pied tamarin *E *Sanguinus bicolor bicolor*																O														
Saddle back tamarin *Saguinus fuscicollis*																O														
Geoffroy's tamarin *Saguinus geoffroyi*				O																		O								
Red-mantled tamarin *Saguinus illigeri*									O	O										G	O									
Emperor tamarin *I *Saguinus imperator*	G			O																O	O							O		
Emperor tamarin *I *Saguinus imperator subgriscens*		O							O																O					
White-lipped tamarin *Saguinus labiatus*				O	O					O		O														G	O			
White-lipped tamarin *Saguinus labiatus labiatus*																														
Red-handed tamarin *Saguinus midas*	G	O								O		O																		

Species	Banham	Belfast	Blair Drummond	Blackpool	Bristol	Chester	Colchester	Cricket	Chessington	Cotswold	Drusillas	Dudley	Edinburgh	Glasgow	Highland	Howletts	Jersey	Knowsley	Longleat	London	Marwell	Norfolk	Paignton	Port Lympne	Twycross	Whipsnade	Windsor	Welsh Midland	Woburn
Black-handed tamarin *Saguinus midas niger*																													
Cotton top tamarin *E *Saguinus oedipus*	G	G			G	G	G	G	G	G	G	G				G		G	G					E	G				G
Weddell's tamarin *Saguinus weddelli*		O																											
New world monkeys																													
Dusky titi monkey *Callicebus moloch*																													
Red uakari *Cacajao rubicundus*																								O					
White-faced saki *Pithecia pithecia*	O									O			G			G								G	O				
Black howler monkey *Alouatta caraya*																								G					
Red howler monkey *Alovatta seniculus*																								O					
White-fronted capuchin *Cebus albifrons*																													
Brown capuchin *Cebus apella*			O	G					O				O								G	O		O					
Black-capped capuchin *Cebus apella apella*															G	G													
White-throated capuchin *Cebus capucinus*			G										O	G															
Weeper capuchin *Cebus nigrivitattus*							O																						
Squirrel monkey *Saimiri sciureus*				G					O	O									O					O	G				
Black-capped squirrel monkey *Saimiri s. boliviensis*	E								O														O						
Long-haired spider monkey *Ateles belzebuth*																													
Long-haired spider monkey *V *Ateles belzebuth belzebuth*							O																						
Marimonda spider monkey *V *Ateles belzebuth hybridus*																								O					
Columbian spider monkey *V *Ateles fuciceps robustus*	O	G																						O					
Black-handed spider monkey *V *Ateles geoffroyi*									O																				O
Geoffroy's spider monkey *V *Ateles geoffroyi geoffroyi*				O																									
Hooded spider monkey *V *Ateles geoffroyi grisescens*																													
Ornate spider monkey *V *Ateles geoffroyi ornatus*																													O
Brown-foreheaded spider monkey *Ateles geoffroyi frontatus*																													
Black spider monkey *V *Ateles paniscus*	G		O																				O		G				
Red-faced spider monkey *Ateles paniscus paniscus*																				O									
Peruvian black spider monkey *Ateles paniscus chamek* *V	O			G																									
Woolly monkey *Lagothrix lagothrica*																								O					

164

Old world monkeys

	Banham	Belfast	Blair Drummond	Blackpool	Bristol	Chester	Colchester	Cricket	Chessington	Cotswold	Drusillas	Dudley	Edinburgh	Glasgow	Highland	Howletts	Jersey	Knowsley	Longleat	London	Marwell	Norfolk	Paignton	Pensthorpe	Port Lympne	Twycross	Whipsnade	Windsor	West Midland	Welsh Mountain	Woburn
Black mangabey *IK *Cerocebus aterrimus*				O	O																										
Sooty mangabey *V *Cerocebus torquatus atys*																							O								
Grass monkey *Cerocebus aethiops*		O	O					O																							
Vervet monkey *Cercopithecus aethiops*		O																													
Schmidt's guenon *Cercopithecus ascanius*										O																O					
Diana monkey *V *Cercopithecus diana*	O	G				O				O							O				O				G	O					
Owl-faced monkey *V *Cercopithecus hamlyni*	O									O							O														
L'Hoest's monkey *Cercopithecus l'hoesti*										O																					
Diademed monkey *Cercopithecus mitis*																							O								
Syke's guenon *Cercopithecus mitis albogularis*																															
De Brazza's monkey *Cercopithecus neglectus*	O			O	O		O			O															G	O			O		
Allen's monkey *Cercopithecus nigroviridis*			O							O																O					
Patas monkey *Cercopithecus patas*					G					O									O	O									O		
Spot-nosed guenon *Cercopithecus petaurista*																															
Talapoin monkey *Cercopithecus talapoin*					G																										
Stump-tailed macaque *Macaca arctoides*										O																					
Crab eating macaque *Macaca fascicularis*			O																				G								
Rhesus macaque *Macaca mulatta*		E																E												E	E
Pig-tailed macaque *Macaca nemestrina*																															
Celebes black ape *Macaca nigra*			O							O					E			G	G	G											
Black ape *Macaca nigra brunnescens*								O																							
Lion tailed macaque *E *Macaca silenus*		G		E	G	O				O																					
Toque monkey *Macaca sinica*																															
Barbary ape *V *Macaca sylvanus*						O				O									O	O								O			
Mentawi Island macaque *E *Macaca pagensis*			O																												
Anubis baboon *Papio cynocephalus anubis*															E																
Hamadryas baboon *R *Papio hamadryas*																							G					E			
Mandrill *V *Papio sphinx*		O			O															E		O									
Eastern bl & white colobus *Colobus guereza*	O				O	O																	G	G							

	Banham	Belfast	Blair Drummond	Blackpool	Bristol	Chester	Colchester	Cricket	Chessington	Cotswold	Drusillas	Dudley	Edinburgh	Glasgow	Highland	Howletts	Jersey	Knowsley	Longleat	London	Marwell	Norfolk	Paignton	Penscynor	Port Lympne	Twycross	Whipsnade	Windsor	West Midland	Woburn
Eastern colobus *Colobus guereza kikuyuensis*	G			G															O	O										
Western bl & white colobus *Colobus polykomos*																		O												
Black and White Colobus *Colobus polykomos polykomos*	O					O							O												O	O				
Silvery leaf monkey *Presbytis cristatus*	G				O																				O					
Javan brown langur *Presbytis cristatus pyrrhus*			G										E												G					
Entellus langur *Presbytis entellus*																		O							O					
Banded langur *Presbytis melaphos*													E																	
Spectacled langur *Presbytes obscura*										O															O					
Douc langur *E *Pygathrix nemaeus*													E																	
Apes																														
Agile gibbon *Hylobates agilis*																							O		G					
Black gibbon *V *Hylobates concolor*																									G					
Black gibbon *Hylobates concolor leucogenys*																									O					
Kloss's gibbon *E *Hylobates klossi*																									O					
Lar gibbon *Hylobates lar*	O		O			O	O	O	O							O			O	O					G					O
Javan grey gibbon *E *Hylobates moloch*													E						O											
Mueller's gibbon *E *Hylobates moloch muelleri*	O																		O		O									
Pileated gibbon *E *Hylobates pileatus*																							O		G					
Siamang gibbon *Hylobates syndactylus*	O								O				E					O							E	G				
Western lowland gorilla *V *Gorilla gorilla gorilla*		G		O	O				G			O	O		E	E	O	O							G					
Chimpanzee *V *Pan troglodytes*	O	E	O	O	E	G				O	O								G		O	O	O	O		G	G			G
Bornean orang utan *E *Pongo pygmaeus pygmaeus*				O	G					O				O											O					
Summatran orang utan *E *Pongo pygmaeus albelii*				O	G									O											O					
RODENTS **Squirrel family**																														
Prevost's squirrel *Callosciurus prevosti*																														
Finlayson's squirrel *Callosciurus finlaysoni*																														
Prarie marmot *Cynomys ludovicianus*	G	O		O	G					O	O											O	O			G	G			
Siberian chipmunk *Eutamias sibiricus*	O					O		O	O										O											
Townsend's chipmunk *Eutamias townsendii*																			O											
Fire-footed squirrel *Funisciurus pyrrhopus*																														

	Banham	Belfast	Blair Drummond	Blackpool	Bristol	Chester	Colchester	Cricket	Chessington	Costwold	Drusillas	Dudley	Edinburgh	Glasgow	Highland	Howletts	Jersey	Knowsley	Longleat	London	Marwell	Norfolk	Paignton	Pensthorpe	Port Lympne	Twycross	Whipsnade	Windsor	West Midland	Welsh Mountain	Woburn
Northern flying squirrel *Glaucomys sabrinus*																															
Woodchuck *Marmota monax*																						O									
Common giant squirrel *Ratufa affinis*																															
Malay black giant squirrel *Ratufa bicolor*																															
Red squirrel *Sciurus vulgaris*																													O		
Eastern chipmunk *Tamias striatus*									O		O																				
Beaver family																															
North American beaver *Castor canadensis*									O	G	O	O																			
Springhare family																															
Springhaas *Pedetes capensis*			O	O																											
Rats and Mice, etc.																															
Oldfield mouse *Peromyscus polionotus*																				O											
Dwarf hamster *Phodopus sungorus*																				G											
Cotton rat *Sigmodon hispidus*																															
Bank vole *Clethrionomys glareolus*							O													G											
Lemming *Dicrostonyx torquatus*																															
Malagasy rat *Hypogeomys animena*															G					O											
Field vole *Microtus agrestis*													O																		
Pallid gerbil *Gerbillus perpalliidus*																				O											
Shaw's jird *Meriones shawii*																				G											
Cairo spiny mouse *Acomys cahirinus*																				G											
Golden spiny mouse *Acomys russatus*																				G											
Common dormouse *Muscardinus avellanarius*																				O											
Nile rat *Arvicanthis niloticus*																															
Harvest mouse *Micromys minutus*																				O											
Norway rat *Rattus norvegicus*									G											G											
Black rat *Rattus rattus*																				G	O										
Edible dormouse *Glis glis*																					O										
Jerboa *Jaculus jaculus vocator*																				O											
Porcupines																															
Brush tailed porcupine *Atherurus africanus*																				O											

Species	Banham	Belfast	Blair Drummond	Blackpool	Bristol	Chester	Colchester	Chessington	Cricket	Cotswold	Drusillas	Dudley	Edinburgh	Glasgow	Highland	Howletts	Jersey	Knowsley	Longleat	London	Marwell	Norfolk	Paignton	Penscynor	Port Lympne	Twycross	Whipsnade	Windsor	West Midland	Welsh Mountain	Woburn
Crested porcupine *Hystrix cristata*				O				O				O								O	O										O
Indian crested porcupine *Hystrix indica*																															
North American porcupine *Erethizon dorsatum*			O																												

Cavys, Capybaras, Pacas and Agoutis

Species	Banham	Belfast	Blair Drummond	Blackpool	Bristol	Chester	Colchester	Chessington	Cricket	Cotswold	Drusillas	Dudley	Edinburgh	Glasgow	Highland	Howletts	Jersey	Knowsley	Longleat	London	Marwell	Norfolk	Paignton	Penscynor	Port Lympne	Twycross	Whipsnade	Windsor	West Midland	Welsh Mountain	Woburn
Rock cavy *Kerodon rupestris*																															
Mara *Dolichotis patagonium*	O	O		O	O			O	O	O										G	O					G	G				
Capybara *Hydrochoerus hydrochaeris*	O	O	O	G			O		O	O										O	O		O			O					O
Spotted paca *Cuniculus paca*				O																											
Agouti *Dasyprocta (hybrid)*					O																										
Orange-rumped agouti *Dasyprocta agouti*			O																O	O	O										
Grey agouti *Dasyprocta fuliginosa*																															
Brown agouti *Dasyprocta punctata*			O																												
Green acouchi *Myoprocta pratti*			O																O												

Chinchillas

Species	Banham	Belfast	Blair Drummond	Blackpool	Bristol	Chester	Colchester	Chessington	Cricket	Cotswold	Drusillas	Dudley	Edinburgh	Glasgow	Highland	Howletts	Jersey	Knowsley	Longleat	London	Marwell	Norfolk	Paignton	Penscynor	Port Lympne	Twycross	Whipsnade	Windsor	West Midland	Welsh Mountain	Woburn
Chinchilla *I *Chinchilla laniger*					O		O												O	O							O				
Mountain vischcha *Lagidium viscaccia*			O																												
Jamaican hutia *R *Geocapromys browni*																	G														
Coypu *Myocastor coypu*				G																	G										
Degu *Octodon degus*																			O												

Mole rats

Species	Banham	Belfast	Blair Drummond	Blackpool	Bristol	Chester	Colchester	Chessington	Cricket	Cotswold	Drusillas	Dudley	Edinburgh	Glasgow	Highland	Howletts	Jersey	Knowsley	Longleat	London	Marwell	Norfolk	Paignton	Penscynor	Port Lympne	Twycross	Whipsnade	Windsor	West Midland	Welsh Mountain	Woburn
Naked mole rat *Heterocephalus glaber*																															

CARNIVORES
Dog Family

Species	Banham	Belfast	Blair Drummond	Blackpool	Bristol	Chester	Colchester	Chessington	Cricket	Cotswold	Drusillas	Dudley	Edinburgh	Glasgow	Highland	Howletts	Jersey	Knowsley	Longleat	London	Marwell	Norfolk	Paignton	Penscynor	Port Lympne	Twycross	Whipsnade	Windsor	West Midland	Welsh Mountain	Woburn
Arctic fox *Alopex lagopus*															O						G										O
Grey wolf *V *Canis lupus*				O				O	O						O				O								E		G		G
Timber wolf *Canis lupus occidentalis*															E											E		G			
Maned wolf *V *Chrysocyon brachyurus*	G	G			G														G	G	G										
Dhole (Asiatic wild dog) *Cuon alpinus*													E																		
Fennec fox *Fennecus zerda*			O																	O											
Hunting dog *E *Lycaon pictus*					G																					E					
Bush dog *V *Spetheos venaticus*				O					O					G											O						
Grey fox *Urocyon cinereoargentateus*																															

168

	Banham	Belfast	Blair Drummond	Blackpool	Bristol	Chester	Colchester	Cricket	Chessington	Cotswold	Drusillas	Dudley	Edinburgh	Glasgow	Highland	Howletts	Jersey	Knowsley	Longleat	London	Marwell	Norfolk	Paignton	Penscynor	Port Lympne	Twycross	Whipsnade	Windsor	West Midland	Woburn
Red fox *Vulpes vulpes*													O																	
Bears																														
Asiatic black bear *Selenarctos thibetanus*						O				O		E																	G	
Spectacled bear *V *Tremarctos ornatus*		G													G															
Brown bear *Ursus arctos*		O		O						O		O														G	G		O	
Syrian brown bear *Ursus arctos syriacus*				O																										
American black bear *Ursus americanus*										O																				E
Polar bear *V *Thalarctos maritimus*		G		O	O		O				O																			
Hyaenas																														
Brown hyaena *Hyaena brunnea*																									G					
Striped hyaena *Hyaena hyaena*																									G					
Spotted hyaena *Crocuta crocuta*		O				O					O																			
Raccoons, Pandas, Civets and other carnivores																														
Red panda *IK *Ailurus fulgens*		G							G		G							G		G				G						
Olingo *Bassaricyon alleni*																														
Cacomistle *Bassariscus astutus*											G																			
Coati *Nasua narica*																													O	
Ring-tailed coati *Nasua nasua*				G	O	O	O		O		O									G	O	O			O					
Kinkajou (honey bear) *Potos flavus*		O		G																O										
Raccoon *Procyon lotor*	O					O	O				O																			
Tayra *Eira barbara*																														
Grisson *Galictis cuja*																														
Pine marten *Martes martes*													O						O	O										
Weasel *Mustela nivalis*																														
Polecat *Mustela putorius*							O						O						O	O									O	
European badger *Meles meles*													O							O										
Striped skunk *Mephitis mephitis*															O							O								
Honey badger (Ratel) *Mellivora capensis*															O							O								
Asian short-clawed otter *IK *Aonyx cinerea*	O			O	O	O	O	O	O	G	O								O	O	G			G					G	
North American otter *Lutra canadensis*	O							O																						
Eurasian otter *Lutra lutra*													O							G									G	

169

	Banham	Belfast	Blair Drummond	Blackpool	Bristol	Chester	Colchester	Cricket	Chessington	Cotswold	Drusillas	Dudley	Edinburgh	Glasgow	Highland	Howletts	Jersey	Knowsley	Longleat	London	Marwell	Norfolk	Paignton	Penscynor	Port Lympne	Twycross	Whipsnade	Windsor	West Midland	Woburn
Blotched genet *Genetta tigrina*																			O	O										
Civet *Vivera civetta*	O			-	O																									
Binturong *Arctitis binturong*	O				O																			O						
Smooth toothed palm civet *Arctogalidea trivirgata*																														
Yellow mongoose *Cynictic penicillata*								O											O	O										
Dwarf mongoose *Helogale parvula*				G								O							G	O										
Banded mongoose *Mungos mungo*	O			G	G		O	O																				G		
Meerkat *Suricatta suricatta*	O	O		O	O	O	O		O	G	O	O	O						G	O		O		O	O				O	
Small Cats																														
Leopard cat *Felis bengalensis*				O				O						G										O						
Caracal *Felis caracal*				O	O			O						G					O					O						
Jungle cat *Felis chaus*				O	O		O	O	O	O		G						O	G			O	O			O				
Pampas cat *Felis colocolo*																														
Puma *Felis concolor*		O			O															O										
Geoffroy's cat *Felis geoffroyi*	O			G						O																				
African wild cat *Felis lybica ornata*																														
Northern lynx *Felis lynx*				O	O							G	G						O											
Northern lynx *Felis lynx lynx*							O											O												
Canadian lynx *Felis lynx canadensis*																														
Siberian lynx *Felis lynx wrangeli*				O				O				G										O								
Pallas's cat *Felis manul*													G																	
Marbled cat *Felis marmorata*													G																	
Black-footed cat *Felis nigripes*	O			O	O								G																	
Indian desert cat *Felis ornata*													G											O						
Ocelot *V *Felis pardalis*	O		O	O	G		O		O	O		G					O				O									
Rusty spotted cat *IK *Felis rubiginosa*	O			O								G											O							
Serval *Felis serval*				O		O	O	G				G	O					O	O	G										
Wild cat *Felis silvestris*				O					O	O							O													
Fishing cat *Felis viverrinus*				G																			O							
Margay *V *Felis wiedii*				G					O	O																				

170

Species	Banham	Belfast	Blair Drummond	Blackpool	Bristol	Chester	Colchester	Cricket	Chessington	Drusillas	Dudley	Edinburgh	Glasgow	Highland	Howletts	Jersey	Knowsley	London	Longleat	Marwell	Norfolk	Paignton	Pensoyor	Port Lympne	Twycross	Whipsnade	Windsor	Welsh Mountain	West Midland	Woburn
Jaguarundi *V / *Felis yagouroundi*				O																										
Temminick's cat / *Profelis temminicki*																								G						
African golden cat / *Profelis aurata*																								O						
Big Cats																														
Clouded leopard *V / *Neofelis nebulosa*										O	G			O								G								
African lion / *Panthera leo*			G	O	O	G	O		O		G	O	O			G	E			O					O	O	G	G	O	E
Asiatic lion *E / *Panthera leo persica*	G																G	G												
Barbary lion (Atlas lion) / *Panthera leo leo*																							E							
Jaguar *V / *Panthera onca*						G	O	O			O						G													
Leopard *V / *Panthera pardus*				O	G					O	O	O	G				O												O	
Persian leopard *V / *Panthera pardus saxicolor*				O	O			O			O						O	O											O	
Amur leopard *V / *Panthera pardus orientalis*									O				G																	
Tiger *E / *Pathera tigris*		G	G	O								E		G	E			O			E				G	G				E
Bengal tiger *E / *Panthera tigris tigris*							O		O																					
Siberian tiger *E / *Panthera tigris altaica*				G	O				O			E			G					E	E									
Sumatran tiger *E / *Panthera tigris sumatrae*			O													O														
Snow leopard *E / *Panthera unica*	E				G	O		O	G		G	G			O		E													
Cheetah *V / *Acinonyx jubatus*		G		G	O				O	G		O		G	O		G	O		E	O									
Seals and Sealions																														
S. American fur seal / *Arctocephalus australis*	O			O																										
Cape fur seal / *Arctocephalus pusillus*														O																
Patagonian Sea lion / *Otaria flavescens (bryonia)*				O				O														O	G							
California sealion / *Zalophus californianus*		G	O	G		G			O			G					O									O	O		O	
Grey seal / *Halichoerus grypus*				O	O																						O			
Baikal seal / *Phoca sibirica*																							G							
Common seal / *Phoca vitulina vitulina*																		O												
Elephants																														
Indian elephant *E / *Elephas maximas*		G		O	O	E		O									O			O			O	E	O	O				
African elephant *V / *Loxodonta africana*					O			O			O		E	G	G			O				O			O			O		
Hyraxes																														
Bush hyrax / *Heterohyrax brucei*																														

171

	Banham	Belfast	Blair Drummond	Blackpool	Bristol	Chester	Colchester	Cricket	Chessington	Cotswold	Drusillas	Dudley	Edinburgh	Glasgow	Highland	Howletts	Jersey	Knowsley	Longleat	London	Marwell	Norfolk	Paignton	Penscynor	Port Lympne	Twycross	Whipsnade	Windsor	Welsh Midland	Woburn
Rock hyrax *Procavia capensis*						O														O										
Horses, Rhinos and Tapirs																														
Common zebra *Equus burchelli*		G			O				O				O					O											O	G
Damara zebra *Equus burchelli antiquorum*			O	O																										
Common zebra *Equus burchelli boehmi*		O			O		O				O												O							
Chapman's zebra *Equus burchelli chapmani*						O	O	O											O	G						O	O			
Grevy's zebra *E *Equus grevyi*	O													G											G					
Hartman's mountain zebra *V *Equus zebra hartmani*																			O	E										
Kulan *V *Equus hemionus kulan*														G																O
Onager *V *Equus hemionus onager*				G																					G					
Przewalski's horse *E *Equus przewalskii*				G								O	O								E	O			E	E		O	G	G
Malayan tapir *E *Tapirus indicus*																					G				E	G				
Brazilian tapir *Tapirus terrestris*				O	O	O		O	O		O	O			O						O	O			G	O				
White rhinoceros *Ceratotherium simum*		O			O		G			G		O				G	G		G		G				E	O	O			G
Black rhinoceros *E *Diceros bicornis*				G																G					E					
Sumatran (Woolly) rhino *E *Dicerorhinus sumatrensis*																									E					
Indian rhinoceros *E *Rhinoceros unicornis*				G																						G				
ARTIODACTYLS **Pig family**																														
Babirusa *Babyrousa babyrousa*														G										G						
Wart hog *Phacochoerus aethiopicus*																								O						
Wild boar *Sus scrofa*										O	O									O										
Collared peccary *Tayassu tajacu*				O	O			O		O	O	O							O	O					O					
Pygmy hippopotamus *V *Chereopsis liberiensis*					O							O								O				O						
Hippopotamus *Hippopotamus amphibius*									O									O						G						G
Camel family																														
Bactrian camel *Camelus bactrianus*			G	O	O	O	O	O		O		O					G	O	O						O	G	G	O		G
Dromedary camel *Camelus dromedarius*	O	O	G	O		O			O													O				O	G			
Llama *Lama glama*	O		O		O		O	O	O	O		O							O	O			O				O	O	O	O
Guanaco *Lama glama guanicoe*				O		O		O	O			O							O						O				O	
Alpaca *Lama glama pacos*				O																				O						

172

Species	Banham	Belfast	Blair Drummond	Blackpool	Bristol	Chester	Colchester	Cricket	Chessington	Cotswold	Drusillas	Dudley	Edinburgh	Glasgow	Highland	Howletts	Jersey	Knowsley	Longleat	London	Marwell	Norfolk	Paignton	Penscynor	Port Lympne	Twycross	Whipsnade	Windsor	Welsh Midland	Woburn
Vicugna *V / *Lama vicugna*	O																		G	G										
Deer family																														
Reeves muntjac / *Muntiacus reevesi*			G	O					O												O	O			G					E
Axis deer / *Cervus axis*		O		O	O	G							G	E						G			E	E					G	E
Fallow deer / *Cervus dama*						G									G						O						E	G	G	E
Barasingha *E / *Cervus duvaceli*																					G		E	E						E
Red deer / *Cervus elephas*													E								G		E						G	E
Wapiti / *Cervus elephas canadensis*				O	O																			G					O	
Persian fallow deer / *Cervus mesopotamicus*																														
Sika deer / *Cervus nippon*		G				G																							G	E
Formosan sika deer *E / *Cervus nippon taiouanus*	G																							G	O		E	G	E	
Hog deer / *Cervus porcinus*			O		O								E								E				G	E				
Calamian deer / *Cervus porcinus calamianensis*													E																	
Sambar deer / *Cervus unicolor*													E												E					
Père David's deer / *Elaphurus davidiensis*		G		G									G	G			G	G							E					E
Roe Deer / *Capreolus capreolus*											O																			
Chinese water deer / *Hydropotes inermis*				O	O																O							E	O	
Pudu / *Pudu pudu*	O			O								O								O	G									
Reindeer / *Ragifer tarandis*				G						O			O							O	O	O			G					
Giraffe family																														
Giraffe / *Giraffa cameleopardis*		G	O	O	O	G		O	G	G				G	G				E	G	G		O			G	G	G	G	G
Opaki / *Okapia johnstoni*				G																G	O									
Bovid family																														
North American bison / *Bison bison*				O	G																O		G						G	G
European bison *V / *Bison bonasus*													G	E							G						E		G	G
Gaur *V / *Bos gaurus*																											O			
Yak / *Bos mutus grunniens*																												G	O	
Zebu / *Bos primigenius indicus*		G																						G						
Nilqai / *Boselaphus tragocamelus*				G										G													E			
Indian water buffalo / *Bubalus arnee*					O																									
Water buffalo / *Bubalus bubalis*														G											E					

Species	Banham	Belfast	Blair Drummond	Blackpool	Bristol	Chester	Colchester	Cricket	Chessington	Cotswold	Drusillas	Dudley	Edinburgh	Glasgow	Highland	Howletts	Jersey	Knowsley	Longleat	London	Marwell	Norfolk	Paignton	Penscynor	Port Lympne	Twycross	Whipsnade	Windsor	West Midland	Woburn
Anoa *E / *Bubalus depressicornis*																			O											
African buffalo / *Suncerus caffer*															G	G							G		G					G
Congo buffalo / *Syncerus caffer nanus*				G																G										
Eland / *Taurotragus oryx*				G											G	E					O		G						O	G
Nyala / *Tradelaphus angasi*																				G					G					
Bongo / *Tradelaphus euryceros*												E								G										E
Sitatunga / *Tragelaphus spekei*	O																			E					E					
Greater kudu / *Tragelaphus strepsicernos*																				G	E				O					
Maxwell's duiker / *Cephalophus maxwell*																														
Addax *E / *Addax nasomaculatus*						G				G										E										
Chousingha / *Tetracernus quadricornis*															E															
Brindled gnu / *Connachaetes taurinus*														O															O	G
Eastern white-bearded gnu / *Connochaetes taurinus albojubatus*				G											G															
Bontebok *V / *Damaliscus dorcas dorcas*																											O			
Blesbok / *Damaliscus dorcas phillipsi*																														
Roan antelope / *Hippotragus equinus*				G																G			G							
Sable antelope / *Hippotragus niger*																				O	O									
Waterbuck / *Kobus ellipsiprymus*																				E					E					
Red lechwe *V / *Kobus lechwe*	G	O			E				E						G															
Kafue flats lechwe *V / *Kobus lechwe kafuensis*				G																				G						
Nile lechwe *V / *Kobus megaceros*																											O			
Scimitar-horned oryx *E / *Oryx damah*				G			G			E										E					E					
Gemsbok / *Oryx gazella*	O																		O	O									O	
Arabian oryx *E / *Oryx leucoryx*																				E	G				G					
Springbok / *Antidorcas marsupialis*	O									O																				
Blackbuck / *Antilope cervivapra*	O			G	G		G			G			E											O					G	
Dama gazelle *E / *Gazella dama ruficollis*																				E										
Arabian gazelle *V / *Gazella gazella arabica*			G	G	G				G												G									
Thomson's gazelle / *Gazella thomsoni*																													E	

174

	Banham	Belfast	Blair Drummond	Blackpool	Bristol	Chester	Colchester	Cricket	Chessington	Cotswold	Drusillas	Dudley	Edinburgh	Glasgow	Highland	Howletts	Jersey	Knowsley	Longleat	London	Marwell	Norfolk	Paignton	Pensthorpe	Port Lympne	Twycross	Whipsnade	Windsor	West Midland	Woburn
Barbary sheep *V *Ammotragus lervia*			O								G	O								O	O							G	G	
Markhor *V *Capra falconeri*			G																											
Ibex *Capra ibex*													O																	
Musk ox *Ovibos moschatus*																											G			
Bighorn sheep *Ovis canadensis*																			G											
Moulflon *V *Ovis musimon*														G							G							G	O	
Chamois *Rupicapra rupicapra*			G																											

175

Part 6
Where To See
Animals in Britain

AVON

Bristol Zoo
Clifton, Bristol, Avon BS8 3HA
Telephone: 0272 738951

How to find it: From the city centre follow signs to Clifton. 2 miles west of Bristol on the B4468

Open: all year from 10.00 a.m.
See p. 66.

BEDFORDSHIRE

Stagsden Bird Gardens
Stagsden, Bedfordshire MK43 8SL
Telephone: 02302 2745

How to find it: Signposted from Stagsden, 15 miles west of Bedford on the A422

Open: 11 a.m.-6 p.m., or dusk.
A fine collection of cranes and pheasants. Also sacred ibis, parrots, waterfowl, and birds of prey.

Whipsnade Wild Animal Park
Whipsnade, Bedfordshire LU6 2LF
Telephone: 0582 872171

How to find it: Leave the M1 at Exit 9 or 12. Signposted on B4540

Open: all year from 10.00 a.m.
See p. 147.

Woburn Deer Park
Woburn Park, Woburn, Bedfordshire MK17 9QN
Telephone: 0525 290666

How to find it: Leave the M1 at Exit 13. Well signposted.

Open: all year from 10.00 a.m.
See p. 155.

Woburn Wild Animal Kingdom
Woburn, Nr Milton Keynes, Bedfordshire MK17 9QN
Telephone: 0525 290407

How to find it: Leave the M1 at Exit 13. Well signposted.

Open: all year from 10.00 a.m.
See p. 155.

BERKSHIRE

Childe Beale Wildlife Park
Church Farm, Lower Basildon, Reading, Berkshire
Telephone: 0491 671325

How to find it: On the Thames between Oxford and Pangbourne on the A329

Open: March-Sept, 10a.m.-6p.m.
Rare breeds of domestic animals, Highland cattle and sheep, peacocks, wild-fowl, cranes, and flamingos share this attractive parkland setting. There are riverside walks, and lakes. The collection also includes tropical fish, tropical birds, and insects. This is the home of the World Pheasant Association collection of pheasants.

Windsor Safari Park
Winkfield Road, Windsor, Berkshire SL4 4AY
Telephone: 0753 569841

How to find it: Leave the M4 at Exit 6, the M3 at Exit 3, the M25 at Exit 13

Open: all year from 10 a.m.
See p. 151.

BUCKINGHAMSHIRE

Waddesdon Manor
Waddesdon, Aylesbury, Buckinghamshire HP18 OJH
Telephone: 0296 651211

How to find it: 6 miles north-west of Aylesbury on the A41

Open: varies. Telephone for details.
A nineteenth century French style chateau, featuring aviaries for tropical birds, and a deer park with Japanese sika deer.

CAMBRIDGESHIRE

Linton Zoo
Mortimer House, Hadstock Road, Linton Nr Cambridge, Cambridgeshire
Telephone: 0223 891308

How to find it: 10 miles south-east of Cambridge on the B1052

Open: 10 a.m.-6 p.m. or dusk.
A mixed collection of zoo animals in 10 acres of grounds. The collection includes lions, tigers, wallabies and bears. There are parrots, and birds of prey, and reptiles, and a good invertebrate section which includes palm spiders and millipedes. A good educational zoo.

The Wildfowl and Wetlands Trust, Peakirk
Peterborough, Cambridgeshire
Telephone: 0733 252271

How to find it: 5 miles north of Peterborough on the A15

Open: 9.30 a.m.-5.30 p.m. or dusk.
A superb collection of waterfowl in impressive wetland surroundings. The collection includes over 600 ducks and swans on the site of a Roman waterway. There are Trumpeter swans, Coscoroba swans, and black-necked swans, as well as flamingos and Andean geese. The reserve covers only 16 acres, but it is home to a host of birds.

The Wildfowl and Wetlands Trust, Welney
Pintail House, Hundred Foot Bank, Welney, Wisbech, Cambridgeshire PE14 9TN
Telephone: 0353 860711

How to find it: North of Ely on the A1101

Open: 10 a.m.-5.00 p.m. or dusk.
An 850-acre reserve, home and refuge to a huge number of captive and migrating birds. It is the winter home for up to 5,000 migrating swans, including Bewick's and Whooper swans; thousands of wild geese also visit the Ouse Washes, and it is a spectacular place to see nesting ducks in the spring, from numerous hides, and a splendid observatory. Also here are redshank, snipe, ruff, pintail ducks, and a host of other waterfowl.

CHESHIRE

Brigdemere Wildlife Park
Bridgemere, Nr Nantwich, Cheshire
Telephone: 09365 223

How to find it: Signposted west of Nantwich on the A51

Open: daily 10 a.m.-6 p.m.
A small mixed collection of zoo animals in 50 acres of attractive pastureland. The collection includes deer, raccoons, foxes, badgers, and rare breeds of domestic animals.

Chester Zoo
Upton by Chester, Chester, Cheshire
Telephone: 0244 380280

How to find it: Signposted 2 miles north of Chester city centre off the A41 ring road.

Open: all year from 10.00 a.m.
See p. 73.

Tatton Deer Park
Knutsford, Cheshire WA16 6QN
Telephone: 0565 54822

How to find it: Between M6 Exit 19 and M56 Exit 7, signposted off A50/A556

Open: all year, times vary.
The 1,000-acre country park at Tatton holds splendid herds of fallow deer.

CORNWALL

Cornish Seal Sanctuary Marine Rescue Centre
Gweek, Nr Helston, Cornwall
Telephone: 0326 22361

How to find it: On the B3291 between Falmouth and Lizard

Open: 9 a.m. summer, 10 a.m. winter
10 pools for sick and injured seals, an aquarium, exhibition centre, and nature trail.

The Monkey Sanctuary
Murrayton, Looe, Cornwall
Telephone: 05036 2532

How to find it: 3 miles east of Looe on the narrow lanes between Looe and Seaton

Open: Easter Friday and Sunday, from 10.30 a.m. During May-September, Sun, Tues & Thurs only. During July and August, Sun, Mon, Tues, & Thurs only.
This collection specialises in keeping and breeding the endangered Humboldt's woolly monkey from South America. Set on the hillside in a beautiful woodland setting, the monkeys are regularly introduced to visitors, and talks are given mornings and afternoons. The monkeys are in tall, well-roped enclosures, and the breeding successes here have been remarkable. Some monkeys have been returned to South America to assist in a reintroduction project.

Newquay Zoo
Trevance Leisure Park, Newquay, Cornwall
Telephone: 0637 873342

How to find it: Just inland from Newquay centre, signposted to Trevance.

Open: Easter to October
A small seaside zoo catering to holiday visitors. The zoo keeps traditional zoo animals – lions, monkeys, parrots, and reptiles. Endangered Diana monkeys have been bred here.

Padstow Tropical Bird Gardens

Fentoluna Lane, Padstow, Cornwall PL28 8BB
Telephone: 0841 532262

How to find it: Close to Padstow centre off the B3276

Open: all year from 10.30 a.m.
A fine collection of birds housed in a walk through tropical house, and among attractive gardens. The collection includes beautiful taccazze sunbirds. There are choughs which are the emblem of Cornwall. A butterfly house provides the opportunity to walk among free flying butterflies and moths.

Paradise Park
Hayle, Nr St Ives, Cornwall
Telephone: 0736 753365

How to find it: Close to the centre of Hayle, signposted off the B3302

Open: all year from 10.00-Dusk
A collection of birds, otters, and rare breeds, with a reputation for breeding rare and endangered species. The collection includes the endangered St Vincent parrot, the Mexican thick-billed parrot, macaws, cranes, and toucans. The park is also home to the Cornish Otter Sanctuary, and features several enclosures of otters. There is also a rare breeds farm and a children's farm.

CUMBRIA

Appleby Castle Conservation Centre
Appleby in Westmoreland, Cumbria CA16 6XH
Telephone: 07683 51402

How to find it: In the centre of Appleby, 12 miles south of Penrith.

Open:
A Rare Breeds Survival Trust collection in the beautiful grounds of Appleby Castle. The collection includes waterfowl, pheasant, rare sheep, and Bagot goats.

DERBYSHIRE

Riber Castle Wildlife Park
Riber Castle, Matlock, Derbyshire DE4 5JU
Telephone: 0629 582073

How to find it: 1 mile from Tansley along Alsers Lane. Signposted in Riber.

Open: all year from 10.00 a.m.
The world's most comprehensive collection of lynx housed in the 20-acre grounds of a 19th century castle. The collection also includes deer, otters, and a variety of rare breeds, as well as a butterfly house. The park has superb views

across the valley from the 835-foot high Riber Hill. Lynx bred here have been released back into the wild in the Vosges Mountains in France.

DEVON

Aqualand
Beacon Quay, Torquay, Devon
Telephone: 0803 24439

How to find it: On the Torquay seafront.

Open: all year from 10.00 a.m.
An aquarium featuring a display of local and tropical marine life, freshwater fish, otters, and turtles.

Bicton Park Bird Gardens
East Budleigh, Bicton, Devon
Telephone: 0395 68074

How to find it: North of Budleigh Salterton on the A376

Open: Easter-October from 10 a.m.
A variety of birds on display in the gardens of Bicton Park.

Buckfast Butterfly Farm
Buckfastleigh Steam and Leisure Park, Buckfastleigh, Devon TQ11 ODZ
Telephone: 0364 42916

How to find it: Off the A38 Exeter-Plymouth road.

Open: Easter-Oct 31st from 10 a.m.
A small but flourishing collection of butterflies and moths.

Dartmoor Wildlife Park & Westcountry Falconry Centre
Sparkwell, Plympton, Devon
Telephone: 075537 209

How to find it: 5 miles north-east of Plymouth, follow A38 to Lee Mill, & lanes north.

Open: all year from 10.00 a.m.
A zoo that specialises in European wildlife, this collection covers 25 acres on the edge of Dartmoor National Park, and includes bears, wolves, seals, and herds of deer. There are also wild cats, foxes, badgers, and a great many birds including eagles and owls. Recent additions have departed from the European theme, and a new enclosure features jaguars from South America. There are falconry displays, and animal contact sessions.

Exmoor Bird Gardens
South Stowford, Bratton Fleming, Barnstaple, Devon EX31 4SG
Telephone: 05983 352

How to find it: Off the B3226 between Blackmoor Gate and Bratton Fleming

Open: all year from 10.00 a.m.

12 acres of landscaped gardens, home to a variety of birds and mammals. There are Humboldt's penguins, swans, waterfowl, toucans, parakeets, and cheer pheasants. There are also guanacos, wallabies, and farm animals.

Paignton Aquarium
South Quay, Paignton Harbour, Paignton, Devon
Telephone: 0803 522913

How to find it: On Paignton harbour.

Open: Easter-30th Sept from 10 a.m.
A small collection of local marine life.

Paignton Zoo
Totnes Road, Paignton, Devon
Telephone: 0803 557479

How to find it: On the A385 Totnes-Paignton road, 0.5 miles from Paignton.

Open: all year from 10.00 a.m.
See p. 128.

Shaldon Wildlife Trust
Ness Drive, Shaldon, Devon TQ14 OHP
Telephone: 0626 872234

How to find it: Signposted from the A379 Torquay-Teignmouth road.

Open: April-Sept 10 a.m., winter 11 a.m.
Once Shaldon Children's Zoo, this small collection includes small mammals and donkeys, as well as some birds and reptiles.

Tamar Otter Park
North Petherwin, Bude, Devon.
Telephone: 0566 85646

How to find it: Signposted off the B3254 Launceston to Bude Road, 5 miles north of Launceston.

Open: April to October from 10.00 am.
An Otter Trust collection of both Asian otters, and British otters bred for release into the wild – the park also features a walk-through deer park with muntjac and fallow deer, two large wildfowl lakes, and a breeding centre for British owls. The otters are fed daily at noon and at 3.30 pm.

DORSET

Abbotsbury Swannery
New Barn Road, Abbotsbury, Dorset
Telephone: 0305 871242

How to find it: Near the Sea Front, 1 mile from Abbotsbury centre.

Open: mid May-mid Sept from 9.30 a.m.

This is the only place in Britain where you can see a flock of mute swans, and the only place where visitors can see breeding swans close at hand. The swans have nested here for over 600 years. The Swannery also includes an 8 mile stretch of valuable wetlands, and is home to many migrating birds.

Lodmoor Country Park
Weymouth, Dorset
Telephone: 0305 775315

How to find it: A short walk from Weymouth seafront.

Open: Easter-September from 10 a.m.

This park includes The Great Shire Horse Centre, a butterfly farm, and the splendid Sea Life Centre which includes the biggest shark exhibit in the country, as well as many other marine creatures.

Lyme Regis Marine Aquarium
The Cobb, Lyme Regis, Dorset
Telephone: 02974 3678

How to find it: On the harbour wall.

Open: May-Oct from 10 a.m.
A collection of local marine life.

Monkey World
Longthorn, East Stoke, Wareham, Dorset BH20 6HH
Telephone: 0929 462537
How to find it: 10 miles west of Poole and 10 miles east of Dorchester, well signposted off the A31, on the Wool and Bere Regis road.

Open: all year 10.00 a.m.-5.00 p.m.
Described as 'giving homes to primate refugees from the conservation war', Monkey World is home to over 150 monkeys and apes in a wooded, 40-acre, hillside setting. The collection specialises in rescuing chimpanzees from the beach photographers of Spain, and rehabilitating them into one of the spacious outdoor enclosures. The new 4-acre chimp compound is the largest in Britain. Laboratory monkeys that have been rescued here include pigtail macaques, crab-eating macaques, and vervet monkeys. The collection also houses hybrid lemurs, ring- tailed lemurs, and Bornean orang utans. The collection works closely with Zoo Check, the organisation which aims to monitor conditions in British Zoos.

Poole Park Zoo
Poole, Dorset
Telephone: 0202 745296

How to find it: South of the A350 on the north side of Parkstone Bay

Open: all year from 10.00 a.m.
A 1-acre zoo with a varied collection of animals, large and small. They include monkeys, small cats, and a variety of parrots and other birds.

Worldwide Butterflies
Compton House, Sherbourne, Dorset DT9 4QN
Telephone: 0935 74608

How to find it: 2 miles west of Yeovil on the A30.

Open: April-Oct from 10 a.m.
A large collection of butterflies and moths in a jungle setting, and free flying in a tropical palmhouse. The centre specialises in breeding buttefrlies from all around the world, and also houses a silk farm.

EAST SUSSEX

Bentley Wildfowl and Motor Museum
Halland, Nr Lewes, East Sussex BN8 5AF
Telephone: 082584 573

How to find it: 7 miles north-east of Lewes, signposted from the A22 and A26.

Open: 18 March-31 Oct, 10.30 a.m.
A large collection of wildfowl that includes Hawaiian geese, mandarin ducks, flamingos, and cranes. White winged wood duck bred here and were reintroduced to the wild in Thailand.

Brighton Aquarium
Marine Parade, Brighton, East Sussex
Telephone: 0273 604233

How to find it: On the seafront.

Open: all year from 10.00 a.m.
A Victorian building that houses hundreds of species of fish and marine creatures, including seals.

The Butterfly Centre
Royal Parade, Eastbourne, East Sussex BN22 7AQ
Telephone: 0323 645522

How to find it: On the eastern end of the promenade.

Open: Palm Sunday-Oct from 10 a.m.
A walk through tropical house with free flying butterflies and moths.

Drusillas Park Zoo
Alfriston, East Sussex
Telephone: 0323 870243

How to find it: At the junction of the A27 and the B2108 to Alfriston

Open: all year from 10.30 a.m.
See p. 86.

Living World
Seven Sisters Country Park, Exceat, Seaford, East Sussex BN25 4AD
Telephone: 0323 870100

How to find it: 2 miles east of Seaford on the A259.

Open: Easter-Oct.
An invertebrate collection with butterflies, bees, scorpions and snails, as well as some fish.

ESSEX

Basildon Zoo
London Road, Vange, Basildon, Essex
Telephone: 0268 553985

How to find it: On the A13 London Road, signposted.

Open: 10 a.m. summer, 11 a.m. winter
A very small mixed zoo with about two hundred or more animals of around fifty species, in a garden setting. There are big cats, and plenty of birds.

Colchester Zoo
Maldon Road, Colchester, Essex CO3 5SL
Telephone: 0206 330253

How to find it: On the B1022 Tiptree-Colchester road, 3 miles south of Colchester

Open: all year from 10 a.m.
See p. 79.

Mole Hall Wildlife Park
Widdington, Newport, Saffron Walden, Essex CB11 3SS
Telephone: 0799 40400

How to find it: South of Newport on the B1383

Open: all year from 10.30 a.m.
A 25-acre park in the medieval moated grounds of Mole Hall. The collection includes many traditional zoo animals, among them deer, serval, jungle cats, monkeys, wallabies, and dingos. There are Canadian otters which have bred here.

GLOUCESTERSHIRE

Berkeley Castle
Berkeley, Gloucestershire

Telephone: 0453 810332

How to find it: 1.5 miles west of the A38 on the B4509

Open: telephone for details
A 12th century castle featuring a butterfly house with many tropical species.

Birdland Zoo Gardens
Rissington Road, Bourton on the Water, Nr Cheltenham, Gloucestershire GL54 2BN
Telephone: 0451 20689

How to find it: A short walk from Bourton centre.

Open: all year from 10.30 a.m.
A 4-acre garden, densely populated with dozens of species of birds. There are penguins, cranes, pelicans, hornbills, many parrots and a walk through tropical aviary.

The Falconry Centre
Newent, Gloucestershire GL18 1JJ
Telephone: 0531 820286

How to find it: 1 mile south-west of Newent off B4221.

Open: varies. Telephone for details.
The largest known collection of birds of prey in the world – there are over 200 birds, and over 50 species represented. Special attention is paid to breeding and rearing birds of prey, and there are also spectacular displays of falconry.

Newent Butterfly and Natural World Centre
Springbank, Birches Lane, Newent, Gloucestershire
Telephone: 0531 821800

How to find it: Signposted from Newent centre.

Open: Easter-Oct from 10 a.m.
A small children's zoo, and butterfly house, also featuring some reptiles and insects.

Prinknash Bird Park
Prinknash Abbey, Painswick, Gloucestershire
Telephone: 0452 812272

How to find it: Between Cheltenham and Stroud off the A46 2 miles north of Painswick

Open: Easter-Oct from 10 a.m.
A 9-acre park opened in 1974 alongside Prinknash Abbey, and home to several hundred birds. The collection features wildfowl including several species of geese and swans, pheasants, and crowned cranes. There are also fallow deer and pigmy goats, and trout ponds where visitors can feed the trout.

The Wildfowl and Wetlands Trust, Slimbridge

Slimbridge, Gloucestershire GL2 7BT
Telephone: 04538 9333

How to find it: Exit 13 or 14 off the M5, A38 to Slimbridge.

Open: all year from 9.30 a.m.

Opened by Sir Peter Scott in 1946, and covering more than 800 acres of wetlands, this has been one of the most important collections of wildfowl in the world. More than 180 species of ducks, geese and swans, captive and wild, inhabit these low-lying fields. Regular visitors include thousands of Bewick swans.

Every species of flamingo is kept here, and four of the six breed regularly. The trust specialises in keeping and breeding endangered species, and among the world's rarest birds kept here are Hawaiian geese, Cuban whistling duck, pink eared duck, and musk duck. There is also a tropical house with hummingbirds, and sunbirds. This is the headquarters of the Wildfowl and Wetlands Trust.

GREATER MANCHESTER

Cannon Aquarium and Vivarium

The Manchester Museum, Manchester University, Oxford Road, Manchester, Greater Manchester M19 9PL
Telephone: 061 275 2000

How to find it: Follow University signs from City Centre. The museum is opposite the University Medical School.

Open: weekdays from 10 a.m.

A small collection of fish and reptiles.

Dunham Massey Hall

Altrincham, Greater Manchester
Telephone: 061 941 1025

How to find it: Signposted from M56 Exit 7, north of the motorway.

Open: varies. Telephone for details.

An 18th century house and deer park featuring a splendid herd of fallow deer.

HAMPSHIRE

The Hawk Conservancy

Weyhill, Andover, Hampshire SP11 8DY
Telephone: 0264 772252

How to find it: Signposted 4 miles west of Andover on A303 to Thruxton.

Open: March-Oct: times vary

Originally Weyhill European Wildlife Park, this collection now specialises in birds of prey, and keeps and breeds a wide variety of hawks, eagles, falcons, and owls. There are regular falconry displays when weather permits, and there are also other birds to see in the 15 acres of the park.

Marwell Zoological Park

Colden Common, Nr Winchester, Hampshire SO21 1JH
Telephone: 0962 74406

How to find it: Signposted from A33 Winchester-Southampton road.

Open: all year from 10.00 a.m.
See p. 123.

The New Forest Butterfly Farm

Longdown, Ashurst, Nr Southampton, Hampshire SO4 4UH
Telephone: 042129 2166

How to find it: Signposted off A35 Southampton to Lyndhurst road.

Open: 24th March-29th Oct from 10.00 a.m.
The first butterfly farm in Britain, this collection is housed in a large, heated, glasshouse. It features both British and tropical butterflies. There are also dragonfly ponds, and other insects and spiders. Many exotic butterflies are successfully bred here.

Paultons Park

Ower, Romsey, Hampshire SO51 6AL
Telephone: 0703 814442

How to find it: Off the A31, close to M27 Exit 2, north-west of Southampton.

Open: March-Oct from 10 a.m.
An 8-acre park with a variety of birds, domestic animals, and exotic mammals including llamas and capybaras.

HERTFORDSHIRE

Knebworth Deer Park

Knebworth, Stevenage, Hertfordshire
Telephone: 0438 812661

How to find it: Off the A1 at Stevenage

Open: varies. Telephone for details
The 250-acre country park at Knebworth holds splendid herds of fallow deer.

HUMBERSIDE

Sewerby Hall Park and Zoo

Bridlington, Humberside YO15 3JH
Telephone: 0262 673369

How to find it: In Sewerby village.

Open: all year from 9.00 a.m.
An 18th century house with a miniature zoo featuring penguins, flamingos, waterfowl, some monkeys, llamas, and farm animals. There are deer in the park.

The Tropical Butterfly Gardens
The Boating Lake, Cleethorpes, Humberside DN35 OAG
Telephone: 0472 602118

How to find it: On Cleethorpes sea front.

Open: all year from 10.00 a.m.
A large and varied collection of butterflies and moths in a huge walk-through tropical house.

ISLE OF MAN

Curraghs Wildlife Park
Ballaugh, Ramsey, Isle of Man
Telephone: 0624 897323

How to find it: Signposted north of Ballaugh on the A3

Open: Easter-Sept from 10.00 a.m.
A 26-acre wildlife park alongside the Ballaugh Curraghs Wetland Nature Reserve, that specialises in wetland species. There are over 100 species here, and they include otters, Pere David's deer, penguins, and capybaras. There is also a monkey island, and a South American lake, and a variety of parrots and other birds.

ISLE OF WIGHT

Flamingo Park
Springvale, Seaview, Ryde, Isle of Wight
Telephone: 0983 612153

How to find it: 3 miles east of Ryde at Nettlestone Point on B3330/B3340

Open: times vary.
A country park overlooking the Solent. The bird collection includes flamingos, parrots, and wildfowl, many of which can be fed from the hand.

Isle of Wight Zoo
Sandown, Isle of Wight
Telephone:

How to find it: On the seafront east of Sandown.

Open: summer from 10.00 a.m.

A small seaside zoo with several mammal species, including large cats, but specialising in reptiles with a good reptile house.

Robin Hill Adventure and Zoological Park
Robin Hill, Newport, Isle of Wight
Telephone: 0983 527352

How to find it: 3 miles south-east of Newport, signposted off the A3056 to Sandown

Open: March-Oct from 10 a.m.
An 80-acre leisure park that combines around 100 or more species of mammals, birds and reptiles with a country adventure park. There are herds of grazing animals, monkeys, and a reptile house holding snakes, and tortoises.

The Tropical Bird Park
Old Park, St Lawrence, Isle of Wight
Telephone: 0983 852583

How to find it: On the south coast, 1 mile west of Ventnor on the A3055

Open: Easter-Oct from 10 a.m.
A collection of more than 400 birds in walkthrough aviaries, and waterfowl on an ornamental lake.

KENT

Blean Bird Park
Honey Hill, Blean, Kent CT2 9JP
Telephone: 0227 471666

How to find it: 3 miles north-west of Blean on the A290

Open: March-Nov from 10.00 a.m.
A collection that specialises in parrots, Blean has the largest breeding group of macaws, cockatoos and parakeets in Britain. In this respect it is an important collection, and visitors can expect to see a host of parrot species. There are more than 600 birds in the park, including pheasants, mynahs, toucans, and owls, as well as all the parrots. There is also a beautiful woodland walk.

Brambles Wildlife Park
Wealdon Forest Park, Herne Common, Canterbury, Kent CT6 7LQ
Telephone: 0227 712379

How to find it: On the A28 between Herne Bay and Canterbury.

Open: Easter-October from 10 a.m.
A 20-acre woodland park with nature trails featuring fallow deer, sika deer, foxes, frogs, toads, and fish. There is also a frog and toad farm.

The Butterfly Centre
Macfarlanes Nurseries, Swingfields, Dover, Kent

Telephone: 0303 83244

How to find it: On A260 Canterbury-Folkestone road.

Open: April-Sept from 10 a.m.
A small tropical butterfly house.

Howletts Zoo Park
Bekesbourne, Nr Canterbury, Kent
Telephone: 0227 728298

How to find it: Signposted from A2 or A257 Canterbury-Wingham road.

Open: all year from 10 a.m.
See p. 100.

Leeds Castle
Maidstone, Kent ME17 1PL
Telephone: 0622 65400

How to find it: 4 miles east of Maidstone close to junction of M20 and A20.

Open: varies. Telephone for details.
Widely billed as 'The Loveliest Castle in the World', Leeds Castle is also home to a variety of exotic birds, including kookaburras, cockatoos, finches, and cranes.

Port Lympne Zoo Park
Lympne, Hythe, Kent CT21 4PD
Telephone: 0303 64646

How to find it: Leave A20 Ashford-Folkestone road, and follow signs to Lympne

Open: all year from 10.00 a.m.
See p. 133.

Wingham Bird Park
Wingham, Canterbury, Kent CT3 1JL
Telephone: 0227 720836

How to find it: On the A257 between Wingham and Sandwich.

Open: all year from 10 a.m.
A small collection of birds in good sized aviaries and beautiful surroundings adjoining a pick-your-own fruit farm.

LANCASHIRE

Blackpool Zoo
East Park Drive, Blackpool, Lancashire
Telephone: 0253 65027

How to find it: Leave M55 at Exit 4. Follow signs to Stanley Park and Zoo

Open: all year from 10.00 a.m.
See p. 62

Bolton Museum Aquarium.
Le Mans Crescent, Bolton, Lancashire BL1 1SE
Telephone: 0204 22311

How to find it: In the town centre.

Open: weekdays from 10.00 a.m.
A wide range of British, tropical, and freshwater fish.

Haigh Miniature Zoo
Haigh Country Park, Aspull, Wigan, Lancashire
Telephone: 0942 831262

How to find it: On the B5238 Wigan-Aspull road, 2 miles north-east of Wigan.

Open: Easter-October from 10 a.m.
A small zoo with a variety of traditional zoo animals including zebras, monkeys, and several birds.

Leighton Hall
Carnforth, Lancashire
Telephone: 0524 734474

How to find it: 3 miles north of Carnforth off A6.

Open: varies. Telephone for details
The gardens of Leighton Hall are home to an extensive collection of birds of prey. Falconry and flying displays are given regularly, weather permitting.

Marineland
The Promenade, Morecambe, Lancashire
Telephone: 0254 414727

How to find it: On the seafront at Morecambe.

Open: Easter-October from 10.30 a.m.
A municipal collection which includes performing dolphins and sealions. The collection also includes an aquarium with local marine life, tropical fish, and alligators.

Southport Zoo
Princess Park, Southport, Lancashire
Telephone: 0704 38102

How to find it: On the seafront, close to the fair, just south of the pier.

Open: all year from 10 a.m.
A 5-acre seaside zoo with nearly eight hundred animals of about 175 species. There is great variety here, and the collection includes large and small mam-

mals, a great many birds, a reptile house and an aquarium. Chimpanzees are a speciality and there is a newly built chimp enclosure.

The Wildfowl and Wetlands Trust, Martin Mere
Martin Mere, Burscough, Ormskirk, Lancashire L40 OTA
Telephone: 0704 895181

How to find it: Take M6 Exit 27, A5209 to Burscough, B5242 to Scarisbrick.

Open: all year from 9.30 a.m.
More than 1,500 ducks, geese, swans, and waterfowl inhabit the 300-acre refuge at Martin Mere. They are overlooked by hides for visitors, and are joined annually by thousands of migrating waterfowl and waders. These include several thousand pink-footed geese, and several hundred Bewick and hooper swans. There are 2 flocks of flamingos, and a splendid visitor centre. This is one of the most important habitats for waterfowl in the North of England, and is one of the 7 collections of the Wildfowl and Wetlands Trust.

LINCOLNSHIRE

The Animal Gardens
North End, Mablethorpe, Lincolnshire LN12 1QG
Telephone: 0521 73346

How to find it: 2 miles north of Mablethorpe centre.

Open: Easter-Oct from 10 a.m.
A 2-acre collection of about 200 animals. The gardens house a variety of birds, Arctic foxes, raccoons, and other mammals, and cares for orphaned or injured birds and seals.

Long Sutton Butterfly Park
Long Sutton, Spalding, Lincolnshire PE12 9LE
Telephone: 0406 363833

How to find it: On the A17 in Long Sutton, east of Spalding

Open: Easter-Oct from 10 a.m.
A butterfly house, insectarium including scorpions and spiders, and pets corner.

Skegness Natureland Marine Zoo
North Parade, Skegness, Lincolnshire
Telephone: 0754 4345

How to find it: On the Skegness sea front.

Open: all year from 10.00 a.m.
A small tropical house and aquarium, and outside a group of seals and penguins.

LONDON

London Zoo
Regent's Park, London
Telephone: 071 722 3333

How to find it: Tube to Camden Town or Regent's Park, then a 10 minute walk. Otherwise buses as marked, or taxi.

Open: all year from 10.00 a.m.
See p. 113

MERSEYSIDE

Knowsley Safari Park
Prescot, Merseyside
Telephone: 051 430 9009

How to find it: Leave the M57 at Exit 8, follow A68 to Prescot.

Open: all year from 10.00 a.m.
See p. 111.

MIDDLESEX

The London Butterfly House
Syon Park, Brentford, Middlesex TW8 8JN
Telephone: 081 560 7272

How to find it: Leave M3 at Exit 1, take A316 to Syon Park.

Open: all year from 10.00 a.m.
One of Britain's first butterfly houses, on the banks of the Thames.

NORFOLK

Banham Zoo
The Grove Banham, Nr Norwich, Norfolk NR16 2HB
Telephone: 095 387 476

How to find it: Signposted from the B1077 / B1113 and the A11

Open: all year from 10.30 a.m.
See p. 56

Kelling Aviaries
Weybourne Road, Holt, Kelling, Norfolk
Telephone: 0263 711185

How to find it: Just north of the A148 Holt-Cromer road, 1 mile north-east of Holt.

Open: all year from 10.00 a.m.
A 4-acre gardens with a large collection of birds, they include several parrots, parrakeets, and cockatoos, free flying tropical birds, and waterfowl. There are some mammals, and a children's pet's corner.

Kilverstone Country Park
Kilverstone Hall, Thetford, Norfolk IP24 2RL
Telephone: 0842 755369

How to find it: Signposted off the A11 Thetford-Norwich road, 2 miles north of Thetford.
Open: all year from 10.00 a.m.
Opened in 1992 on the site of what was formerly Kilverstone Wildlife Park, this country park makes much of the features of the old zoo, including some splendid squirrel monkey islands. The collection also includes Brazilian tapirs, llamas, wallabies, maned wolves, and agoutis. Sadly the splendid collection of rare and endangered Latin American primates that had been so painstakingly gathered together at Kilverstone have gone, but there is still a good group of marmosets and tamarins. The park is the only British collection to keep the red handed tamarin. Grazing animals include blackbuck and scimitar horned oryx, and there are impressive flocks of waterfowl. The setting is a 25 acre estate in the valley of the River Thet.

The Norfolk Wildlife Park
Great Witchingham, Norwich, Norfolk
Telephone: 0603 872274

How to find it: 12 miles north of Norwich on the A1067

Open: all year from 10.00 a.m.
See p. 126.

Thrigby Hall Wildlife Gardens
Filby, Great Yarmouth, Norfolk NR29 3DR
Telephone: 0493 77477

How to find it: On an un-numbered lane just south of Filby.

Open: all year from 10.00 a.m.
A collection that specialises in the animals of Asia, Thrigby includes a variety of mammals, birds, and reptiles. The collection boasts snow leopards, gibbons, porcupines, tigers, caracals, and binturongs.

NORTHAMPTONSHIRE

Coton Manor Gardens
Coton, Northamptonshire

Telephone: 0604 740219

How to find it: 6 miles north-west of Northampton on the A428 then 1 mile on lanes north-eastwards.

Open: Easter-Sept Times vary
A manor gardens including flamingos, wildfowl, and cranes.

Lilford Park
Lilford Hall, Nr Oundle, Peterborough, Northamptonshire PE8 5SG
Telephone: 08015 648

How to find it: On A605 between Oundle and Thrapston.

Open: Easter-October from 10 a.m.
The aviaries at Lilford park were built more than a century ago, and now they hold more than 100 species of birds. The park covers 240 acres, and there are flamingos, owls, a variety of pheasants, and birds of prey, as well as some mammal species.

NOTTINGHAMSHIRE

Wetlands Waterfowl Reserve and Exotic Bird Park
Loundlow Road, Sutton-cum-Lound, Nottinghamshire
Telephone: 0777 818099

How to find it: 3 miles north of East Retford. A638 to Sutton then lanes east.

Open: all year from 10 a.m.
A 32-acre wetlands reserve. The collection includes flamingos, wildfowl – geese, swans, and ducks, and several species of aviary birds, such as parrots. There is also a children's farm.

OXFORDSHIRE

The Cotswold Wildlife Park
Burford, Oxfordshire OX4 4JW
Telephone: 0993 823006

How to find it: Off A361 Lechlade-Burford road, 2 miles south of Burford.

Open: all year from 10.00 a.m.
See p. 82

SHROPSHIRE

Shropshire Country World
Yockleton, Shrewsbury, Shropshire SY5 9PU
Telephone: 074384 217

How to find it: 4 miles west of Shrewsbury on B4386

Open: Easter-Oct from 10 a.m.
A collection of domestic and farmyard animals that also includes a tropical butterfly house.

SOMERSET

Cricket St Thomas
Chard, Somerset TA20 4DD
Telephone: 0460 30755

How to find it: 2 miles east of Chard on the Crewkerne road.

Open: all year from 10.00 a.m.
See p. 84

The Tropical Bird Gardens
Rode, Bath, Somerset BA3 6QW
Telephone: 0373 830326

How to find it: On the A36 between Bath and Warminster.

Open: all year from 10.30 a.m.
A 17-acre collection of birds that includes nearly 200 species in beautiful surroundings. There is a pets corner, and an ornamental lake, and well planted gardens.

STAFFORDSHIRE

Drayton Manor Park and Zoo
Tamworth, Staffordshire B78 3TW
Telephone: 0827 287979

How to find it: On A4091, 2 miles south of Tamworth

Open: Easter-Oct from 10.30 a.m.
A mixed and traditional collection of zoo animals in the grounds of Drayton Manor Park, a family leisure park. The collection includes penguins, lions, tigers, sealions, and a reptile house.

SUFFOLK

Norton Tropical Bird Gardens
Norton, Bury St Edmunds, Suffolk IP31 3LE
Telephone: 0359 30957

How to find it: 9 miles east of Bury on the A1088

Open: all year from 11.00 a.m.
More than 100 species of birds including flamingos, parrots, cranes, and waterfowl.

The Otter Trust
Earsham, Bungay, Suffolk NR35 2AF
Telephone: 0986 3470

How to find it: 1 mile west of Bungay on A143

Open: April-Oct from 10.30 a.m.
A collection that specialises exclusively in keeping and breeding European otters.

Tropical Butterflies of Barrow.
Barrow, Bury St Edmunds, Suffolk IP29 5BG
Telephone: 0284 810859

How to find it: Between Newmarket and Bury off the A45

Open: Easter-Oct from 10.00 a.m.
Free-flying butterflies in a tropical hot house.

SURREY

Birdworld and Underwaterworld
Holt Pound, Farnham, Surrey GU10 4LD
Telephone: 0420 22140

How to find it: 3 miles south of Farnham on the A325

Open: all year from 9.30 a.m.
An 18-acre park which is home to a huge variety of birds. The collection includes ostriches, pelicans, hummingbirds, and tanagers. Underwaterworld is an aquarium with tropical freshwater and marine fish.

Chessington World of Adventures
Leatherhead Road, Chessington, Surrey KT9 2NE
Telephone: 03727 27227

How to find it: Signposted from M25 Exit 9. 5 miles north of Leatherhead on A243

Open: all year from 10.00 a.m.
See p. 70. See p. 70.

Gatwick Zoo and Aviaries
Charlwood, Crawley, Surrey RH6 OEG
Telephone: 0293 862312

How to find it: Signposted 3 miles west of Gatwick Airport.

Open: Easter-Oct from 10.30 a.m.
A small 10-acre zoo featuring many species of birds and small mammals. Notable is the monkey island with spider monkeys and squirrel monkeys.

SUSSEX

The Wildfowl and Wetlands Trust, Arundel
Arundel Castle Park, Mill Road, Arundel, Sussex BN18 9PB
Telephone: 0903 883355

How to find it: 1 mile NE of Arundel, signposted.

Open: all year from 9.30 a.m.
A 55-acre reserve, home to more than 1,000 ducks, geese, swans, and water-fowl. There are observation hides that overlook the reed beds and the wader scrapes. In the centre is Swan Lake. Many of the ducks and geese will feed from your hand. There is also a theatre and a viewing gallery. Many migrating birds join the captive birds every year, and you may see teal, water rail, snipe, and green sandpiper, among many others.

TYNE AND WEAR

The Wildfowl and Wetlands Trust, Washington
Washington Waterfowl Park, District 15, Barmston, Washington, Tyne and Wear NE38 8LB
Telephone: 091 416 5454

How to find it: Signposted just outside Barmston village.

Open: all year from 9.30 a.m.
This is one of Europe's largest collections of wildfowl, with over 1,200 water birds of more than 100 species represented. The park covers 100 acres, and 70 of these are set aside for wild birds which can be watched from hides. The collection includes a splendid flock of Chilean flamingos, and there is a viewing gallery which affords view over the whole collection. Like all the Wildfowl and Wetlands Trust's reserves, this reserve pays great attention to breeding and conserving rare and endangered wildfowl.

WARWICKSHIRE

Stratford upon Avon Butterfly Farm
Tramway Walk, Stratford upon Avon, Warwickshire CV37 7LS
Telephone: 0789 299288

How to find it: Over the Avon, walking distance from the centre.

Open: all year from 10.00 a.m.
Said to be 'the largest butterfly farm in the world', this collection includes hundreds of butterflies, a tropical house, and 'Insect City'.

Twycross Zoo
Twycross, Atherstone Warwickshire CV9 3PX
Telephone: 0827 880250

How to find it: 6 miles north of Atherstone on the A444

Open: all year from 10.00 a.m.
See p. 139.

WEST MIDLANDS

Birmingham Nature Centre
Pershore Road, Edgbaston, Birmingham, West Midlands B5 7RL
Telephone: 021 472 7775

How to find it: At the south-west entrance to Cannon Hill Park

Open: March-Oct from 10.00 a.m.
A small collection of British & European animals

Dudley Zoo
2 The Broadway, Dudley, West Midlands
Telephone: 0384 52401

How to find it: Just north of Dudley centre

Open: 9.00 a.m. Mon-Sat. 10.00 a.m. Sun
See p. 88.

WILTSHIRE

Longleat
Longleat Park, Warminster, Wiltshire
Telephone: 098 53328

How to find it: Between Warminster & Frome. Signposted off A362 or B3092

Open: all year from 10.00 a.m.
See p. 120.

WORCESTERSHIRE

Spetchley Deer Park
Spetchley Park, Spetchley, Worcestershire
Telephone: 0905 65 213

How to find it: Off M5 Exit 7, signposted off A422.

Open: Telephone for details.
Red deer and fallow deer in the park gardens.

West Midlands Safari and Leisure Park
Bewdley, Worcestershire
Telephone: 0299 402114

How to find it: Off A456 between Kidderminster and Bewdley.

Open: April-Oct from 10.00 a.m.

See p. 144.

YORKSHIRE

Flamingo Land
Kirby Misperton, Malton, Yorkshire YO 17 OUX
Telephone: 065386 287

How to find it: 2 miles west of the A169 between Malton and Pickering.

Open: April-Sept from 10.00 a.m.
A 375-acre family leisure park, which includes a host of rides, a monorail, and a mixed zoo integrated among the attractions. The collection includes elephants, lions and tigers, and sealions. There are several herds of grazing animals, and a popular baboon island which holds an active society of baboons on a high rock. The zoo occupies about 120 acres of the park, and there are over 1,000 animals.

Harewood Bird Gardens
Harewood Estate, Leeds, Yorkshire LS 17 9LF
Telephone: 0532 886225

How to find it: On the Leeds-Harrogate A61 road.

Open: Easter-October from 10 a.m.
The gardens of Harewood House were landscaped by Capability Brown, and 4.5 acres are now set aside as bird gardens. The collection is one of the most important bird collections in Britain, featuring more than seven hundred birds of over 150 species. There are penguins, a varied collection of pheasants, and a tropical house with hummingbirds, tanagers, and a host of parrots. There are also some reptiles, and some mammals on display.

SCOTLAND

Blair Drummond Safari and Leisure Park
Nr Stirling, Scotland FK9 4UR
Telephone: 0786 841456

How to find it: 7 miles north of Stirling on A84

Open: Summer from 10.00 a.m.

See p. 64.

Camperdown Wildlife Centre
Camperdown Country Park, Coupar Angus, Dundee.
Telephone: 0382 623555

How to find it: Signposted off the A923 north of Dundee.

Open: All year from 10.00 am.

A municipal wildlife park, owned and subsidised by Dundee County Council as an educational resource (the park is host to 40,000 school children a year), this is a seventeen acre, well laid out park with a surprising collection of wildlife. The emphasis is on indigenous and European species, and the collection includes bears, lynx, several species of deer, otters, martens and waterfowl, as well as rare breeds and farm animals. There are also Siberian chipmunk, flying squirrels, beaver, various mice and voles, Arctic fox and a pair of grey wolves.

Edinburgh Butterfly Farm

Melville Nurseries, Lasswade, Edinburgh, Scotland
Telephone: 031663 4932

How to find it: Follow A7 from Edinburgh centre, and A6094 to Lasswade.

Open: All year from 10.00 a.m.
The only butterfly farm in Scotland; in the grounds of Dobbics Garden Centre.

Edinburgh Zoo

Corstorphine Road, Murrayfield, Edinburgh, Scotland
Telephone: 031 334 9171

How to find it: On A8 Edinburgh-Airport road, 2 miles from city centre.

Open: All year from 9.00 a.m. Mon-Sat, and 9.30 a.m. Sun
See p. 90.

Glasgow Zoo

Calder Park, Uddingston, Glasgow, Scotland G717RZ
Telephone: 0417711185

How to find it: Signposted from A74 and M74, 8 miles east of city centre.

Open: All year from 10.00 a.m.

See p. 95.

Glengoulandie Deer Park

Aberfeldy, Tayside, Perthshire, ScotlandTelephone: 08873 509

How to find it: 8 miles north-west of Aberfeldy on B8460

Open: April-Oct from 9 a.m.
A deer park featuring red deer and other European species in a splendid Highland setting.

The Highland Wildlife Park

Kincraig, Kingussie, Aviemore, ScotlandTelephone: 054 04 270

How to find it: Well signposted off the A9 at Kingussie.

Open: Telephone for details.
See p. 98.

Sea Life Centre
Loch Creran, Barcaldine, Strathclyde, Scotland
Telephone: 063172 386

How to find it: On the A828 Oban-Fort William road, 1 mile west of Barcaldine

Open: Mid Feb-Nov from 9 a.m.
One of Europe's most modern marine aquaria with a huge collection of marine fish and invertebrates from around the shores of Britain. The collection includes a tidepool exhibit, and seals with underwater viewing.

The Wildfowl and Wetlands Trust, Caerlaverock
Caerlaverock, Eastpark Fn, Dumfriesshire, Scotland DG 14RS
Telephone: 038777 200

How to find it: Signposted from Dumfries on the North Solway.

Open: 16 Sept-30 Apr from 9.30 a.m.
More than 1,300 acres of the North Solway shore has been gazetted as a nature reserve by the Wildfowl and Wetlands Trust, and is open to visitors during the winter months. Thousands of barnacle geese visit these wetlands as their main wintering ground, and there are pink-footed geese, greylag geese, Bewick swans and whooper swans, as well as thousands of wading birds, and several raptors. Excellent observation hides and towers provide visitors wiih ideal opportunities to watch the birds.

WALES

Anglesey Sea Zoo
The Oyster Hatchery, Brynsiencyn, Anglesey, Wales LL61 6QT
Telephone: 0248 71411

How to find it: Signposted from Brynsiencyn.

Open: Feb-Nov from 10.00 a.m.
Reputedly Wales's largest aquarium, this varied collection specialises in marine life from around the North Wales coast, and exhibits invertebrates and fish in theme-tanks to illustrate their lifesiyle and habitats.

Butterfly Palace
Ffordd Penmynydd, Menai Bridge, Aiiglesey, Gwynedd, Wales LL59 5RP
Telephone: 0248 712474

How to find it: Well signposted from the Menai Bridge.

Open: During the season from 10 a.m.
A walk-through tropical butterfly house, with other insects including stick insects, and wood ants.

Cardigan Wildlife Park
Coedmore, Cardigan, Dyfed, Wales

Telephone: 0239 614449

How to find it: 1 mile south of Cardigan on the A478

Open: All year from 10.00 a.m.
A 200-acre park that opened in 1978 and specialises in the wildlife of Wales (and Northern Europe). The collection includes a diverse range of birds and mammals, and there are nature walks and fishing on the River Tefi.

Fairbourne Railway and Butterfly Safari
Beach Road, Fairbourne, Gwynedd, Wales LL38 2PZ
Telephone: 0341 250084

How to find it: 10 miles west of Dolgellau on the A493

Open: Easter-Sept. Times vary.
One attraction along a steam railway ride is the butterfly safari which includes a butterfly house, and small mammals such as ring- tailed lemurs, leopard cats and racoons.

Manor House Wildlife and Leisure Park
St Florence, Carew, Dyfed, Wales
Telephone: 0646 651201

How to find it: 2 miles west of Tenby on the B4318 to Carew

Open: Easter-Sept from 10 a.m.
A 12-acre zoo set in beautiful woodlands, with a varied collection that includes guanacos, banded mongoose, otters, coatis, chimpanzees, and capuchin monkeys. There is also a reptile house, an aquarium, and a pet's corner, and several species of birds.

Penscynor Wildlife Park
Cilfrew, Neath, South Wales, Wales
Telephone: 0639 2189

How to find it: 2 miles north-west of Neath, signposted off A465.

Open: All year from 10.00 a.m.
See p. 131.

Solva Nectarium Butterfly Farm
Solva, St David's, Dyfed, Wales
Telephone: 0437 721323

How to find it: Signposted from A487, St David's Head road.

0pen: Easter-Sept from 10.00 a.m.
Tropical butterflies and insects on display.

The Welsh Hawking Centre
Weycock Road, South Glamorgan, Wales CF6 9AA
Telephone: 0446 734687

How to find it: Signposted from Barry on the A4050

Open: All year from 10.30 a.m.

A collection that specialises in keeping and breeding birds of prey – over 200 birds are kept here, including falcons, eagles, and owls. Falconry displays are given regularly, weather permitting.

The Welsh Mountain-Zoo
Colwyn Bay, Clwyd, Wales
Telephone: 0492 2938

How to find it: Signposted from Colwyn Bay centre off the A55

Open: 9.30 a.m. summer, winter 10 a.m.
See p. 142.

CHANNEL ISLANDS

Jersey Zoo
Les Augres Manor, Trinity, Jersey, Charinel Islands
Telephone: 0534 61949

How to find it: 5 miles north of St Hellier, well signposted.

Open: All year from 10.00 a.m.
See p. 105.

Le Friquet Butterfly Farm
Le Friquet Road, Castel, Guernsey, Charinel Islands
Telephone: 0481 54378

How to fnd it: Signposted from Castel centre.

Open: Easter-October from 10 a.m.
A variety of European and exotic butterflies in a free flying tropical house

NORTHERN IRELAND

Belfast Zoo
Antrim Road, Belfast BI36 7P
Telephone: 0232 776277

How to Find it: Signposted north of Belfast on the A2 Antrim road.

Open: All year from 10.00 am
See p. 59.

REPUBLIC OF IRELAND

Dublin Zoo
Royal Zoological Society of Ireland

Phoenix Park,
Dublin 8
Telephone: Dublin (0103531)771425

How to find it: Well signposted at the north end of Phoenix Park

Open: All year from 9.30 am weekdays, 11.00 am Sundays.
One of the oldest zoos in Europe, Dublin Zoo opened in 1830 and was the first Zoo in the British Isles to admit paying visitors. The Zoological Society received its Royal Charter from the young Queen Victoria. Today it occupies 30 acres of Phoenix Park, and holds a wide variety of animals, befitting a national collection. Despite financial crises that have mirrored those at London, the zoo has continued to grow, recently opening a new monkey house. The zoo is beautifully landscaped around a large central lake, and species to look out for include the snow leopards, douc langurs, giraffes, tapirs and elephants. The zoo is proud of its lions in a large open enclosure (the MGM lion was a Dublin lion).

Fota Wildlife Park
Fota Island,
Carrigtwohill,
County Cork
Telephone: Cork 812 736

How to Find it: 10 miles NE of Cork. Turn for Cobh from Rt N.25 Cork-Ross-lare/Wexford road.

Open: Mid March-End of September from 10.00 am weekdays, 11.00 am Sundays.
Fota is the country home of the Royal Zoological Society of Ireland. It is a 70 acre walk-round estate specialising in species that can be shown with natural barriers (like monkey islands) or with minimal fencing such as giraffe, zebra, and ostrich. Fota opened in 1982 and is world famous for its extraordinary breeding successes with cheetah; over 80 have been born here. There are also scimitar horned oryx, lion tailed macaques, and a good bird collection including penguins, flamingos, and macaws. Wallabies and lemurs roam free throughout the park.